Life and Works
of Saadat Hasan Manto

Life and Works
of Saadat Hasan Manto

Edited by
ALOK BHALLA

INDIAN INSTITUTE OF ADVANCED STUDY
RASHTRAPATI NIVAS, SHIMLA-171005

© Indian Institute of Advanced Study 1997

First published 1997

All rights reserved. No part of this book may be reproduced in any form, or by any means, without the written permission of the publisher.

Published by the Secretary
Indian Institute of Advanced Study
Rashtrapati Nivas, Shimla

Typeset at the Indian Institute of Advanced Study, Shimla
and printed at Replika Press Pvt. Ltd., Delhi.

Contents

Introduction	ix
Manto Reconsidered *Gopi Chand Narang*	1
Melodrama or…? A Note on Manto's "In This Maelstrom" *Muhammad Umar Memon*	13
A Dance of Grotesque Masks: A Critical Reading of Manto's "1919 Ke Ek Baat" *Alok Bhalla*	28
The Craft of Manto: Warts and All *Keki K. Daruwala*	55
Lord Shiva or The Prince of Pornographers: Ideology, Aesthetics and Architectonics of Manto *Harish Narang*	69
The Theme of Piety and Sin in "Babu Gopinath" *Varis Alvi*	90
Surfacing from Within: Fallen Women in Manto's Fiction *Sukrita Paul Kumar*	103
Manto and Punjabi Short Story Writers *Tejwant Singh Gill*	113
Manto's Philosophy: An Explication *Ashok Vohra*	129
The World of Saadat Hasan Manto *Shashi Joshi*	141

Manto in English: An Assessment of Khalid Hasan's Translations *M. Asaduddin*	159
Saadat Hasan Manto: A Note *Bhisham Sahni*	172
A Reading of 'Pandit' Manto's Letter to Pandit Nehru *Abdul Bismillah*	175
Manto: The Image of the Soul in the Mirror of Eros *Devender Issar*	184
Manto—The Person and the Myth *Shamim Hanfi*	191
Saadat Hasan Manto: Idealogue and Social Philosophy *Tarannum Riaz*	201
A Note On Some Myths About Manto *Indra Nath Chaudhuri*	215
Contributors	221

Acknowledgements

A few years ago, a seminar on Saadat Hasan Manto would have been inconceivable. The established literary critic found his vision of life at the criminal edges of cities brutal, the anxious ideologue through the mockery of the politics of identity scandalous and religious preacher considered his agnosticism shameful. It was, therefore, courageous of Professor Mrinal Miri to agree to hold a seminar on Manto at the Indian Institute of Advanced Study. I am grateful to him and the staff at the Institute for help and support.

Many of the papers presented at the seminar were in Urdu and Hindi. I must thank Harish Narang, M. Asaddudin and Ahsan Raza Khan for translating them into English in the shortest possible time.

This volume would never have got done without the intelligent and careful support of my wife, Vasundara.

Introduction

The papers collected in this volume were presented at a seminar on the life and works of Saadat Hasan Manto held at the Indian Institute of Advanced Study at Shimla in May 1996. It is, perhaps, worth recording that the seminar was the first serious one of its kind held on Manto either in India or Pakistan. The fact that the work of Manto had never before been the subject of extensive discussion amongst Urdu, Hindi, Punjabi and English literary and social critics is surprising, because he is acknowledged by everyone in the Indian subcontinent to be a writer of extraordinary brilliance, who had the courage to present his milieu in ways which were radically different from writers who were his contemporaries. The seminar was, however, also memorable because it attracted, along with literary critics, scholars of history, sociology, political science and philosophy.

While it has generally been acknowledged that Saadat Hasan Manto was one of the finest writers of our age, it is surprising that neither his life nor the vast range of his writings have received the scrupulous critical attention they deserve. His life has been the subject of countless anecdotes about his eccentricities and temper, his fierce relationships with everyone he knew and his pitiless appraisal of strangers, his acerbic wit and the fluent ease with which he wrote. No one has, however, written a comprehensive biography which carefully locates him in a historical period when our confidence in a trustworthy society of common decencies was badly shaken, and at the same time, attentively considers his readings and sources, his friendship and betrayals, his religious and political presuppositions or his restless shifts from Delhi to Bombay and finally to Lahore.

Discriminating biographical studies of Manto are necessary, if we have to understand why his work is so crowded with physical things that men either collide with them or stumble over them and are always defeated by them, or why his stories are marked by the sense that we are foredoomed to a life of solitude, pain and sorrow. Thus, we must know more about Manto's life within the moral and political economies of the urban centere of colonial India in the first half of the twentieth century and amongst people who lived either in their liminal spaces, or in their criminalised dens, or in their enclaves of glamorous culture. Critical biographies, which place Manto beside his contemporaries whose social sympathies were more limited, could help us realise that, because he had the singular gift of traversing across each of these spaces, he could record with empathy the lives of the marginalised and the brutalised, and at the same time attack with sardonic humour the carelessness of the privileged.

Finally, the most important contribution biographical studies of Manto could make is to help us understand why a man like him, who had spent all his life expressing his abhorrence of everything that was merely religious and political, and in condemning ideas that did not emerge from the sensuousness of lived actuality as a swindle, persuaded himself to migrate to Lahore after 1947. After all even in Pakistan he didn't abandon his cynical belief that there was nothing which reason could do to prevent men and women, Hindus and Muslims equally, from living like fools. It would be useful to know how Manto, once he settled in Pakistan, tried to resolve the apparent contradiction between an Islamic legal state which sought to throw a protective boundary exclusively around people who professed to belong to certain sects of Islam, and his own inherited sense that citizenship is the right of anyone who has lived for a long time within a certain territorial boundary and feels at home within its cultural space.

If the records of Manto's life are fragmentary, scattered and ahistorical, a large part of the critical commentaries about his writings are perfunctory, sentimental and unscholarly. Most of the critics who deal with his stories before the partition, concentrate on a handful of well-known ones about prostitutes, alcoholics and self-loathing writers in order to draw from them jejune morals about the worthiness of the down-trodden in a callous age and the writer's need to descend into the abyss for knowledge. Manto is perhaps at heart a moralist, but he isn't naive. Indeed, his strength lies in his ability to gaze hard at the real world without sentimentality, illusions or hope. Even if there are fleeting moments in his stories when a prostitute dreams of a gentler world or a slum-dweller forgets the stink from the urinal nearby, there is hardly a story of his which doesn't make one shudder or leave one with a feeling of shame and disgust. He is painful precisely because he doesn't suggest a religious, political or ethical solution to misery. The tone of his stories is sardonic and nasty, the actions of many of his characters are loathsome and the sufferings he describes are not a part of some useful ethical scheme to persuade us to act justly but sufferings which will not let us rest in peace.

Manto's stories about the horrors of the partition of India have received thoughtful critical attention from a variety of people trying to make some sense of a world in which men drift, for no reason at all, and again and again, into cruelty and mindless slaughter. Part of the fascination with these stories seems to lie in the fact that, while other writers about the partition often find a place in their narratives for moral men who refuse to abandon their belief that it is better to suffer wrong than to inflict it on others and who refuse to accept a politics without rules of virtuous conduct, Manto mockingly asserts that all civil societies are designed to legitimise our worst impulses and rejects man as a creature who has any ethical sense. These stories are nightmares because they reveal that atrocities can be committed, not only by men who have lived for so long in violent streets that they have adopted the norms of survival in such streets, but by any one of us, against randomly chosen victims, in the name of the finest political principles and God. What is scandalous about Manto's partition stories is his radical erasure of all social, moral or religious reasons which normally inform civilisations. It is not surprising, therefore, that his stories are fragmentary and discontinuous. They merely record instances of terror and cries of pain, violations and pleas for mercy, brutal sexuality and cynical laughter. As fragments they offer no consolation, no hope of emergence into a saner and kinder world. Instead, they prophesy endless days of misery, torture, ruin, madness and waste.

Manto's primary argument is not only the Hobbesian one that when men are freed from responsibilities they become predators, but also that in a world which is as heartless and selfish as ours there is no reason for mercy and pity to create a safe ground for the frailty of goodness to survive. He shocks us even more when we realise that the lives he wants us to witness are being lived at precisely the same historical moment in which Gandhi is pointing to immediate examples of moral courage and pleading for a politics of virtuous regard for all creatures who share this earth with us.

I hope, therefore, that this volume will encourage scholars to write comparative and historical studies which will place Manto within the literary and political currents of his time. Indeed, I am sure that future studies will pay close attention to the complex moral impulses which govern Manto's literary works, as well as make careful analysis of the texture of his tales—the concrete images he uses to create a relentless world, the harsh rhythms of his prose, the grating roughness of his diction—in order to show how successful he is in forcing us to consider the pain of living in colonial India.

—Alok Bhalla

Manto Reconsidered

GOPI CHAND NARANG

Saadat Hasan Manto (1912-1955) has the distinction of being a much maligned and yet widely read short story writer in Urdu. No other Urdu fiction writer has so ruthlessly exposed the hollowness of middle class morality and unmasked its sordid aspects with such telling effect. A master craftsman and a short story writer *par excellence,* he blazed a trail of glory in Urdu fiction unmatched by any other writer. His way of telling a story may well appear to be simple, but the treatment of his subjects and themes, and the light he shed on human nature were marked by refreshing, rather devastating originality. His stories, one after another, sent shock waves through complacent minds. So much so, that some of them were even branded as obscene or lewd, and he was unceremoniously expelled from the fraternity of newly emerging progressive Urdu writers. He was considered a reactionary and even degenerate in his thinking. He was hauled up before the law courts on the heinous charge of peddling pornography, not once but several times. No abuse was too great for him and no humiliation too small. The 'progressives' as well as the traditionalists bestowed these largesses on him in generous measures. But this in no way blunted the rapier-sharp thrust of his pen, nor diminished the boldness of his thinking. Manto spent the last years of his life in great penury. Poverty, lack of a regular income and excessive drinking removed him from our midst at the young age of forty-three.

It is well known that Manto's characters mostly comprise of fallen and rejected members of society, the so-called fallen and rejected who are frowned upon for their depravity. Undoubtedly, his best stories, and the ones for which he is remembered most, are those in which he depicts, with great mastery, fallen women and prostitutes against the backdrop of filthy lanes and slums. Here touts and pimps rub shoulders with tarts, drawing customers into their coils. The stories unfold their lives layer by layer, offer one revelation after another. Manto takes no sides, holds out no pleas. He only reconstructs the spectacle of life as it passes before him. With ruthless objectivity, he unmasks those hypocrites who masquerade as the custodians of society and who day and night dole out, parrot-like, moral homilies, but are in fact the lords of oppression and solely responsible for the degradation of women. Spurned by society, these women are ground between two millstones. Manto does not go into the reasons for their downfall, nor does he lament over their loss of innocence and grace. He only gives us a glimpse of that humane space which they have vicariously created for themselves in this hell for their survival. Most of his characters are condemned to a sordid existence, yet they transcend it.

While rereading Manto after a long lapse of time, a few things strike the mind rather sharply. Manto was a supreme rebel, he was up against *doxa*, be it in arts, literature, customs, manners, social norms, morality or whatever. Anything that was conventional, familiar, acceptable, or belonged to the realm of the so-called *ashrafiya* (the elite, bourgeoisie), was rejected by him and he rebelled against it vehemently. At the core of his creative effort lies a total rejection of all forms of *doxa*, and a radically different view of literature and reality which sent shock waves through his readers as well as his contemporaries. He was way ahead of others, and perhaps no other fiction writer of Urdu in his time was as clear about the nature of literature as he was. The predominant climate in Urdu at that time was utilitarian and didactic as propounded by Hali in his *Maqaddama* and taken to ecstatic heights by Akbar Allahabadi and Iqbal. Manto, while defending his writing, said that it was painful for him to record that "After Iqbal, may his soul rest in peace, it is as if Providence has put locks on all doors of literature and handed over the keys to just one blessed soul. If only Allama Iqbal were alive!" (Comments on the court case regarding "Boo," in *Dastavez*, p. 57). At another point, regretfully he quips, "Most of the respectable journalists who are considered to be custodians of literature are in fact fit to be termed, *tila furosh* i.e., peddlers in drugs for potency" (ibid, p. 57).

Manto was dragged to the courts, time and again, and his patience was stretched to the utmost. On such occasions, while facing a utilitarian readership and an equally ill-informed judiciary, he seems to give the impression that for a while he too favoured the reformist role of literature:

> If you cannot tolerate my stories, this means the times are intolerable. There is nothing wrong with my stories. The wrong which is ascribed to my stories, is in fact the rot of the system. ("Adab-e-Jadeed," 1944, included in *Dastavez*, p. 52).

He goes on:

> If you are opposed to my literature, then the best way is that you change the conditions that motivate such literature (ibid, p. 53).

Manto here seems to be supporting the view that if social conditions change, the need for literature to attend to the woes of fallen women will be obliterated. In yet another defence, he emphasises:

> Maybe my writings are unpleasantly harsh. But what have humans gained from sweet homilies? The neem leaves are pungent but they cleanse the blood. ("Afsana Nigar Aur Jinsi Mailan," The Story Writer and the Subject of Sex, in *Dastavez*, p. 83).

But these were simply positions of defence to absolve himself of the charges that were levied against him and thwart the warrants of prosecution. In actual fact, by his terribly dispassionate realism and totally uncompromising attitude, he had introduced Urdu fiction to an absolutely new concept of art, i.e., the relative autonomy of aesthetic effect not subservient to any of the demands of *ashrafiya* morality or social reform. When free from the exigencies of the judiciary and the prosecution, he elucidated his point of view much more convincingly. He knew that the questions he was involved with were much deeper. They touched the labyrinths of the human psyche, and were perennial questions to which there are no simple answers. Thus:

> If humanity could have listened to the exhortations that stealing or lying is bad, then one Prophet would have been enough. But the list of Prophets is large...We writers are no Prophets, whatever we understand, true or false, we present to our readers; we do not insist that the readers should accept it as the only truth...We criticise the law, but we are not law-makers, we criticise the political system, but we do not lay down the system; we draw the blue-prints but we are not builders; we speak of the malady, but we do not write out prescriptions (ibid, pp. 81-82).

In yet another essay, "Kasoti" (Touchstone), he said:

> Literature is not a commodity like gold or silver which has a rising or falling index. It is made out like an ornament, so it has some adulteration. Literature is not pure reality. Literature is literature or non-literature. There is no via media, as man is either man or an ass (*Dastavez*, p. 84).

It need not be over-emphasised that Manto's concerns were different from those of his contemporaries. He thus ushered in an altogether new form of realism, which the Urdu literati took time to understand and accept. Having assimilated his Russian and French masters at an early age, Manto knew that the fire that raged within him was of a different order. In 1939, when he was barely twenty-seven, he wrote to Ahmad Nadeem Qasmi, "Whatever the situation, I remain restless. I am not satisfied with anything around me. There is something lacking in every thing" (*Nuqoosh*, Manto Number). It is in this context that his delineation of fallen human beings and his constructions of fictional situations need to be reassessed. The obvious, the familiar, or the conventional face of reality, i.e., the *doxa*, never triggered his creativity, rather he always endeavoured to expose it. While giving an address at Jogeshwari College, Bombay, a few years before the partition, he had said in his peculiar style:

> In my neighbourhood if a woman is daily beaten by her husband and if she cleans his shoes the next morning, she is of no interest to me. But if after quarrelling with her husband, and after threatening to commit suicide, she goes to see a movie, and her husband is terribly worried, I am interested in both of them. If a boy falls in love with a girl—it is no more important to me than somebody catching a common cold...The polite, decent women and their niceties are of no consequence to me.

Obviously Manto's fancy thrived on his disdain of *doxa*. Given his urge to look at the other side, the non-conventional, the basic question about the core characters of Manto, especially his fallen women, is whether they are only what they seem to be? Isn't it a paradox of Mantoiana that the fallen characters of Manto were misunderstood during his lifetime, and they continue to be misunderstood even after his death, though the nature of misunderstanding in either case is different. During his lifetime, Manto was opposed tooth and nail, and all that was written about him was trivial and perfunctory. The criticism of Manto was undiscriminatory, bordering on total rejection. The climate changed after his death. If he was totally rejected before, he was eulogised after his death. The rejection all along was for reasons sentimental and highly subjective. So was the later eulogisation. Both lacked an objective, scrupulous, critical base in literary appreciation. Generally, the eulogisation of Manto was due to his representation of the subaltern, the socially degraded, and the perennial flesh trade and women's right to it. The later Mantoiana suffers from a glut of this kind of eulogisation, with the result that the image of Manto, which has gained currency, underscores Manto as a writer of prostitutes, pimps and perverts; as one who rejoices in the portrayal of the seamy side of life. This perhaps calls for some reassessment.

It may be recalled that Manto time and again laid stress on the maxim that "A *veshya* is a woman as well, but every woman, is not a *veshya*" ("Ismat Furosh," Prostitute, in *Dastavez*, p. 92). He says, "We do not go to the prostitutes' quarters to offer *namaz* or *dorood*, we go there because we can go there and buy the commodity we want to buy" ("Safed Jhoot," in *Dastavez*, p. 73).

Manto's concern is not the commodity, but the pain, the suffering, and the loneliness of the human soul that sells it. The two are not the same. You can pay for the commodity, but you cannot set a price on the dignity of the human soul. Manto laments the attitude that for many people the very existence of a woman or the very nature of the man-woman relationship is obscene. If this were so, why did God then create woman? He is equally critical of the man-made codes of morality that do not equate the two. He asks, "Isn't morality the rust on the razor-edge of society which is simply there because it is left there thoughtlessly"? He makes it abundantly clear that he is not a sensationalist: "Why should I take off the *choli* of society, it is naked as it is; of course I am not interested in covering it up either, because that is the job of tailors, not of writers" ("Adab-e-Jadeed," New Writing, *Dastavez*, p. 53).

It is no coincidence that time and again Manto's insights scan the interior landscape of these fallen and marginalized women. He strongly believed that a majority of these women, though they plied the trade, in fact despised it and possessed hearts purer than those of men who came to buy them (*Dastavez*, p. 88). The semantic field of Manto's characterisation needs to be examined afresh. His themes are intricately intertwined with the anguish, the suffering, and the loneliness of the soul he is trying to chart. It is not the body but the *being*, the inner-self, or the air about the 'misery-ness' of the misery which Manto tries to recapture and recreate. It shouldn't, thus, be out of place to take a fresh look at some of the core protagonists of Manto's stories.

In "Kali Shalwar" (Black Shalwar), the most touching part is where Sultana, having been deceived by both the *Khuda* (God) and *Khuda Bakhsh* (her man) and having lost her business after moving from Ambala Cantonment to Delhi, feels forsaken and forlorn:

> Early in the morning, when she came out into her balcony, a weird sight would meet her eyes. Through the haze she could see the locomotives belching out thick smoke which ponderously rose in columns towards the grey sky, giving the impression of fat men swaying in the air. Thick clouds of steam would rise from the railway lines, making a hissing sound and then dissipate in the air in the twinking of an eye. Sometimes a detached bogey, getting an initial push from the engine, kept running on the track by its own momentum. Sultana would feel that an invisible hand had also given a push to her life and then left her to fend for herself. Like the bogey which switched from one track to another under a locking device manipulated by an invisible cabinman, an invisible hand was also changing the course of her life. And then a day would come when the momentum would be spent up and she would come to a dead stop at some unknown spot where there would be no one to take care of her (*The Best of Manto*, ed. and trans. by Jai Ratan, p. 15).

There are moments in a *veshya*'s life when she is only a woman, a tender-hearted woman. On such occasions the archetypal image of woman shines through Manto's writings. Sughandhi in "Hatak" (Insult) is a frail, yet strong woman. Madho, her lover from Poona, has been making a fool of her by taking advantage of her and even fleecing her of her earnings. Sugandhi, though clever, is not really so clever, since she can be fooled by simple words of love and affection, and Madho is a past master at this game.

> Every night her new or old lover would say, "Sugandhi, I love you." And Sugandhi, although she knew that the man was telling a lie, would melt like wax, deluding herself in the belief that she was really being loved. Love—what a beautiful word it was! How she wished that she could dissolve the word and rub it over her skin, letting it seep into her being.
>
> So overpowering was her desire to love and be loved that she tried to put up with the vagaries of all the men who came to her. Among them, were the four men whose photographs now adorned her wall. Being herself essentially a good soul, she failed to understand, why men lacked this goodness of heart. One day when she was standing before the mirror the words escaped her lips: "Sugandhi, the world has given you a raw deal."
>
> (ibid, pp. 27-28).

Isn't the whole concept here built around the archetypal mother-image of woman? Doesn't *prem* incarnate (love) permeate her total existence, everything that is within and without; doesn't it draw the being into its fold and put it to sublime sleep attuned to the music of the eternal lullaby? This feeling of deep compassion, *karuna* or *mamata*, by whatever term you call it, flows through the whole narrative, till Sugandhi is rejected by a *seth* in the middle of the night. Shocked and dejected, having finally seen through the hypocrisy of man, she takes out her rage on Madho who happens to be visiting her at that time. Anguish and loneliness once again rend the soul, there is emptiness all around. The metaphor of a lonely shunted train deserted on the rails of life is once again invoked in this story with telling effect thus:

> Sugandhi looked up startled, as if she had come out of a reverie. The room was steeped in an eerie silence—a silence she had never experienced before. She felt as if she was surrounded by a vacuum—as if a train on a long haul,

after depositing the passengers en route was now standing in the loco shed, looking deserted and forlorn. An emptiness seemed to have taken root in her heart (ibid, p. 38).

The most baffling and unusual story is, "Babu Gopi Nath," in which a neo-rich man is fond of the company of pimps and hangers-on, and *peers* and *faqirs,* because he maintains that if one wants to deceive oneself, then there is no better place to go to than the *kotha* of a *veshya* (den of a prostitute) or the *mazaar* of a *peer* (mausoleum of a saint) since these are the places that thrive on sham and deceit. At the *kotha*, they sell the body, and at the *mazaar* they sell God. Babu Gopi Nath is involved with the young Zeenat, a Kashmiri girl, utterly naive and uncouth, who could never learn the tricks of the trade. Babu Gopi Nath is trying to find a man to wed Zeenat so that she can have a home. To achieve this end, he is prepared to go to any length and spend all his wealth. It is an unusual situation. On the one hand, there is an undercurrent of dark humour in the naivety of Zeenat, and the cleverness of pimps and hangers-on; and on the other, it is the benevolence of Babu Gopi Nath that permeates the events. One cannot help thinking that in Babu Gopi Nath, Manto has created a male protagonist, who is in fact an embodiment of the qualities of the mother-image. The situation is full of irony, and it is through Babu Gopi Nath that the milk of compassion and the spirit of sacrifice and service flow through the story and render it unique.

If there is a female parallel to Babu Gopi Nath, who else could it be but the humane and motherly Janaki (in the story of the same name) who, though not in the profession, is passed on from one man to another, and yet is full of the tender feelings similar to that of *mamata* for the men she comes across. She hails from Peshawar where she was committed to Aziz. She cares for Aziz day and night. She tends to his needs, takes care of his food and clothes, nurses him through his illness and lives with him. She comes to

Bombay looking for a job and in the course of events gets involved with Saeed. This is resented by Aziz. Eventually Saeed also forsakes her, but in turn she gets involved with yet another person, Narain. She adores him and bestows the same care and affection on him. Men may come and men may go, but Janaki remains the same, a fountain-head of love and devotion, a goddess who nurtures her men.

This leads us to consider if there wasn't a cherished mother-image lurking somewhere in the labyrinth of Manto's unconsious. None of his biographers has dwelt on his relationship with his mother, but whatever sketchy information we have confirms that he had a harsh and cruel father, and a host of step-brothers. Maybe, the only thing that made up for this deprivation was the affectionate care of his loving mother, Babi Jan. One gets the feeling that Manto was profoundly familiar with suffering from his earliest days. Imploringly, at one point, he says, "O God, take me away from this world! I cry where I should laugh, and I laugh where I should cry" ("Pas-manzar," Context, in *Dastavez*, p. 159). His *dukha, udasi* and *karuna** seem to have a Buddhist ring. But for Manto, perhaps, suffering, compassion and love were different faces of the same reality. "Suffering is ordained, a predicament," Manto says, "Suffering (*alam/dukha*) is you, suffering is me, suffering is Saadat Hasan Manto, suffering is the whole universe" ("Kasooti," p. 86). He perceived one through the other. Repeatedly, he stresses that the body can be bartered or branded, not the soul ("Ismat Furosh," *Dastavez*, p. 90). He elaborates that many of the women in the flesh trade are god-fearing, devotionally attached to icons and images, and observe religious rituals. Maybe because religion is that part of their selves which they have saved from the trade and through which they redeem themselves.

Nonetheless, Mozel is entirely different as she pokes fun

---

* The term *karuna* is used by Waris Alvi for Manto, but in a different context. (see Monograph on Manto published by Sahitya Akademi, New Delhi, 1994).

at religious observances, whatever their form. This is yet one more example of Manto's dialogic art in the sense Bakhtin uses it. Isn't it amazing that one comes across such a large variety of men and women in Manto's fiction? Mozel is a bohemian girl of Jewish descent; vivacious and carefree, she is full of ridicule for religion that divides man from man. She makes fun of the turban, *kesha* (hair) and other manifestations of Trilochan, who is a Sikh. But the same playful Mozel comes to Trilochan's rescue when riots break out in Bombay, and without caring for her personal safety, saves Trilochan's fiancèe, Kirpal Kaur, and in the process becomes a victim of the killers. One can see that once again a woman of doubtful character rises to the occasion and, through her compassion and devotion, delivers the persons around her from destruction.

In this context, it is needless to belabour "Boo" (Odour), one of Manto's best-known stories. Suffice it to say that this story of consummate copulation can refreshingly be read as a story of the cycle of seasons, falling raindrops and the soaking of the virgin mother earth, i.e., the union of the elements where Randhir is *Purush* and the Ghatin girl *Prakriti*, who lies dormant, but is the giver and receiver of pleasure in abundant measure.

"Sharda," "Fobha Bai," and "Burmese Girl" are some of the other stories where the protagonists are moved by the same underlying force of benevolence. In "Burmese Girl," we have a fleeting glimpse of a girl who shares a flat with two young boys for a few days and is soon gone like a whiff of soft breeze. Despite her short stay, she leaves behind sweet memories of setting the house in order and infusing the whole place with an atmosphere of affection, charm and motherliness. But before the boys get to know her better, she is gone. In comparison, Sharda and Fobha Bai (dialectal variation of Shobha Bai) are actual mothers. Sharda is the complete embodiment of womanhood as she is simultaneously a mother, a sister, a wife and also a whore, and none of these roles is in conflict with one another. Fobha Bai has tragic strains in her, as she has to sell herself in the city to protect the mother within her by sustaining a young son back home. But the son dies, and with his death the woman, who sold herself for his sake, is also devastated. Similarly in "Sarak Ke Kinare" (By the Roadside), motherhood is accomplished, but remains unfulfilled in the sense that as an unwed and forsaken woman, she cannot bring up the child. In the dead of night, the child is left by the roadside. Manto raises the question, "Is the coming together of two souls at a single point and the giving up of everything in a cosmic rhythm mere poetry? No. Certainly, this is the merging of two souls, and their rising to enfold heaven and earth and the whole universe. But then why is one soul left behind wounded, simply because she helped the other to rise to the heights of the cosmic rhythm?"

This is the kernel of unmitigated suffering, the predicament from which there is no escape. The infinite sorrow in Manto at the deeper level sustains his creativity, through which are constructed his fallen women. Once, opening his heart to Ahmed Nadeem Qasmi, he wrote: "I, in fact, have reached a point in my thinking where faith or disbelief becomes meaningless. Where I understand, I do not understand. At times, I feel as if the whole world is in the palm of my hand, then there are times when I feel insignificant, as insignificant as an ant crawling on the body of an elephant" (*Nuqoosh*, Manto Number).

Manto, in his finer moments, is attuned to the symphony of the mystery of creation, and in this symphony his dominant note is the note of sorrow. The sorrow of existence, the loneliness of the soul, and that unfathomable suffering, *dukha*, which is part of the music of the infinite. Many of his protagonists turn out to be more than life-size, more durable, more lasting than mere frail men and women of flesh and blood. They become the embodiment of something more pervasive, more universal; that is, of benevolence or compassion incarnate, the sublimest of the sublime, of the fountain-head of *mamata* and *karuna* which flow through the emotional space of Manto's narrative, and with which we all identify.

Melodrama or....?
A Note On Manto's "In This Maelstrom"

MUHAMMAD UMAR MEMON

It is somewhat puzzling that Saadat Hasan Manto had called his play "Is Manjdhar Men" (In this Maelstrom) a melodrama. But is it? All the ingredients of melodrama are absent in this play. There are no monstrously evil villains, propelled by fiendish hate, to be sure, and the main characters, even though some of them appear less fully developed, show an amazing complexity and depth. Moreover, the very subject of this play defies, by its own incontrovertible inner logic, any attempt to place the work in the genre of melodrama. But did Manto really fully appreciate the implication of melodrama as a dramatic form or was he using the word in its more common and pejorative connotations of something non-erious, sensational and outlandishly sentimental; something naive, infantile and frivolous, something to laugh at, something that only parodies and mimics life in the crudest of fashions for cheap, emotional gratification?

I know Manto-lovers won't take it kindly, but I am inclined to think that in this play, Manto does not appear to have grasped the dramatic form of melodrama, either to its function or to its creative possibilities. This despite the fact that among Urdu writers, Manto is perhaps the most conscious of the technical demands imposed by narrative art: and also despite the fact that "In this Maelstrom" is a very sophisticated piece of writing.

That Manto, who could stare down the moralist, the critic, and the law with audacious courage when it came to defending his choice of subject-matter, would take a dim view of his play does seem puzzling. But it can be explained.

Until Eric Bentley came to vindicate it and earn for it a

measure of respectability in the late 1960s – too late, alas! for Manto—the form of melodrama had all along suffered a bad reputation in the western literary world. The continued prejudice against it, the bad name given to it, was the result, in most part, of the shallow and pedestrian nature of popular Victorian melodrama. Just how shallow and pedestrian is it? Scan through the plots of some such dramatic pieces given by James L. Smith in his *Melodrama,* and you will know. But what was essentially a Victorian expression and possibility, determined by specific social factors, became the normative principle in defining the term as "a dramatic piece characterized by sensational incident and violent appeals to emotions, but with a happy ending" (*Oxford English Dictionary,* as quoted in Smith, p. 5). Smith quotes a lengthy passage from Frank Rahill's *The World of Melodrama* which would be profitable to reproduce here by way of a working definition of the genre:

> Melodrama is a form of dramatic composition in prose partaking of the nature of tragedy, comedy, pantomime, and spectacle, and intended for a popular audience. Primarily concerned with situation and plot, it calls upon mimed action extensively and employs a more or less fixed complement of stock characters, the most important of which are a suffering heroine or hero, a persecuting villain, and a benevolent comic. It is conventionally moral and humanitarian in point of view and sentimental and optimistic in temper, concluding its fable happily with virtue rewarded after many trials and vices punished. Characteristically it offers elaborate scenic accessories and miscellaneous divertisements and introduces music freely, typically to underscore dramatic effect (Smith, p. 5).

In the Urdu literary world, on the other hand, where most literary conventions, forms, and terms borrowed from the West have been generally understood in their western—though perhaps at times also in a somewhat etiolated—sense, one can hardly expect significant strides towards redefining "melodrama" beyond its inherited meaning. The more so because Urdu culture and humanities just do not have a viable tradition of stage drama and other theatrical arts. Even now, when radio and television have popularized play-writing, one is struck by the generally low quality of plays and their conspicuous lack of any sense of the medium. There haven't been good plays in Urdu, much less good "melodramas." The only thing vaguely resembling melodrama—not in the sense of a dramatic form, but in the sense of a grossly exaggerated and fanciful piece of writing—are the historical romances by Abdul Halim Sharar (1860-1926).[2] Here, however, every norm of fiction-writing is flouted with impunity, but the raw material is not unlike that from which, in a different time and place, a Victorian would have woven tapestry after dazzling tapestry of melodramatic colours.

Perhaps it will be profitable at this point to briefly recapitulate the main arguments of Eric Bentley as set forth in his *The Life of the Drama*.[3] An exposition of his views will, it is hoped, help determine the nature of "In this Maelstrom" more precisely.

Bentley thinks that melodrama and tragedy, though certainly not identical, and granted that a sharp line could not always be drawn between them, do have a lot in common. Melodrama represents the primitive, the child in us, and, therefore, the most spontaneous, direct, and uninhibited way of working off emotion; tragedy, on the other hand, deals with maturer emotion and is artistically more restrained. "Melodrama is human but it is not mature. It is imaginative but it is not intelligent" (p. 217). Being human, of course, does not place melodrama above tragedy, but it does rescue it from the abyss of pedestrianism in which it had been thrown by the Victorian dramatist.

Why the melodrama has been regarded unfavorably is due, first, to the very bad examples of it produced by the Victorian writer. But "it is unfair," remarks Bentley, "to judge anything by its weakest link" (p.196). And Smith is simply echoing Bentley's view when he says, "Any art form deserves to be judged by its highest, not by its lowest achievements" (p.14).

Second, and more importantly, we judge it negatively because of the widespread tendency to regard emotion as necessarily bad emotion, to be wary, therefore, of all emotion, and consider the ability to work it off uninhibitedly as somehow demeaning. To cry is to be a child; and, let's accept it, all we want from a melodrama, indeed all it can give us, is a "good cry." A culture that places so little value, or perhaps none at all, on tears is not likely to highly regard a literary form whose important function is to make us cry and help release tension.

Having divested "cry" of its negative contemporary animus and produced an eloquent defense of "tears," Bentley next argues that all the other standard features of a typical melodrama—i.e., pity, which is, ultimately, self-pity; fear; exaggerated (though he prefers uninhibited) action and language etc.—are likewise not quite so fanciful and, therefore, unnatural as they are assumed to be. Theirs is the reality of a child or an adult in dreams. Nonmagnified feelings are more an ideal than a fact of life. *Reality is magnified feelings.* In Bentley's sense, then, melodrama is more natural than Naturalism itself which is "more sophisticated," but not necessarily "more natural" (p. 216).

Some standard features of melodrama: according to Bentley are: "Goodness beset by badness, a hero beset by a villain, heroes and heroines beset by a wicked world" (p. 200). However, the two most important elements are *pity* for the hero and, by extension for onself; and *fear,* often irrational fear, of the villain. While the former represents the weaker side of melodrama, the latter represents the stronger. Finally, *exaggeration* is highlighting pity and fear, both in action and dialogue.

Manto's "In this Maelstrom" is not a melodrama for a number of reasons. While there may be some *pity* for the central character, Amjad—though pity alone does not, indeed should not, qualify a work as a melodrama—there is no fear of the villain. The villain is just not there, let alone being superhuman or diabolic. Though melodramatic vision is paranoid (Bentley, p. 202), one doesn't have to be persecuted by a real flesh and blood villain; even the landscape can oppress and persecute. Manto's landscape, though, is invested with breathtaking *beauty*. More importantly, this beauty is not presented as axiomatic. It derives, dialectically, inch by inch as it were, from the generally positive manner in which the characters react and respond to it. Then again, while a typical melodrama rarely moves beyond *pity* and *fear*, "In this Maelstrom" is not tamed, bound or otherwise defined by these categoties. Although, we do feel a certain sense of pity for Amjad, we feel a greater sympathy for his wife Saeeda and wish for her beauty and youth, now hopelessly wasting away, to blossom. Thus, whatever pity we feel for Amjad is ultimately sublimated— or perhaps muted—by our still greater feelings of support and happiness for Saeeda and Majeed. "We...grieve not," in the words of William Wordsworth, "rather find/Strength in what remains behind."[4]

The characters, too, are not the stock characters of a melodrama. Neither cast according to the "Progressive" formula, nor defined by *bourgeois moeurs*, they vibrate with a life all their own. They are imbued with remarkable individuality and amazing independence of will, and reveal a complex psychology in their thoughts, feelings, and actions, with few, if any, parallels in Urdu drama. Thus Amjad, who has picked Saeeda from among countless other women to be his wife, knows that his choice doesn't ultimately, amount to more than the impulse to pick up the finest thing in the market. As for loving her—that, he freely admits to Asghari, he doesn't. Still this does not stop him from wondering, "I can't understand why I want to keep her [i.e., Saeeda] shackled in chains whose every link is as uncertain as my life." Well aware of the burgeoning, illicit love between his wife and younger brother, he appears to be strangely free of even the slightest trace of jealousy, so unlike, one might almost say, of South Asian males.

I do not agree with Mumtaz Shirin's contention that

Saeeda is less a character than a "symbol of beauty." She is an aesthetic attribute. But she is also much more. She is both attractive and aware of her tremendous attraction for men. Nothing so extraordinary perhaps. Where, however, she eminently disqualifies herself as a young stereotypical South Asian young Muslim woman is when she "unabashedly," though not without disarming directness and honesty, mentions to Asghari the desires raging inside her, and catalogues her frustrations. She says:

> I'm young, I'm pretty. Inside me are numberless desires. For seventeen long years I've nurtured them with the nectar of my dreams. How can I stifle them'...Call me weak, a coward, or even immoral...I confess I cannot tear down the garden of my youth, where the vein of every leaf and flower throbs with the hot blood of my unfulfilled desire...

And Asghari, the maid: her frequent caustic jibes at the crippled Amjad, in spite of her knowledge of the extremely brittle state of his mind; her scathing, abrasive wit; and, above all, her hesitation in accepting Amjad's love, in spite of being herself in love with him—all these raise her above the meek and obsequious world of a South Asian domestic to the plane of a fairly complex personality.

Finally, Majeed. Although as a character he is not fully developed, but in coveting the wife of his own brother, he appears to be refreshingly untypical.

Melodrama is often characterized by its use of an exaggerated—i.e., heightened, lyrical—form of language. A declamatory, excessively rhetorical style of speech is no doubt noticeable in a couple of long-winding speeches by Amjad addressed to Saeeda at mid-point in the play and to Asghari the maid at the end; and in a single piece where Saeeda addresses Asghari. But in all these instances, the elevated rhetoric appears called for by event and situation, which it dialectically supports and enhances. It does not appear tired, crude or otherwise organically *non sequitur*. Moreover, "Intensity of feeling," as Bentley has it, "justifies formal exaggeration in art" (p. 204). A brief sequence of emotionally charged utterances would be inadequate ground to place the work in the category of melodrama.

Finally, one thing is sure: we certainly do not get a "good cry" out of the play. What we do get is the calm of a sobering moment in which our momentarily frozen senses—because of two suicides at the end—gradually thaw out to a sense of beauty and blossoming optimism toward life's continuity which is far in excess of our initial shock at the twin suicides. We come to accept, almost, the suicides as the necessary price life must pay to remain on-going, continuous, whole.

Manto probably didn't have before him examples of good melodrama; of its "highest achievements," as Smith would say. But he certainly had good sense. Why, then, did he characterize a serious and far-reaching work of his as being the equivalent of "sob stuff," a "tear jerker," and a "poor man's cathartic laugh"?

For the answer we will have to determine the theme of the play, for it is here and not in its incidental likeness to this or that melodramatic element that we can hope to find the most cogent proof of its not being a melodrama.

This play underscores the relationship between a married woman and an unmarried man. In Manto's society, just as, I believe, in most societies, this type of relationship is not looked upon kindly and remains, without mincing words, downright illicit. This particular relationship is made more complicated by the fact that the woman's husband has been rendered impotent following a train wreck prior to consummating the marriage, and her lover, with whom she hasn't yet entered into a physical relationship, is none other than her crippled husband's younger brother. Manto, of course, isn't interested in celebrating promiscuity *per se*. He, therefore, neither jeers at the invalid for his loss of manhood, nor, on the other hand, helps initiate the lovers in the ways of pleasure. By avoiding any explicit or implicit reference to actual sexual contract—though not, perhaps, to the fact of sexual attraction—between the lovers, he seems to give us a clue to his profounder purpose, which is to transcend the confining circumstances of self-indulgent sensual love itself and give it a creative, complementary role integral to the wider scheme of things; to produce, in other words—and here I may be repeating Mumtaz Shirin's very astute observation—a philosophy of life and existence.

It is in the scheme of things that healthy and whole parts of nature must come together to renew and continue life, while its decaying parts must inevitably fade out of existence. By eliminating the weak and the broken and in letting the healthy and the whole prosper, Nature simply acts out its own laws, without implying contempt or disgust for the ones soon to be eliminated. And the coming together of two parts is, basically, a coming together of two cognate parts.

The invalid husband himself gradually comes to have more than a fair inkling of this inexorable natural logic. When, therefore, at the end of the play, Amjad commits suicide, we do not react with shock or disbelief, or otherwise mourn his death. We interpret the incident—tragic, no doubt—as a necessary point in the continuum of life, a point which will help revitalize and preserve it. It is also, by extension, the point where conventional morality, fed liberally on religious ethics, must unavoidably take a back seat to humanism. This humanism is based upon the primacy of instinctual forces in human nature and asserts its belief in the healing possibilities for our wounded civilization afforded by an entirely new relationship between sexes. If, according to Nietzsche, art's perfection, beyond good and evil, lies in affirming, blessing, and deifying existence, this play by Manto seems to do just that.

Now the greater or at least a significant part of Manto's themes deals with what is only fact, with "nothing but the truth."[5] If we do not like a given fact, so much the worse for us. When the moralist, the critic, and the law got on his tail, it was not because Manto was distorting or falsifying reality. It was because he was presenting a reality whose very presence involved a judgment of these self-righteous people as accomplices in a conspiracy of silence and latitudinarianism, a conspiracy which hated the effect but did nothing to eliminate the cause. Whether a pimp, a pinko, a floozy, a conman, an underworld character, or the sudden awakening into manhood of an adolescent body *a la* Alberto Moravia, or, finally—and this certainly does not exhaust the list of Manto themes—a chance, illicit sexual encounter between an urban man and a mountain woman —all are real. *Facts!* Manto's society never liked these characters, feelings, experiences. But they were there and could not be simply willed away. The society was thus in time forced to strike its own *modus vivendi* with them: a toleration of something relegated to the blurry, hazy fringe of consciousness.

What, however, could not be so easily relegated to the blurry fringe of consciousness was adultery in a "respectable" married woman. And even if the society did not like her, the prostitute performed a socially useful function: she bore enormous demands on her accommodating flesh and, thus, helped the society uphold its so-called "honour." Had she not been conveniently there, the sprightly youth of the nobility would have, in all likelihood, looked elsewhere in the direction of "respectable" women to vent his passion. So, even if no love was lost between society and the whore, the former was only thankful to the latter, however obliquely and grudgingly, for her chastening presence.

Regardless of the subtler and, ultimately, positive dimensions of Manto's philosophy in the play at hand, this philosophy, if not actually founded upon, at least made use of what, eventually, could not be interpreted as anything but extra-marital sexual relationships. This the society was ill-equipped to handle, condone or tolerate. Of all evils, this alone threatened to destroy most fully the fabric of Muslim life as defined by Islamic precepts. Let us not forget that the play was written in what is now the Islamic Republic of Pakistan. It was a society which would have most certainly reacted differently than early twentieth-century England did when D.H. Lawrence took to living with Frieda Weekley, the as yet undivorced German wife of his own mentor.

It was this threat, and society's inability to deal with the nature of forbidden love with empathy and detachment, that, I am strongly inclined to believe, led Manto to dub the play a melodrama. And, although, Manto most certainly hadn't meant to promote adultery, he was smart enough to know that his society was not likely to read his play any other way. And, so, fully aware of the work's far-reaching, profound import, but also of its scandalous properties, he proceeded to take the unintended, nevertheless very real, sting out of it by presenting it as a joke, something bizarre one must laugh at, something that isn't real, something that just parodies life. Everyone knows Manto was haughty, but he was also clever. His cleverness lay in getting the message across but avoiding the dire consequences that might follow. This, perhaps, also explains the presence of a barely perceptible jocular, almost comic vein in some of the dialogue, which, unfortunately, has escaped the notice of even such an astute Manto critic as the late Mumtaz Shirin.

I am not unware of the implications of camouflage for art, whatever the reasons impelling the writer to employ it. If Manto used it knowingly, he compromised his art to that extent. But here there may be another possibility: the philosophy which he vaguely, intuitively, artistically knew to be true, hadn't quite reached the status of a deep conviction, the point where the writer must place his confidence in the truth of his vision and unequivocally reject what is not supported or accepted by it as true. Hence the ambivalence in his attitude. It denied him the confidence to proudly own up the consequences of the very humanistic vision of life embodied in this play. This seems more likely the reason. Manto was not known to turn his back, cower, flee, or compromise.

Had Manto known the possibilities of a good melodrama, would he still have called "In this Maelstrom" one? I suspect not. Whatever else it may be—Shirin thinks it verges on tragedy—even by the most stringent application of the

A Note on Manto's 'In this Maelstrom' 23

canons of the genre, "In this Maelstrom" is certainly not a melodrama. Its very theme goes far beyond the stuff even the best melodramas are made of. I have in the foregoing deliberately refrained from expounding the meaning of the play. Most of what I might have said, would have amounted to no more than a mere rehashing of the ideas of Mumtaz Shirin (1925-73), Urdu's finest literary critic. She was the first to notice the subtler meanings of "In this Maelstrom" and its striking resemblance to D.H. Lawrence's last novel *Lady Chatterley's Lover*. If we are to understand the play at all, an understanding of these "subtler meanings" is essential. So, I think, it is only fair that, I let Shirin speak directly. In what follows, I translate the relevant part from the article, "Manto Ki Fanni Takmil" (Perfection of Manto's Art) which appears in her collection of critical essays *Mi'yar*.

Two works from Manto's last period exemplify, in my opinion, the perfection of his literary art...: "Sarak ke Kinare" (By the Roadside) and "Is Manjdhar Men" (In this Maelstrom). Both offer a sense of perfection; universal breadth and profundity; and a philosophy of life and existence. Earlier on, Manto's attitude was largely negative and destructive in regard to society and life, which he depicted with relentless, brutal realism. Gradually this was replaced by an increasing regard for the positive and life-affirming values. Finally, it seems Manto had come to realize, with unmistakable clarity, that the creative vision of a truly great writer was founded, ultimately, on affirmation of life and existence.

If one could understand the deeper meanings of "In this Maelstrom," one would inevitably know that here Manto has shown the negative elements—i.e., those lacking vitality—hurtling down their path to annihilation, and brought together those positive elements which both renew and promote life.

Apparently, the subject of this play resembles that of D.H. Lawrence's in *Lady Chatterley's Lover*. Even the characters are, more or less, the same: a husband, crippled shortly after marriage; his young, beautiful, and healthy wife; an equally healthy young man who can offer her life's vigor and vitality; and a maid who feels sympathy and a certain attraction for the invalid. But Manto's presentation, compared with Lawrence's, is both of a higher order and artistically more polished, regardless of the fact that one is a novel and the other is a play. It offers a philosophy, which is lacking at least in this work of Lawrence who had otherwise moulded a veritable philosophy around the subject of "sex." In *Lady Chattreley's Lover,* Lawrence stresses the elements of harmony and perfection in physical relationships—and no more; Manto, on the other hand gives his subject an unmistakable aesthetic quality and attitude. And even though he, too, extrapolates the same meaning from *vigour of life* as does Lawrence, namely, sex is the font of life's vigour and vitality, he also stresses those other elements which give life a sense of beauty, wholeness, and perfection.

Beauty is thus a positive element in "In this Maelstrom," and so are youth, love, physical health, pleasant feelings and the ability to love. These elements are present, more or less, in the wife and her husband's younger brother. Evidently, this is not the case with the husband who, following the accident which has left him paralyzed, becomes a negative element, no longer able to either affirm or support life. Here it is worth mentioning that unlike Lawrence, Manto's treatment of the invalid husband is blissfully free of any undertone of contempt. On the contrary, he fully sympathizes with this character; indeed, he even assigns the extreme anguish, torment and struggle of this character a prominent place in the play.

The husband fully realizes that his wife has a perfect right to be amorously inclined towards his brother, who alone can truly give her the healthy and positive love she deserves; that it is only natural that the two gravitate towards each other; and that, finally, with his crippled body, psychological impediments, and feeling of inferiority he has become a negative element whom one can pity but not love. Love he finds only in the maid who is herself unworthy of being loved, and ugly to boot—ugliness being in itself a negative attribute. While both these negative elements can come together, their union is not likely to produce anything positive. "That is the reason why, when they finally do unite, it is in death and not in life...Compared with Saeeda and Majeed as characters, they are powerful and touching no doubt, but negative all the same.

Although Amjad does not have the stature of a truly tragic hero (for this play by Manto goes a touch beyond melodrama to almost the point of tragedy), his pain and his tragic death do not fail to evoke in us the feelings of pity and horror necessary for tragedy. Still, Amjad is a passive, almost masochistic character. His impotence is nowhere more vividly portrayed than when he asks Saeeda to lie down on the bed and proceeds to act out in his imagination the events that normally transpire on the wedding night. At first joyous and exhilarating, this imaginary scene quickly dissolves into one of utter failure and devastation. And although he tries to keep himself amused and derive some joy out of life, following his own paralysis, these abilities progressively decline. The presence of towering mountains and beautiful natural scenes around him—though no longer accessible—significantly add to his pain and misery. Likewise, Saeeda's breathtaking beauty, too, becomes a source of unmitigated torment for him. Being an extremely sensitive person, he quickly lapses into a state of mind in which he is constantly assailed by thoughts of defeat and destruction, death alone offering the only possible release.

Saeeda appears less a character than a symbol of beauty—the beauty which Amjad had wanted to possess but which turned into a source of suffering. She certainly isn't lacking in sympathy for her husband; indeed she even tries to curb to a certain extent her natural attraction for Majeed; however, her inner moral struggle appears superficial and muted, while Majeed, in spite of being Amjad's brother, shows not even the slightest trace of any struggle at all. All he wants is to escape his maelstrom, and does not hesitate to announce to Saeeda, without remorse or qualms, that Amjad is well on his way to death and that life has its own special, vital demands that can be met in their union.

Therefore, in spite of being relatively less significant, the characters of Saeeda and Majeed become symbols of life's renewal and vitality. Certainly it cannot be considered an artistic flaw on Manto's part that he chose to give them less importance. In Emile Brontë's incomparably brilliant novel *Wuthering Heights,* too, the characters (i.e., young Catherine and Earnshaw) who are a source of life's renewal appear altogether ordinary and commonplace when compared to the towering, passionate, and powerful personalities of Heathcliff and Catherine. However, these two plain and utterly ordinary characters display that healthy equilibrium which is all too necessary for life.

And, although, "In this Maelstrom" presents Amjad's tragedy, at the end of which death emerges dominant and triumphant, it also offers, through Saeeda and Majeed's inevitable union, a subtler allusion to the affirmation of life. Here, then, it can be reasonably assumed, Manto's creative vision has become expansive enough to transform the individual and the particular into the general and the universal.[6]

NOTES AND REFERENCES

1. London: Methuen, 1973.
2. For further information on him and his works see Ralph Russell, "The Development of the Modern Novel in Urdu," in T.W. Clark, ed., *The Novel in India, its Birth and Development* (London: George Allen and Unwin, 1970), pp. 122-32; and Muhammad Sadiq, *A History of Urdu Literature* (London: Oxford University Press, 1964), pp. 329-34.
3. 1964 rpt.; New York; Atheneum, 1967.

4. Lines from his *Ode to Innocence*.
5. Alllusion to a short story by Manto, for which see Faruq Hassan and Khalid Hasan, eds., *Nothing But the Truth* (Montreal: Dawson College, 1978).
6. *Mi'yar*, Lahore: Naya Idarah, 1963, pp. 274-80. Translated by Muhammad Umar Memon.

A Dance of Grotesque Masks: A Critical Reading of Manto's "1919 Ke Ek Baat"

ALOK BHALLA

1

Manto's first set of stories about the partition, like "Toba Tek Singh," "Thanda Gosht" or "Siyah Hashye," written soon after 1947, are vituperative, slanderous and bitterly ironic. They are terrifying chronicles of the damned which locate themselves in the middle of madness and crime, and promise nothing more than an endless and repeated cycle of random and capricious violence in which anyone can become a beast and everyone can be destroyed. Manto uses them to bear shocked witness to an obscene world in which people become, for no reason at all, predators or victims; a world in which they either decide to participate gleefully in murder, or find themselves unable to do anything but scream with pain when they are stabbed and burnt or raped again and again. Manto makes no attempt to offer any historical explanations for the hatred and the carnage. He blames no one, but he also forgives no one. Without sentimentality or illusions, without pious postures or ideological blinkers, he describes a perverse and a corrupt time in which the sustaining norms of a society as it had existed are erased, and no moral or political reason is available.

Manto wrote a second set of stories about the partition between 1951 and 1955. Unfortunately, these stories are neither as well known and documented, nor as systematically analysed as the previous ones. They are, however, significant stories because, together with the earlier ones, they create out of the events that make up the history of our independence movement, an ironic mythos of defeat, humiliation and ruin. If the first set of stories are fragmentary, spasmodic and unremittingly violent, the second set of stories are more complex in their emplotment and more concerned with the deep structural relationship between the carnage of the partition and human actions in the past. While rage and hopelessness still mark the second set of stories, and fear and violence still bracket the beginning and the end of each one of them, the past is more intricately braided into the texture of the main narratives than it is in the first set of stories, and the incidents are more symbolically charged. They should, perhaps, be classified as historical tales which seek to give a "retrospective intelligibility" (Ricoeur, p.157) to the terror of the partition. Each of them tries to locate, at every instance and right down the chronological line from 1947 back to the beginnings of the nationalist struggle, those rifts, breaks and fissures in our social, political and religious selves which always enabled the monstrous to slip into our living spaces.

If the first set of Manto's stories about the partition are derisive tales of a degenerate society, the second set of stories are both parables of lost reason and demonic parodies of the conventional history of the national movement. The triumphant romance of nationalism, in the official Indian and Pakistani historiography, ends with the victory of a sovereign people (even if they are themselves divided by religion) over an illegitimate colonial power, as well as, with the establishment of law governed societies. For Manto, however, 1947 is not a celebrative, an epiphanic, moment. It is, rather, the culmination of a regular and repeated series of actions—I should like to call them "bloody tracks"—which invariably disfigure all the geographical and temporal sites of the nationalist struggle (I am fully conscious of the melodramatic wildness of the phrase, as well as, its dark opposition to the calmer and more wonder-filled notion of "pilgrim tracks" in the Gandhian discourse on nationalism which led towards the ethically good). As he looks back, after the partition, over the years during which the nationalist struggle was waged, he finds countless examples of characters, ideas and actions which always end in vileness, stupidity and cruelty. Indeed, for him, the "teleological drive" (Ricoeur, p. 157) of the entire nationalist past is towards the carnage of the partition. Unlike other writers who saw the violence of the partition as an aberration in the peaceful and tolerant rhythms of our social and religious life, and so turned to the past for consolation and retrieval of values, Manto refuses to believe that the past was another kind of place and another kind of time (for other stories see my *Stories About the Partition of India*). The partition, he is convinced, is not an unfortunate rupture in historical time, but a continuation of it. Each of the bloody tracks backwards into time makes him realise that violence is the characteristic of every chronological segment of the history of India from the beginning of the century to 1947; the nasty, the intolerant, the vengeful is always there at every moment; the "doctrine of frightfulness" (Gandhi's phrase quoted in Draper, p. 211) is not only an aspect of colonial rule, but is also a structural part of the struggle against it. The Gandhian intervention at each instance is merely a temporary and precarious recovery of the ground for virtue, clarity, will and peace. Manto, however, makes it clear that the "punctuated equilibrium" (Stephen Jay Gould's phrase) that Gandhian politics occasionally succeeds in achieving, is inevitably swept aside and rejected as a sign of weakness, hypocrisy and naiveté. Violence always takes over every significant segment of the nationalist past and transforms India before 1947 into a place which is as strange, pernicious and foul as the present—a place where one can see nothing more than a dance of grotesque masks.

2

The story, "1919 Ke Ek Baat," was written in 1951 and published in a volume entitled *Yazid*. The title of the story demands some attention. The casual inconsequentiality of the phrase "Ek Baat" deliberately confronts our presuppositions about the events which happened in 1919 which, officially sanctioned nationalist historiography assures us, foredoomed the British empire. In all the official and popular historical versions, 1919 is a sinister year which finally revealed to everyone that Britain's claim to being an enlightened culture was a sham and that its real intention in India was to continue to inflict "racial hatred" on its people. By keeping the date 1919 in the title agnostically unqualified by any modifiers, Manto makes it clear that he has neither chosen the date arbitrarily nor has any interest in displacing our commonly shared assumptions about what the date signifies in the history of British colonialism. Indeed, Manto affirms unambiguously that for him 1919 signifies the loss of the legitimacy of the British rule, by making the narrator say at the very beginning that, had Sir Michael O'Dwyer not lost his head, 1919 would never have become a "blood-stained" moment in the history of colonial India.[1] But, the incongruity in the title between the story as being nothing more than an account of a randomly selected incident and the momentousness of the historical events which encircle it, makes one suspect that, while Manto may not be concerned with redrawing the "map of truth" (Kermode, p. 130) of the year 1919, he is interested in offering an impertinent, even scandalous, reading of a well known temporal segment of the nationalist discourse.

Further, the title, when considered along with the date in which the story is told in the text (which is the same as the year in which it was published, i.e. 1951), indicates that Manto is deliberately structuring an entirely fictional event, a "feigned plot" (Ricoeur, p. ix), which pretends to be an authentic eye-witness account of happenings in real time, within two different conjunctions of historical facts. The first frame is, of course, provided by the partition and the entire inventory of dates, names, murders and slogans that gives it its factuality. The crazed presence of the partition, Manto seems to insist, intrudes into any interpretative account of our nationalist history.

The second frame is constructed out of a densely vectored series of events in 1919, like the Rowlatt Acts and the violent protests against them from Bombay and Ahmedabad to Delhi, Lahore and Amritsar, General Dyer's arrogance and his callous genocide, Gandhian satyagraha and its sad failure to prevent enthusiastic mobs from doing rather "heinous deeds" (Gandhi's characterisation of mob violence in a letter to J.L. Maffey, Collector of Ahmedabad, on April 14, 1919 but without any knowledge of the shootings at Jallianwalla Bagh the previous day).[2]

It is evident that Manto's intention is to persuade us to read the "odd" incident described in his story within the spaces created by those two sets of historical facticities. He invites us, I think, not only to puzzle out the meaning of the bizarre fictional incident narrated by the storyteller without asking about its truthfulness, but also to recognise that there is a profound link between the two historical dates that frame the incident. From his position as a cultural and existential exile in Lahore in 1951, he wants to suggest that, while 1919 doesn't cause or predict in any mechanical way the horrors of the partition, it contains, what Paul Ricoeur calls, the initial conditions that make them possible; 1919 is merely a part of the sequentiality of events that lead up to 1947. To use Ricoeur again, one could argue that Manto thinks that once 1947 has happened, one can retrospectively find in the fragmentary and disconnected incidents of 1919—amongst other historically significant dates in the nationalist history explored in other stories—a narrative which could be said to prefigure the brutality of the partition. (Often in history, Ricoeur says, "Action is not the cause of result—the result is part of the action," p.136). In making such a connection between 1919 and 1947, Manto seems to indicate that his real purpose in recording an incidental story is to pass a "teleological judgement," not on the British and their indefensible colonial adventure, but on us as Hindus, Muslims and Sikhs. 1919, as he reads the year from his perspective as a reluctant and confused migrant to Pakistan in 1951, seems to be a part of a chronicle which foretells our doom as a civilisation. It is, as if, Manto is on a historical quest backward in time from 1951, and what he finds on his journey back to 1919 is one of the many "bloody tracks" in our national past.

3

The story is told five years after the partition by an unnamed narrator to an unidentified listener on a train which moves across unmarked political and geographical space. Given that the story is, as the narrator repeatedly and insistently reminds the listener, being told a few years after the partition, the lack of geographical markers and of national demarcations is as significant as the definite time which frames the entire text. Both the narrator and the listener speak quite specifically about the fate of Amritsar between 1919 and 1951, but Manto's text itself quite deliberately obliterates the cartographic spaces across which the travellers themselves are moving. What is important here is not the fact of liminality, which is common to all journeys, but the erasure of political boundaries. Fernand Braudel insists that a civilisation is as much a "cultural area," or a set of achievements and activities within identifiable spaces, as it is an understanding about the modes of living on earth which have slowly accumulated over long durations of time (Cf. *On History*). Manto's travellers, who don't have religious, national or cultural identities, move across a blank geographical space. Given that the journey is being undertaken after 1947 when so much religious and cultural pride was being attached to boundaries, I suspect that by obliterating all signs of territorial demarcations, Manto wants us to understand that maps don't bestow virtue, that sharply defined religious enclaves don't ensure the sanctity of moral practices within them and that the separation of communities from each other doesn't legitimise their cultures. He also wants to render it impossible for any group to make self-righteous claims about its own innocence of intentions or to pretend that its own acts of violence were merely acts of retaliatory revenge. In 1947 it was very clear that many people, irrespective of their claims to a particular nationality, had behaved both foolishly and pitilessly. What they had succeeded in creating were not cultural spaces, but their own kingdoms of death, their own areas of moral void, where there were no distinctions between the religious and the vile, the killers and the victims; their actions had not only dehumanised them, but had also contaminated and humiliated everyone. It is quite appropriate, therefore, that in Manto's fable the travellers start out, like millions of refugees and migrants during the partition, from somewhere and are carried forward by the sheer momentum of circumstances towards nowhere; their journey itself has neither a locality, a purpose or a meaning.

4

Before trying to make sense of the dismal tale told by the narrator, it is worth recalling that the story itself is being written by Manto. In 1951, he is in Lahore. If the narrator is a battered refugee in search of a home, Manto is an anguished migrant who has found a destination but who knows that his days of melancholy will never end. He had lived in Lahore once. But his memories, his companions and his writings belong to other cities—cities which are now in another country. He knows that the cities where he had forged his identity as a writer and as a person have become inaccessible and have changed in unrecognisable ways. The place he has now moved to, Lahore, is not home; it is merely a place to which he has been forced by circumstances to escape to. So is Pakistan, which for him is nothing more than a new name for an old geographical space. Unfortunately, Lahore is incapable of offering him either consolation or hope. The longer he lives there, the more he realises, as his stories like "Shaheed Saz," "Dekh Kabira Roya," "Savera," "Jo Kal Aankh Meri Khuli," or "Mere Sahib" also reveal, that it is a city where the dementia of the past is exaggerated by the miasmic corruption of the present, and where everything promises to add in more extravagant ways to life's misery in the future. Unlike Intizar Husain, for whom migrancy and exile are the conditions which define a Muslim and so enable each believer to regard his particular migration out of a stable community into liminal spaces as a secular variation of the grand and sacred narrative about *hijrat*, Manto is far too horrified by the actuality of the sufferings of the migrants themselves, be they Hindus, Muslims or Sikhs, to see in their journeys into exile anything more than an endless repetition of the days of solitude, exhaustion and waste that they have already endured. If, as Salman Rushdie says, "exile is a soulless country," Manto knows from his own personal experiences that the cartographers of that sad place are cynics and bigots, fools and brutes, merciless killers and rapists, and that its boundaries are drawn by smoke, massacres, ash, rubble and the shattered skulls of children. All he can now do, as a migrant, an exile and a refugee in Lahore in 1951, is 'To meditate amongst decay, and stand / A ruin amidst ruins" (Byron).

5

I should, perhaps, notice here the first words of the narrator with which the story opens: "*Yeh 1919 ke baat hai Bhaijan ...*" (In 1919, it so happened *bhaijan ...*).Of course, every traditional *afsana* or *dastan* begins in a similar manner. On the one hand, therefore, the narrator seems to be following the conventional formula for hooking a listener by beginning abruptly and arbitrarily so as to arouse his curiosity. What is significant, however, in the political context of the narrative, is not the acknowledgement of the traditional forms of storytelling, but the fact that the narrator begins to speak, as the train moves across blank spaces, at a particular moment of our history when our assumptions about our sense of our selves had been shattered and the presence of other human beings had become suspect and dangerous.

There is no cause for the narrator to speak; no one has asked him a question and no one has invited him to give an answer or an explanation. Indeed, as we know from the other stories about the partition, it would have been safer for him to remain silent.[3] Yet, he does begin to speak, hesitantly and cautiously at first, then in broken and disconnected sentences as he begins to feel safe. He gives bits and pieces of information about himself and makes fragmentary historical references. His sentences still trail away into silence and all that remains between each sentence fragment is the relentless fury of the iron wheels of the train on iron rails. He picks up his sentences again as if trying to overcome his own internal doubts, apprehensions and fears. It is obvious that it is an effort for him to fill the silence between the people in the compartment with his words and his story. But slowly his voice overcomes the empty space, the mistrust and the dread that separate him from his fellow passengers.

His opening words are the first tentative moves to restore the realm of human speech which had till recently become the site of screams and rage, of cries of supplication and pain, and of hysterical slogans filled with hate and curses (Manto had recorded the ruin of language a few years earlier in the strange fragments about the partition published under the title "Siyah Hashye"). As the narrator emerges into language and begins to discover the elementary structures of stories, he acquires a sense of himself and the listeners as human presences who are similar in kind. Language which had earlier transformed people into phantoms, once again begins to fulfil, however tentatively and momentarily, its primary function of establishing a human community. Yet, since Manto's text tells a story of doom, at the end language crumbles back into silence and all that remains once again is the hallucinatory clatter of iron wheels on iron rails.

Further, the narrator addresses the listener, without first asking him about his religion and national identity or revealing his own, as *bhaijan* (literally, brother). He does so, not only at the beginning, but with a certain insistence, throughout the story. The narrator's use of the word *bhaijan* is deliberate, since in another context he uses the more familiar and colloquial word *yaar* (friend) to address another person in the story. Of course, the narrator is making use of the strategy which storytellers often employ to intercalate the listener into the narrative. Given, however, the fact that 1947 also represents the culmination of a long sequence of efforts to dismember a cohesive society and the sense of kinship between people of different religions, the narrator's attempt to establish brotherhood with the listener should be read as a gesture of in-gathering and of community making. Since the listener quietly accepts the narrator's call to brotherhood as a proper rite of address, the word *bhaijan* seeks to re-establish the grace of companionship (Hannah Arendt's phrase) destroyed by the partition. At the end of the tale, however, this act of communion turns out to be misleading and false. The listener not only suspects the veracity of the narrator's tale, but also fails to find in it anything which would console him for all the dislocation he has suffered or offer him hope for a different future. Unsure about the meaning of the story he has heard, all that remains for him is derision and bewilderment.

Contrary to the deliberate manner in which the geopolitical space is left unmapped, the chronological sequence in the story is carefully crafted. While the story itself is narrated in 1951, it has two temporal locations—a few days in 1919 and 1947. Given the fact that the story is really a meditation on the partition and the reasons for the violence which accompanied it, Manto's main concern is with showing that, though the massacres of 1919 and of 1947 occurred in radically different political circumstances and had different victims and killers, their ethical causes and consequences were similar—as they always are in every condition in which people use force to achieve the ends they desire. The use of mindless power, both in 1919 and 1947, converted living things into corpses as ruthlessly as it transformed those who employed it into grotesques (I am using here Simone Weil's formulation). In Manto's understanding, 1919 haunts 1947 as its malignant shadow.

Unlike Manto, however, the narrator of the tale is blind to the relationship between the incidents of 1919 which preoccupy his fascinated attention and the violence of the partition. The listener, too, is spellbound by the narrator's story and his own dreams of violent revenge and is, therefore, unable to see the bloody tracks that lead from the stupidity of mob violence in the streets of Amritsar in 1919 to the massacres of 1947. Both the narrator and the listener are so deeply entrapped in their own dark fantasies of suffering and retaliatory justice that they neither offer an explanation for the horrors they have witnessed nor find a vision of a more hopeful future. The scepticism of the listener, however, which calls to question many of the interpretations of the narrator's tale, enables us to break the hypnotic control of the storyteller and his tale, and thereby makes it possible for us to pass a reflective judgement both on the fictional and the historical events described.[4]

6

In order to reveal that the ethical presuppositions regarding violence which govern the events of 1919 and 1947 are the same, Manto employs a complex narrative strategy. He tells two stories simultaneously which demand to be read against each other—the enigmatic story told by the narrator and the nationalist story. Both begin with the Rowlatt satyagraha and Jallianwalla Bagh and end with freedom and the holocaust of the partition. The first is, of course, the fictional incident which the narrator describes to the listener. It demands that we pay attention to the sequence of events and the chronological order in which they occur because, like the listener, we have no knowledge of them prior to their being narrated. The events, which the narrator is so passionately concerned with, happen in Amritsar over four days—from the 9th to the 12th of April, 1919. The dates are important because they show that Manto's primary interest is not with the reprehensible genocide by General Dyer at Jallianwalla Bagh on 13th April 1919, but with the protesters against the Rowlatt Act and their actions a few days before April 13th.

The second story, which is familiar both to the narrator and the listener, though each of them has his own way of understanding it, is inscribed within the narrator's story. The narrator assumes that, since the listener's experiences in the past are similar to his own, he also shares with him an elementary knowledge of the facts that make up the history of the nationalist movement from 1919 to 1947. He, therefore, tells the second story with the help of bits and pieces of information marking only important dates and names. These fragments of historical data are scattered at random throughout his own narration of the fictional tale. The problem for the listener, however, is that since the nationalist story is inextricably woven into the fictional tale, the reliability of the narrator's version of the events is suspect. Manto, I think, wants the listener, and by extension the reader, to continuously check each of the references the narrator makes against known and verifiable facts, in the same way as he wants the listener to resist the temptation of accepting the fictional tale by the narrator as being truthful. It is by following the intricate manner in which the two stories are woven into each other that Manto's intentions become clear. The careful way in which important dates are noted suggests that at the heart of Manto's text is neither euphoria over the freedom of India nor anger over the brutality of Jallianwalla Bagh, but the barbarity of the partition in 1947 and the stupidity of violent street politics in 1919.

The first fragmentary sentence by the narrator ("It happened in 1919...") is intentionally ambiguous. By placing the actual year 1919 and all that we (along with the listener) are presumed to know about it within a fictional frame, the narrator not only brings to our attention both the historical narrative and the invented story, but also makes us wonder about the epistemological relation between the two. The narrator's strategy is clever and tantalising. We don't know if we are being invited to suspend disbelief and enter a fictional realm which uses historical references primarily to achieve the effect of reality, or if we are being asked to think about the manner in which the events of 1919 are a part of the structure of the fictional narrative and constitute the meaning of the text.

Immediately after the curious opening statement whose intention is not clearly graspable, the narrator drops the fictive narrative. Unselfconsciously, he slips into a long and rambling account of the nationalist movement from March-April 1919 to 1947, cobbled out of bits and pieces of factual information, memories of actual events witnessed and personal opinions regarding their importance in the last few decades of the colonial period. Our initial response to all that he has to say in quick succession about Gandhi, Dr. Satyapal, Dr. Kitchlew, Sir Michael O'Dwyer, General Dyer, the Rowlatt Acts, or the great communal killings of 1947, is that he is only going over a history that we already know—that he is merely offering, like a dull story-teller on a long train journey, a meandering entry into the fictional world that he actually wants to reveal to us. We give—along with the listener—our lazy consent to the truthfulness of his account because, at first glance, it doesn't seem to be different from the standard inventory of names and places which mark the years between 1919 and 1947 in all the familiar romances about our nationalist history in approved text-books.

It is not surprising that the first factual detail the narrator gives us is about the arrogant stupidity of Sir Michael O'Dwyer and his decision to arrest Gandhi under the Defence of India Act. He reiterates the popular belief that O'Dwyer's act led to the massacres at Jallianwalla Bagh and to the eventual downfall of the British empire. In doing so the narrator makes O'Dwyer into the familiar villain of any nationalist romance. Since a nationalist romance is self-justificatory, and like the mythical figure of *ouroboros*, it "reconstitutes itself by swallowing its own tail" (Jerome Bruner, p. 19), we don't pay much critical attention to the perfunctory reference to O'Dwyer and the exemplary interpretation of the entire incident by the narrator. We accept the narrator's version as a part of a teleologically driven history, in which the inevitable victory at the end condemns the British as the enemies of freedom and offers consolation to those who had endured pain in order to obtain it. As in any nationalist fable, we are neither tempted to pay sufficient attention to the facts which are being offered, nor to consider the manner in which they are being interpreted, nor to judge the end to which they are being presented. We are lulled by the fact that the ritual invocation of the perfidy of O'Dwyer has been uttered, and the suffering of those who had struggled against him and his kind has been vindicated.

The moment, however, we remember that the story is being told in 1951 by a narrator who sees himself as an aimless and bitter wanderer after the partition, the references to 1919, O'Dwyer and others cease to be a part of a triumphant nationalist fable about reprehensible colonialists and innocent Indians. Instead of being intelligible and followable as a simple tale of victory of good over evil, it becomes entangled in a complex network of political ideas, moral problems and actual historical actions which demand "hermeneutic alertness" (Jerome Bruner's phrase, p. 10). We are forced to look for answers to questions about the colonial period and the freedom movement which are comprehensible both within the actual historical context as well as the fictional narrative. We wonder, for example, who the narrator is? What is his national or religious identity? Whose national narrative is he concerned with when he talks about the end of the British empire and freedom? In what historical context are we being required to interpret the events of 1919? What do the narrator, the listener and Manto think about the right of a people to resist laws framed by a foreign power? What means do they think are ethically permissible to resist such laws? Who were, according to them, responsible for the great religious killings of the partition?

Thus, the chronology of the fictional narrative dislocates all that O'Dwyer and 1919 signify in the history of colonial India. Read in this manner, the opening fragment, instead of being a part of the banal repetition of the nationalist's history which is already known and exists before Manto's story, becomes a part of the new scandalous history of the independence movement and the partition which Manto really wants to tell. Manto's subversive narrative doesn't end with freedom in 1947, but crumbles into fear and silence. It shows that for him there is no ethical difference between the degenerate logic of the colonial administration, the blind fury of the mobs of 1919 and the murderous fanatics of 1947—they are all a part of the same awful history of massacres.

Wedged in between the two fragmentary sentences about the "agitation" (Manto uses the English word) in Punjab against the Rowlatt Acts and the ban on Gandhi's entry into the state, is a reference to Amritsar. The narrator, suddenly and without any demand for clarification by the listener, interrupts his opening sentence to specify that his concern is not with what happened in Punjab as a whole but only with events in Amritsar. The narrative placement of Amritsar in the fissure between two broken sentences which together claim that the decline of the British empire began in April 1919 is worth noticing. In the fictional narrative, if April 1919 is identified as the chronological origin of the challenge to colonialism, Amritsar is the place in the political map of India where the legitimacy of a foreign law is radically questioned for the first time. Both the narrator and the listener accept this interpretation in an unproblematic way. In doing so, they give their unquestioning acquiescence to the version of the nationalist romance in which Amritsar is only recalled as a place where first Sir Michael O'Dwyer misread the mood of the crowd which had taken out a procession on Ramnaumi day on April 9th, and then General Dyer shot down unarmed citizens who had gathered peacefully in an open field to celebrate Baisakhi on April 13. For them, Amritsar is simultaneously a place where Hindus, Muslims and Sikhs had agitated together against a foreign power and where the British had added another "bloody page" to their dark history of colonialism. The moment, however, we recall Manto's narrative strategy, this simple structuring of the conflict of 1919 turns out to be naive and seriously flawed. Manto makes it impossible for us to forget our own complicity in the violence that swept across the Indian subcontinent between 1919 and 1951. Thus, Manto temporarily suspends the flow of the narrative in order to focus our attention on Amritsar. The city itself is bracketed by references to two contrary tendencies that invariably marked the freedom movement—the passion of the mobs which lead to widespread violence and Gandhian satyagraha with its ethical commitment to peaceful means and self-sacrifice. Amritsar was as much a site of contestation between the two modes of political action as any other city in the country. The nationalist romance, as we know, is amnesiac towards the former and is content to repeat the truth of the latter as a ritualistic mantra without elaborating on how it actually worked in practice. Since Manto is looking for reasons why we, as Hindus, Muslims and Sikhs, failed to adhere to the most elementary principles of our religious thought and killed each other with the ferocity of beasts, it is not surprising that he chooses as a narrator an ordinary man, who is ambivalent towards the moral implications of the action that must be undertaken to achieve freedom. The narrator, as the rest of the story makes clear, is respectful towards Gandhi and is yet fascinated by the politics of violent revenge; he wants to believe that the protesters in Amritsar were peaceful, but longs to justify those who fought the British in the streets. It is this ambiguity of response that makes the story he has to tell worth listening to, because it gives an insight into some of the reasons for our descent into communal frenzy and murderousness in the 1940's.

Further, Amritsar of 1919 is framed by the narrator within two distinct experiential moments in the history of the city. Both these moments lie outside the fictional narrative. The first experience that frames Amritsar and which, of course, Manto shares with the narrator, is the traumatic one of the partition and the communal carnage that followed. Amritsar of 1951 is represented as a city of death and sorrow—a city of where life is nasty, brutish and uncertain. The narrator, like Manto, sees himself as an exile from it and knows that it is impossible for him to ever return to it.

The second moment in the communal history of Amritsar, which is used by the narrator to frame the imaginary story he wants to tell, in spite of his own encounters with horror, is about life in a society of rich heterogeneity. Manto, himself, I suspect, is more antagonistic towards Amritsar before 1919. His general cynicism would never have permitted him to see any place as an example of an ideal community—though he may have permitted himself to concede to the narrator that, in contrast to what Amritsar did become, it wasn't really such a bad place to live in for anyone.

For the narrator, however, Amritsar before 1919 is a model of a desired community. He speaks of it nostalgically as a place where Hindus, Muslims and Sikhs were aware of their different traditions and yet had an inward regard for each other as members who shared similar conditions of living, being and suffering—where they felt no sense of estrangement from each other and couldn't imagine any cause for it in the future. Such an acknowledgement of Amritsar as a place of communal peace is significant since it is made in 1951 by a narrator who has been a witness to religious killings. Speaking out of his own intense sense of bewilderment, the narrator is quite deliberately constructing a communal history of the city in such a way as to call into question the basic assertions of the proponents of the two-nation theory who claimed that for historical reasons it was both impossible for the Hindus and the Muslims to find civic spaces where they could live together and to make a common political cause against the British. It is quite obvious, however, that for the narrator the notion that the two communities were irreconcilably different is an illusion. That is why in his very next narrative move, he confidently asserts that none of the communities had any hesitation either in acknowledging Gandhi as a Mahatma or in accepting the leadership of Dr. Kitchlew and Dr. Satyapal without being concerned with their religious identities.

If, as the narrator insists, the enmity between the Hindus and the Muslims was neither natural nor culturally fated, then why did the partition occur? It is the search for an answer to that question which makes the reference to Gandhi's role in the protests against the Rowlatt Acts and the priority he is accorded in the chronology of the story worth considering in detail. Perhaps the first thing one needs to comment upon is the fact that the respectful invocation of Gandhi is by a man who has suffered during the partition. In a story about the politics of debasement and hate, for the narrator Gandhi remains, even years later, a Mahatma, a figure of *humanitas*, a man who is recognised as an example of virtue by everyone because he understands that freedom and equality require nothing more than the capacity to be responsible towards oneself and attentive towards others.[5] After the partition, the narrator refers to Gandhi in an attempt to recover out of the ruins some shards of dignity. Yet, as the story unfolds, we realise that since the story the narrator really wants to tell us is about the failure of just vengeance, the presence of Gandhi is meant to be seen as a sign of our civilisational failure which is so profound that nothing can save us.

The second noticeable thing about the Gandhian movement in the text is that its emphasis on clarity of thought, elegance of rational conduct and dignity of co-operative living, is negated by the melodrama of the fictional narrative which follows it with its celebration of mass enthusiasm, casual bravado, and dangerous voluptuousness. For the narrator and the listener, Gandhi is, in spite of their professed admiration for him, ethically and politically incomprehensible; a shadowy presence who disappears once the momentum of a story about a desperate "martyrdom," with an aura of scandalous eroticism, picks up.

Historically, in 1919, Gandhi was so appalled by the mindless violence of the protests against the Rowlatt Acts in Lahore, Ahmedabad, Calcutta, Gujranwalla etc., that he broke down in public in Ahmedabad on the 14th of April and undertook a three day penitential fast to atone for the acts of his followers. Significantly enough, though his fast began on the 14th of April, he had no knowledge of the shootings at Jallianwalla Bagh the day before. Further, from March to May 21, 1919, he issued a series of twenty-one "Satyagraha Pamphlets" in which he repeatedly appealed to people that a satyagraha did not admit of violence. He urged Hindus, Muslims and Sikhs to desist, even under the gravest provocation, from acts of pillage, incendiarism, extortion, murder and rape. Searching for ways of enabling people to realise that they had the right to define themselves as autonomous individuals who could be free only if they made the ethical a part of their political actions, he urged them to take vows of self-suffering and humiliation, prayer and self-discipline, *abhayadan* (the assurance of safety to the innocent as a sacred duty) and religious tolerance. Only then, he was convinced, we could see ourselves and each other as members of a community instead of brutes in a crowd and participants in a *duragraha*. A satyagraha vow was a deliberate, self-critical and thoughtful act which could not be made without a profound awareness of the presence of the other and of his right to be different. It not only restored to each one the right to choose responsibly for himself, it also laid down a minimum moral programme for everyone which was achievable in daily practice.

Since Manto's fictional story is not about nostalgically recovering the past, but about the inconsolable grief over our collective descent into Hobbesian jungles, it is not surprising that the narrator quickly forgets Gandhi. As the narrator continues with his tale, we realise that for Manto the presence of Gandhi is only a temporary stay against insanity. The narrator, oblivious of everything he had said in his historical preamble to the story, begins to gleefully describe the street politics of Amritsar before the 13th of April which he had witnessed. In his version, Amritsar becomes a city of labyrinths, rumours and desperate actions. Crowds surge through its streets looking for victims so that they can exorcise their own sense of humiliation and defeat.

For the narrator, the marauding crowds, which he reads in terms of popular images borrowed from the French Revolution, are signs of the resurgence of vitality, a return of courage. He fails to understand, despite his horrified sense of the partition, that mob actions are always random, unpredictable and callous, that they have the terrifying fluidity of nightmares. Unlike the disciplined ethicality of the responses of the satyagrahis, the behaviour of mobs is invariably foolish and cruel because those who are swept away by frenzy have neither the time for thought nor the patience for justice (cf. Simone Weil, p. 34). According to Manto's text and the available historical records, the furious excitement of the mobs in Amritsar soon after the arrest of Gandhi and the expulsion of Dr. Satyapal and Dr. Kitchlew, was archetypal. Convinced of their own righteousness and charged with a sense of grievance and shame, they roamed the city streets in search of a *pharmokos*, a sacrificial victim whose murder would give them a sense of power (cf. Northrop Frye, p.149). Given that the preferred victims of lynch mobs during riots are often women (Hans Magnus Enzensberger, p. 22), it is not surprising that Miss Sherwood became their most famous victim. The attack on her was used by the British to legitimise all their mythic fears of vicious Indian hordes and redeem their own retaliatory brutality a few days later at Jallianwalla Bagh. While Gandhi saw the ill-willed animosity towards Miss Sherwood as a sign of the "mental lawlessness" (*The Collected Works of Mahatma Gandhi*.Vol. 15, p.230) of the weak, there were some like the narrator who regarded it as a necessary act of murder in any struggle for political redemption.[6] What startles one about the narrator's confession is not merely the fact that he has forgotten his earlier expressions of admiration for Gandhi—a moral amnesia he shares with many—but the specific context of his own tale in which he recalls Miss Sherwood and the gratuitous violence of his tone.

According to the actual historical accounts, Miss Sherwood was a doctor who had worked for fifteen years for the Zenana Missionary Society in Amritsar. On April 10th, after hearing about the riots in the city, she had gone on her bicycle to the five schools under her charge so as to send the six hundred or so Hindu and Muslim girls home. It was during her rounds that she was attacked by the mob. She was beaten mercilessly by young men who shouted slogans in favour of Gandhi and freedom (a fact not recorded by the narrator). Later, she was carried into the house of a Hindu shopkeeper, where her wounds were washed and she was protected from further attacks by people who came back to kill her (for details of the incident see Draper, pp. 65-66).

The narrator's reference to Miss Sherwood comes, not at the point where it ought to have in the historical chronology of events, but at a moment of crisis in the fictional story when political violence, racial contempt, verbal derision and coarse eroticism become indistinguishable aspects of each other. There is a long and difficult sense of emptiness after the narrator finishes describing the story of Thaila, the protagonist, who attacks some British soldiers in the streets of Amritsar on 10th April 1919, and is shot dead by them. For the narrator, it is a tale of unacknowledged martyrdom in the cause of freedom. For a more objective critic of the story, however, it is a predictable adolescent romance full of bravado and enthusiasm but of little political significance. In the embarrassed silence that follows the end of the story, the listener feels as if the wheels are repeating, with dull mechanical regularity, the last phrases of the narrator, "Thaila is dead, Thaila is buried...Thaila is dead, Thaila is buried..." These fragmentary phrases, echoed by the clatter of wheels, seem to reduce the story of Thaila to a mundane and inconsequential incident. Ironically, the narrator fails to see that there is a disturbing gap between his own expressed admiration for Gandhi and his agony over the death of Thaila, and that there are two political possibilities indicated within his own narrative. Thaila's spontaneous decision to kill a British soldier may be full of exultation and energy, but it can't be read as an act which is either personally redemptive or nationally desirable. He is a drunkard, a braggart, a gambler and a bully. There is nothing in the story to indicate that he is a man concerned with national questions. He acts merely on the impulse of the moment. It is, therefore, surprising to find that Leslie Flemming, in her study of Manto, is oblivious to Manto's ironic rage and applauds Thaila as a political activist and bemoans his fate. To do so is not only sentimental nonsense, but is also, in Gandhian terms, an abdication of ethical and political will to the whims of a hooligan (*The Collected Works of Mahatma Gandhi*, No. 15, p. 234). If Thaila has political legitimacy and is a martyr, then so is Dyer; both are mirror images of each other, for the will to power of one is countered by the will to destruction of the other. Thaila doesn't have the intelligence to ask if freedom is worth having at the cost of such murders; Dyer lacks the moral grace to consider if the Empire is worth saving. In Manto's demonology of the nationalist movement, they are both nasty examples of what William Blake identifies as the that grotesque condition when "the soul drinks murder and revenge applauds its own holiness."

There is a further slippage between Gandhian ethicality and politics, and the narrator's unreflecting modes of thought and action. The narrator tells the listener in grave tones that the most tragic aspect of his tale is yet to follow. Immediately afterwards, however, he forgets his rage over Thaila's death. Instead, he begins to describe in sensuous details, the *mujra* Thaila's sisters used to perform for the entertainment of their customers in Amritsar. The listener feels uncomfortable as the narrator loses himself in his recollections of the night world of a sexual epicure. The narrator, however, is incapable of noting that there is little difference between his desire to 'colonise' and 'raid' the bodies of the dancing girls for his own delight and the coercive politics of the Empire. It is beyond his capacities to acknowledge, what moral politicians from Gandhi to Simone Weil have consistently pointed out, that the voluptuary and the coloniser are the same; and that both are so intoxicated by their power to possess and defile their victims that they themselves become grotesques.

After a while, the narrator emerges from his sexual fantasia and resumes his story. He describes how, soon after Thaila's death, some British soldiers heard about his sisters and demanded that they dance for them. He bitterly condemns those Indians who told the British soldiers about Thaila's sisters as "toadies" who, like all collaborators, always put themselves "voluntarily at the service of vile power" (the formulation is Kundera's, p. 125) in order to increase the pain of the defeated. It is during the description of this lurid incident that he suddenly recalls the historically factual attack on Miss Sherwood and inscribes it into his fictional narrative. It is, perhaps, worth noting here that in the larger framework of Manto's text, attacks such as the one on Miss Sherwood were for Gandhi a violation of *abhayadan*, which was not only an important duty of a satyagrahi, but was also the "first requisite of religion" (*The Collected Works Of Mahatma Gandhi*. Vol. 15, pp. 222). The narrator, who has already forgotten Gandhi, unexpectedly bursts into rage, and in an act of compensatory retaliation calls her a *chudel* (a bitch). His verbal assault is, of course, a sign of the fact that he is still so deeply marked by his memories of social defilement that he hopes to recover for himself some sense of pride. The irony is that while he curses Miss Sherwood and is touched by the fate of Thaila's sisters, he fails to see that the entrapment of the dancing girls is not only similar to the predatory attack on the English woman but is also one of its causes. What is shocking, however, is that he forgets that between 1947 and 1951 enraged mobs of Hindus, Muslims and Sikhs had applauded public acts of sexual debauchery and had justified them as fair compensation for their political and religious humiliation at the hands of each other. To take only one example out of many, Kamalabehn Patel recalls that "200 women were made to dance naked for the whole night" in the central hall of the Durbar Sahib in the Golden Temple in Amritsar, and that many people had "enjoyed the unholy show."[7]

While the narrator effaces an obscene present, his memories are still haunted by a past in which nostalgia and pain, loss and desire are strangely mingled. When he resumes his story, at first he offers a fairly conventional comment about the inability of people to believe that even dancing girls can have feelings. Then, he adds, with seeming innocuousness and without any challenge by the listener, that "this country has no sense of self-respect." The statement becomes treacherous, however, the moment we recall that it is being made in 1951 by a narrator who doesn't know where he belongs. In the absence of the name of the nation, we wonder if the country he refers to is India or Pakistan? We also wonder if he is so profoundly lost in the shadowlands of memories that he unselfconsciously assumes that, as in the past, the two new countries shall continue to share the same civilisational space and a common history—and hence, of course, be equally involved in the present shame? The ambiguity of the narrator and the listener towards the formation of the two nations is bewildering. Indeed considering that one reason for the violence of those days was to ensure that the demarcation between the two countries was deeply and ineradicably engraved in the minds of the people, the forgetfulness of the narrator and the listener adds to the phantasmagoria of the story and of the times.

The narrator's tale has two different, but equally scandalous endings. In the first version, Thaila's sisters rip off their clothes, dance naked before the British soldiers and then give a sexually graphic speech, charged with nationalist rhetoric, about their brother's sacrifice for his country's freedom. Mixing politics, eroticism and death, they ecstatically invite the soldiers to "pierce" their "beautiful perfumed bodies" with the "hot irons" of their lust. They also, however, request the soldiers to let them "spit on their faces." After a pause, the narrator, with tears in his eyes, adds that the soldiers responded to the passionate defiance of the sisters by shooting them dead. In the second version, which the narrator admits is more truthful when he is questioned by the listener, the sisters perform a *mujra* for the entertainment of the soldiers. The ending of the first version satisfies the narrator's offended pride, while the ending of the second corresponds to his sense that the times are utterly depraved. What he doesn't realise is that ethically there is no difference between melodramas of retaliatory violence or of base surrender; that both are without meaning, without purpose and without end; that as Blake says, "The beast and the whore rule without controls..."

For Manto, the writer, contemplating the partition from Lahore in 1951, there is a physical, moral and political logic which links the profane desires of the narrator, the massacre at Jallianwalla Bagh, the prurient delights of the British soldiers and the fatal fraternities of mobs from 1919 to 1947. Together, they form a random anthology of incidents in an awful and inexorable tragedy of a degenerate society. All he can do, as he records these tales, is to lament—and lamentation, as we know from religious and psychological sources, is that state of inconsolable sorrow in which one feels that nothing more purposeful will ever offer itself again.

REFERENCES

1. The Congress report on Jallianwalla Bagh concludes that O'Dwyer "invariably appealed to passion and ignorance rather than to reason" (p. 7). It adds that "he invited violence from the people so that he could crush them" (p. 23).

The report also records a meeting between Raizada Bhagat Ram and O'Dwyer which gives some indication of the latter's frame of mind during the Rowlatt satyagraha. Bhagat Ram told O'Dwyer that the meetings had been peaceful and added, "To my mind it was due to the soul force of Mr. Gandhi." Hearing that, O'Dwyer raised his fist and said, "Raizada Sahib, remember, there is another force greater than Gandhi's Soul-force" (p. 44). *Punjab Disturbances*. Vol.1.

The official British report also condemned Dyer's acts as "inhuman and un-British" (p. xxi), but added that "he acted honestly in the belief that what he was doing was right...(p. xxii)." The Indian members of the British Commission refused to endorse these views. *Punjab Disturbances 1919-20.* Vol. 2.

2. On 18 April 1919, Gandhi admitted that his call for civil dis-

obedience against the Rowlatt Acts was a "Himalayan blunder." Cf. Judith Brown, *Gandhi : A Prisoner of Hope*.

3. In the stories about the partition by Manto and others (as in numerous accounts of the Jewish holocaust—and incidentally, in spy-fiction), speech can often lead to betrayal and death. This is, of course, contrary to the assumption of saner societies in which speech enables the world to come into being and ensures the on-goingness of life.

4. It is perhaps worth recording that, while there are countless stories in which hypnotic or mesmeric control leads to brutal death (e.g. Poe or Dickens etc.), tales of enchantment can also result in redemptive release from irrational fears or social rage (e.g. *The Arabian Nights* at one end and Freud at the other).

5. The Hunter Commission report also records that in Punjab in 1919 Gandhi was respected as a *rishi* by the Hindus and as a *wali* by the Muslims. *Punjab Disturbances*. Vol 2, p. 36.

6. General Dyer, for instance, told the Hunter Commission, "I felt women had been beaten. We look upon women as sacred..." He added, that the street where Miss Sherwood had been beaten "ought to be looked upon as sacred..." (p. 61). *Punjab Disturbances*. Vol. 2.

7. Kamalabehn Patel, "Oranges and Apples," *India Partitioned*. Vol. 2. Ed. Mushirul Hasan.

WORKS CITED

Arendt, Hannah. *Between Past and Present*. Harmondsworth: Penguin, 1977.

Bhalla, Alok. *Stories About the Partition of India*. New Delhi: Harper Collins, 1995.

Braudel, Fernand. *On History*. Trans. Sarah Matthews. Chicago: University of Chicago Press, 1980.

Brown, Judith. *Gandhi: A Prisoner of Hope*. New Delhi: Oxford University Press, 1989.

Draper, Alfred. *Amritsar: The Massacre that Ended the Raj*. London: Macmillan, 1981.

Enzensberger, Hans Magnus. *Civil War*. Trans. Piers Spence and Martin Chalmers. London: Granta Books, 1994.

Flemming, Leslie. *Another Lonely Voice: The Life and Works of Saadat Hasan Manto*. Lahore: Vanguard, 1985.

Freud, Sigmund. " Mourning and Melancholia," *Collected Papers*. Vol. 4. Tans. Joan Riviere. London: Hogarth Press, 1925.

Frye, Northrop. *An Anatomy of Criticism*. New York: Atheneum, 1969.

Gandhi, Mohandas Karamchand. *The Collected Works of Mahatma Gandhi.* Vol. 15. Ahmedabad: Navjeevan Press, 1965.

Gould, Stephen Jay. *Bully for the Brontosaurus: Reflections in Natural History.* New York: Norton, 1991.

Hasan, Mushirul. *India Partitioned: The Other Face of Freedom.* Two volumes. New Delhi: Roli Books, 1995.

Husain, Intizar. *Leaves and Other Stories.* Trans. Alok Bhalla and Vishwamitter Adil. New Delhi: Harper Collins, 1993.

Kermode, Frank. *The Genesis of Secrecy: On the Interpretation of Narrative,* Cambridge, Mass.: Harvard University Press, 1979.

Kundera, Milan. *The Art of the Novel.* Trans. Linda Asher. New York: Harper and Row, 1986.

O'Dwyer, Michael. *India As I Knew It.* Delhi: Mittal, 1988.

Punjab Disturbances: 1919-1920. Two volumes. 1920; rpt. New Delhi: Deep Publications, 1976.

Ricoeur, Paul. *Time and Narrative.* Vol. 1. Trans. Kathleen McLaughlin and David Pellauer. Chicago: University of Chicago Press, 1984.

Weil, Simone. *Intimations of Christianity Among the Ancient Greeks.* London: Ark Paperbacks, 1987.

The Craft of Manto: Warts and All

KEKI N. DARUWALLA

Knowing how easily hagiography comes to us, and how nonchalantly we take to adulation—like *kaaz* and *murghab* to water—I propose to take a wry and a rather astringent look at Saadat Hasan Manto. Hagiography, let me hasten to add, would be the wrong term to apply to an unbelieving, hard-drinking rationalist like Manto. His claim to literary apostlehood is understandable. But an attempt needs to be made to balance things out: between his cynicism and the sentimentality that still creeps in; the down to earth story let down by the lack of all sense of place; the obsession with the partition that ignored the political movements that led to it; the uncertain landing after an imaginative leap.

But before we take these up, the essentials need to be put down. Saadat Hasan's commitment to truth was so passionate and complete, that it has to go unchallenged. His worst enemies can't accuse him of sectarianism. And he was totally unselfconscious about his impartiality towards the Hindu and the Muslim—there was no deliberate attempt to match Sikh atrocities with Muslim ones to arrive at some phoney balance. He was above such obvious artifice. His heart was in the right place invariably, and his scorn for the hypocritical and the sanctimonious was unmitigated. And he made the fanatics look not only evil, but also foolish. His social realism has been much talked about. In fact, his entire oeuvre fits so snugly into the slot that one can't even think of putting a different tag on it.

And yet when he lets his hair down as in "Siyah Hashye" Black Marginalia, he can surprise you with the reach of his imagination and the heights it could scale. "Siyah Hashye" could pass off as "existential belle letters" as such pieces were called in USA once. The half page story "Fifty-Fifty" shows Manto taking an imaginative leap that would put him at par with the most new fangled of the moderns. It is a surreal story about a man spotting a big wooden box, presumably in a riot. Since he can't lift it alone, he asks for help and the two of them take it to a safe place and fight over the supposed booty. The man wants to give the helper only one fourth. The other wants fifty-fifty. Then they open the box and a man comes out of it. "He was holding a sword in his hand and he immediately cut the two men into halves, fifty-fifty." This piece is worthy of a Borges or a Cortazar.

Manto rose to fame due to the brilliance, the uniqueness of his vision and the controversial nature of his writing. The Indian middle class, ever prone to a mix of prudishness and hypocrisy in the thirties and forties was shocked out of its wits. And Manto, of course, revelled in whatever shocked them, be it "obscenity" or sudden violence, or the dramatic and brutal manner in which he unmasked hypocrisy. It appears he spent a literary lifetime revelling in his role as the *enfant terrible* of Urdu literature. And there was, of course, the love-hate relationship with the Progressive Writers Union. Like all writers, he was trapped by his times. In 1933, four young progressive writers namely Sajjad Zahir, Ahmed Ali, Rashid Jahan and Mahmud uz-Zafar, all of whom were dissatisfied with the mildly reformist approach to fiction of Premchand and his followers, brought out together an electrifying collection of short stories entitled *Angare* (Live Coals).[1] The stories, which included one by Manto, "were consciously revolutionary, openly ridiculing religion and suggesting the oppressiveness of traditional and social institutions, especially those relating to women."

Meanwhile, in London, in November 1934, some Indian students led by Mulk Raj Anand and Sajjad Zahir, moved by the anti-fascist activity of European writers, had organised the Indian Progressive Writers Association. Later, Sajjad Zahir and Ahmed Ali established the All India Progressive Writers Association, holding its first meeting in Lucknow in April 1936, a meeting presided over by Premchand. As Leslie Flemming shows both the manifestoes issued in London in 1935 and Lucknow in 1936, espoused

(a) nationalism, and (b) literature as a force for social uplift in India. The Lucknow manifesto stated, "We want the new literature of India to make its subject the fundamental problems of our lives. These are the problems of hunger, poverty, social backwardness and slavery."[2] The first issue of *Naya Adab* (April 1939) defined progressive literature as follows: "In our opinion progressive literature is that literature which looks at the realities of life, reflects them, investigates them and leads the way toward a new and better life..."

The Russian influence on Manto is well-known. He after all started his literary career as a translator of Russian stories. Thus, the crucible in which his writing was cast was mainly influenced by the French realists—Maupasant and Balzac— and the Russian writers from Tolstoy to Gorky.

The critical attention he received got focussed on his sensational stories like "Bu" (Odour) or "Thanda Gosht" (Cold Meat) due to which, and for other reasons, he fell out with the progressives. Thus, the critical attention was directed to the more virulent and shocking aspects of his writing, the sudden violence and the seamy side of life that he portrayed, especially of the *demi-monde*. The partition stories also took a fair share of critical attention. The characters that peppered his stories were out of the ordinary, often coming from the detritus of society. The whore, the pimp, the street *dada* jostled for place with those who fought for freedom. And there were, of course, the religious bigots, both Hindu and Muslim, whom he reviled. His characters, thus acted as magnets for criticism, both for and against. His themes—the loss of innocence (but not of grace)—attracted the critics. So did his vision later, terrifying, and nihilistic yet moral in its own unique way. His stories on the partition and on prostitutes had a rivetting political and social relevance. If his craft attracted the critic's eye, it was more in passing. It is this aspect which I propose to take up.

Manto wrote the classical short story, directed to a purpose, with a well-fleshed middle and definitive ending. The character played an important part.

The modern short story which can be just the presentation of a mood, or a sense of loss; where the ending, such as there is, is left hanging in the air like a wisp of mist in the moutains; where the past of the character does not have to be delineated, had not caught up with Manto as yet.

Looking at the plot structure of many of his stories one notices the flaws—the vagueness in regard to detail, the predetermined end, at times an overdose of melodrama perhaps unconsciously imbibed through his association with the film world. Sometimes even normal logic is not adhered to, and hence verisimilitude becomes a victim. One gets the impression that events are being channelized pell-mell, without much regard to their verisemblance, to a preordained end. The fates decree, as it were, and the furies drag the story by the hair to the guillotine.

"Swaraj Ke Liye," (The Price of Freedom) is a story about two young ardent Congressites, Shahzada Ghulam Ali and Nigar, who fall in love. The story is set in Amritsar quite a few years after the Jallianwalla Bagh massacre. Ghulam Ali makes a name as a fiery young Congress worker. Every few days a 'dictator' is appointed to the Congress camp and Ghulam Ali is the 40th 'dictator' to take over since his predecessors have been sent to prison. In this position one does not last for more than a few days before being sent to jail. The scene is set. Post Jallianwalla Bagh Amritsar and two fervent Muslim Congress workers. Then enters the Baba. He heads an ashram and carries a halo about him. All political movements in Amritsar take place with his blessings. One is not left guessing about what Manto thinks of ashrams: "I had seen many ashram inmates in my time. There was something lifeless and pallid about them, despite their early morning cold bath and long walks. With their pale faces and swollen eyes, they somehow always reminded me of cow's udders." To a full-blooded man like Manto this is how an ashramite would appear.

The artifice creeps in when it is the Baba who joins Ghulam and Nigar in wedlock. How a Hindu Baba, heading an ashram, joins two Muslims in marriage is never explained, perhaps because it is not explainable. The Baba asks Nigar to join the ashram and makes a long speech at the wedding where he states that the sexual link was not as important as it was made out to be in a marriage. "A true marriage should be free of lust," he says. The sanctity of marriage was more important than the gratification of the sexual instinct. All this stirs Ghulam Ali who states, trembling with emotion, "I have a declaration to make. As long as India does not win freedom, Nigar and I will live not as husband and wife but as friends." He asks Nigar whether she would like to mother a child who would be a slave from the moment of his birth? She wouldn't. After marriage Ghulam Ali is bundled off to jail for eight months. After he returns they obviously live together, but with sexual abstinence. The return to conventional life is humdrum and boring, compared to the excitement of their days with the Congress. Many years later, the narrator meets him and finds that he is now doing well and owns shoe shops. However, he does not stock rubber footwear. Ghulam Ali hates rubber, the reason being the use of condoms which he and Nigar resorted to in order to keep their vow to the Baba that he would not father a child in an enslaved India. Later he gives up condoms and has children but the bitter antipathy against rubbers lingers. The story ends with his child coming into the shop with a balloon, and Ghulam Ali in a tantrum, pouncing on the balloon and bursting it and throwing the ugly rubber out of the shop.

The story reflects detailed, almost blow-by-blow plotting, and also shows Manto's cockiness which seems to declare that he can carry off almost anything. But the basic flaw in the story remains—the Baba being substituted for the Qazi. A Hindu Baba was perhaps needed because he had to talk about freedom and perhaps hint at sexual abstinence. That is one thing a Qazi won't do at a *nikah*. Manto's distrust of ashrams also comes through when he talks about Nigar joining the ashram. "Why should she, who was herself pure as a prayer, raise her hands to heaven?" The ending, of course, is superb—the child's balloon being pricked but one can't forget the flaw in the story—the Hindu Baba marrying two Muslims and preaching sexual abstinence in the bargain. There is critical speculation to the effect that the Baba really stands for Gandhiji. He is held in great respect and his views are similar to Gandhi's. All one can say here is that if Manto had to induct Gandhi into the story, he should have managed it with greater finesse.

Another trait of Manto's is the total lack of any local detail, whatsoever. His sense of geographical spaces was vague and undefined. He was born in Amritsar, yet the only reference you get in his stories based in Amritsar, is possibly Jallianwalla Bagh. *Coocha* and *galli*, lane and *mohalla*, street and road—everything is nameless, paved with anonymity. What does this reveal? Either he was too impatient to plot and work out an idea carefully. That would have meant visually capturing an area and putting in the details—all of which can get a little tedious for the writer, and certainly for an impatient genius.

The second alternative is to concede that he was too arrogant to bother about such detail as names and places. Worse still, he may have even thought that this was not necessary.

For me, setting the scene is very important. Either you create a place out of your imagination and fill in the detail as you wish. That can be very exciting at least to start with. Or you research and stick to detail. Manto does neither and that's a pity. You lose out both on authenticity and local flavour. If he thought that all that there was to a short story was to work out an idea, then he did poor service to his craft and his art.

His Jews, Anglo-Indians, Christians and Parsis are stereotyped and two dimensional. Take "Mozel," a story set in Bombay, about a Jewess, Mozel, and Sardar Trilochan Singh who falls in, and then out, of love with her. And there is Kirpal Kaur whom Trilochan finally falls in love with and whom Mozel saves. Now Manto lived for years in Bombay. You could have expected some detail. At the height of the riots, Mozel simply clad in a kaftan sets out with Trilochan to rescue Kirpal Kaur. Not one place is ever named, as if Manto was writing in a nameless limbo. Kirpal Kaur lives in a *mohalla* with her blind mother and crippled father. Her brother Niranjan "lived in another suburb". Mozel works "in one of the big department stores in the Fort area." Here at least he pin-points something. When the two set out to save Kirpal, who lives in a Muslim locality, this is how Manto describes it, "They came to a street which led to the *mohalla* where Kirpal Kaur lives." Now if that's all the local flavour you need, then someone sitting in Bhiwandi could write a story about a Warsaw Ghetto during the Nazis.

Except for Mozel the other characters are two dimensional and lifeless. Mozel's end is heroic and bloody, and the other characters seem to be there to provide a chance for her to carry her part through. It could be said that Mozel was Manto's answer to the general denigration of and the onslaught on the Jews. But this would be far fetched.

There is a terrifying image at the end—three gunny sacks dripping blood. And there is humour. When Trilochan Singh kisses Mozel on the lips for the first and the only time, she says, "Phew. I already brushed my teeth this morning. You needn't have bothered." Manto's intentions are transparent. Here he sets out to prove that this scantily clad Jewess, who is free with her love, is a bolder and better person than the rest of the characters put together.

Manto's sympathies with the waifs and strays of our society are obvious. At times a surge of compassion seems to spark off a story. Some of those are unsuccessful. His heart is in the right place and he writes against the male's exploitation of the wife, the woman, the prostitute. But strong feeling does not necessarily make for strong art.

Take one of the worst examples of Manto writing —at least as he comes out sieved through translation. The story I refer to is "By the Roadside" (Sarak Ke Kinare) and is included in Khalid Hasan's anthology of Manto's stories. The story starts as follows:

Yes, it was this time of year. The sky had a washed blue look like his eyes. The sun was mild like a joyous dream. The fragrance from the earth had risen to my heart, enveloping my being. And, lying next to him, I had made him an offering of my throbbing soul.

He had said to me: "You have given me what my life had always lacked. These magic moments that you have allowed me to share have filled a void in my being. My life would have remained an emptiness without your love, something incomplete. I do not know what to say to you and how, but today I have been made whole. I am fulfilled. Perhaps I no longer need you."

And he had left, never to come back.

Now this is as bad a start as you can ever get. Nothing is defined. There are cliches like "The sun was mild like a joyous dream" which perhaps hints at an early winter sun. Were they living in a house, a *kholi*, a *chawl*? What had the fellow walked out of? And where had the bugger gone—to the war? to the high seas? To the next kotha?

The dialogue is as phoney as it can get. He says, "These moments we have shared have filled my emptiness. The atoms of your being have made me complete. Our relationship has come to its pre-ordained end." Firstly no one talks like this. Secondly, there is no logical nexus between his having become "complete" through "the atoms of her being" and their relationship coming to an end.

She protests. He answers, "The honey which bees suck from half-opened flowers can never adorn the flowers or sweeten their bitterness." This is worse than some third rate serial on Zee TV or Doordarshan.

The story is supposedly written by a woman who is betrayed, or rather deserted by her man. But there isn't a single feminine touch to the writing. In fact Manto loses his concentration, as for instance, in the following passage: "A woman can weep. She cannot argue. Her supreme arguments are (sic) the tears which spring from her eyes." This is not how a woman would write. This is exactly how a male from Punjab would write.

Worse follows. When the man is about to go he says, "If you must leave, I cannot hold you back, but wrap these tears in the shroud of your handkerchief and take them away and bury them somewhere, because when I cry again, I would know that you once performed the last rites of love." This is Manto's compassion getting mixed up with sentimentality at its worst.

The story "Sarak Ke Kinare" (By the Roadside) is about a man who walks out on his woman perhaps without realising that she is pregnant. It ends with a postscript:

> The police have found a new-born baby by the roadside. Its naked body had been wrapped in wet linen with the obvious intention that it should die of cold and exposure. However, the baby was alive and has been taken to hospital. It has pretty blue eyes.[3]

Here the end seems premeditated. Manto seems to have worked backwards. Whatever precedes the end has been put together in a slam bang fashion to ensure the surprise ending, if it can be called a surprise. A short story needs a lot of staff work, as we say in bureaucratic parlance. A lot of details have to be filled in to set the scene as it were, and get it right. Manto's staff work often failed him.

I must, however, add that Urdu scholars tell me that this is one story where Manto completely veered away from his usual style. The style is remarkable for its high pitched lyricism and the story could almost be taken as a prose poem if we allow our imaginations some liberty. But in translation the lyricism does not come through.

Meldrama creeps in often, for instance in "Thanda Gosht" (Cold Meat) where Kalwant Kaur finds her rioting lover, Ishwar Singh, unable to perform in bed. His foreplay turns her on. "Ishar Sian, you have shuffled me enough, it's time to produce your trump," she says languidly. He tells her why he can't. He had slaughtered six members of a family with his *kirpan* and the seventh, a beautiful woman, he carried away only to discover during the sex act that she was already dead. Here the bizarre and the melodramatic dovetail into each other as Ishwar Singh withdraws from or consumates necrophilic sex. Kalwant Kaur stabs him in fit of jealous rage even before he makes his near necrophilic confession. The story is dramatic enough, as it is. That final dagger-thrust was unnecessary. Why should she stab him at all? Why must sexual death be duplicated by physical death or hurt?

There are occasions when Manto does not seem to know when to stop. The story "Khuda Ki Qasm" (I Swear by God) is told by a liaison officer who supervises the recovery of abducted woman, and so comes to India often. In Jalandhar he notices a near mad Muslim woman in dire straits looking out desperately for her missing daughter. The officer, for some reason, tries to convince the old unkempt woman that her daughter is dead. He hopes thereby to facilitate her return to Pakistan. The woman retorts that no one could kill her daughter because she is so beautiful. So beautiful that no one could dream of even lifting his hand against her.

Then, on one of his trips, the liaison officer sees the old woman at the Farid Ka Chowk at Amritsar, still searching for her daughter. He wants to persuade her to accompany him to Pakistan. As he crosses the road to talk to her, he notices a couple passing by. "The woman's face was covered with a short veil. The man accompanying her was a young Sikh, very robust and handsome..." The Sikh recognizes the mother and points her out to the woman. She lifts her veil to take a look at the old woman and the liaison officer sees her "exquisitely (sic) beautiful, rosy face framed within her white chaddar."[5]

"Your mother," the Sikh tells her. But her daughter squeezes his arm and says "Let's go." The mother recognizes her and cries out to the officer that she has seen her daughter. Seeing how she has been ignored by the daughter he tries to convince her that her daughter is dead. "I swear in the name of God she is dead," he says. "Hearing this the woman fell in a heap on the ground."

Now that last bit was unnecessary. The agony of it all had been brought out through the beautiful daughter spurning her mad mother who has been brought to this state in the endless search for her daughter. Why does Manto have to wring out more pathos by killing the poor woman at the end? The story does symbolize the death of relationships as Leslie A. Flemming avers. But the relationship is already dead when the daughter turns her face from the mother. It is her collapse which is unnecessary. She would have become an even more tragic figure if she had wandered around like a ghost, looking for her daughter. Physical death, in any case, was not a scarce commodity during the partition. It was all around.

And one feels quite petty in pointing out one odd detail. No Muslim woman would dare wear a veil in Amritsar in March 1948 (there were no Muslim women in Amritsar by 1948). The veil would have attracted hooligans. It would have also been an open invitation to the police to seize her and deport her to Pakistan. No burkas were seen in East Punjab in 1948.

Yet Manto's compassion is palpable throughout the story which starts with a general discourse on the fate of abducted woman on both sides of the new border. Manto works himself into a passion when he thinks of raped women now big with child. "Who would be the owner of what lay inside these stomachs? Pakistan or India?...And who would bear the responsibility of these nine months of travail? Pakistan or India? Will all this be duly recorded in the account books of man's inhumanity or nature's callousness? But was there any page still left blank to make more entries?"[6] There is passion here and compassion and the wrenching exposure of filial indifference and ingratitude. And yet the death of the old mother was not necessary.

The surprise has to be left till the very end, of course, and in his bid to shock there is a sudden eruption of violence and death at the end of the tale. In "Sau Candle Power Ka Bulb" (A Hundred Candle Power Bulb) a prostitute who is kept working overtime by her pimp, and hence unable to sleep, smashes his head with a stone and then snores away peacefully. The ending in "Mozel" is in keeping with the heroic endings of our Bombay films. The thing to note is that violence is often used by Manto to round off a story effectively.

A question which has not, perhaps, been probed is the insularity one encounters in Manto. Politically, he hardly ever reaches beyond Jinnah and Gandhi, Jallianwalla Bagh and the partition. He lived in momentous times—the Spanish Civil War, the Great War, the rise of fascism, the Jewish holocaust. They were times of doctrinal wars— Nazism and Facism versus Communism. And the democracies had, of course, taken all three of them on. He worked for a time with the All India Radio, and so should have been sensitive to events on the world stage. For instance, Iqbal was alive to every global cross current. But in Manto's corpus there is hardly any such mention, as if the doors of his mind were closed to what was happening in Europe or Asia or North Africa.

This is not strictly true. As shown in his "Chacha Sam Ke Nam Khatoot," (Letters to Uncle Sam) or his letter on Kashmir, Manto was very alive and sensitive to political currents. But unless they referred to either the freedom struggle on the subcontinent, or to the stupidity of the partition, they never made an appearance in his fiction.

Secondly, the Lahore Resolution on the formation of Pakistan, was passed by the Muslim League in 1940. Surely, Manto must have seen the writing on the wall. A sensitive person, as all good writers are supposed to be, was expected to see what this would lead to. For instance, English poetry of the thirties broods all along and is sprayed with premonitions of the coming war. But Manto, in his stories written right till 1946, seems oblivious of things to come, as if he never sensed or saw the shadow advancing over the Indian subcontinent.

And yet there are stories where he transcends it all. "Hatak" (Insult) is an absolute shocker, where Sugandhi after driving out her worthless lover, Madho, lies down with her mangy dog in her bed. Though the last half of the story moves on an emotional high, it can never be called melodramatic. The story builds its own explosive dynamism as it goes along. Sugandhi moves from passivity to action.The end is nihilistic as Sugandhi ends up in utter moral despair. A note of utter despair is also struck in regard to human relationships.And Manto has been very careful about his craft. The detail has been filled in meticulously. Take this description of Sugandhi's room:

> In one corner of the room on a wooden bracket lay her cosmetic-rouge for her cheeks, red lipstick, face power, combs, metal hairpins. A parrot lay asleep in a cage hanging from a long peg, its neck hidden in the plumage on its back. Pieces of raw guava and rotten orange peels lay scattered inside the cage, mosquitoes and moths hovering over them. Near the bed stood a cane chair, its back soiled by the oily heads constantly resting against it. By the side of the chair rested a beautiful teapoy on which lay a portable gramophone, covered with a tattered piece of black cloth and used gramophone needles lay scattered all over the floor. Right above the gramophone hung four framed photographs. A little apart from these photographs, facing the door hung a glossy picture of Lord Ganesha, almost hidden under a layer of fresh and dry flowers. The picture had been peeled off from a bale of cotton cloth and framed. Near the picture was a small alcove in which was kept a cup of oil and a small clay lamp. In the stuffy, airless room the flame of the lamp stood up straight like a sandal paste mark on a devotee's forehead. Ashen residues of burnt joss-sticks lay curled on a wooden bracket.[4]

This is Manto at his best, the mind keen and alert and carrying on a dialogue with the surroundings, as it were. "Siraj" is the story of a betrayed woman who finds herself in a whore-house after the man she eloped with walked out on her. She comes to Bombay, and despite her "profession" keeps her virginity intact. Then she goes back to search for her betrayer, walks out on him and takes to the "profession." It is a perfect story with a surprise, psychological twist at the end. In many of his stories, including "A Matter of Honour," "Kali Salwar" (The Black Trousers) or "Naya Kanoon" (The New Constitution), one encounters a perfection of sorts. "The New Constitution" can be called a parable not only on the 1935 Government of India Act, but also on the 'Gradual' home rule being doled out in driblets by the British to the Indians. It is deservedly treated as a classic.

There are quite a few others of such ilk. Many of his bad stories one can put down to the pressures of penury and meeting deadlines, or drink, which killed him at the young age of forty-three. Quite a few of his stories glitter even today like perfectly cut diamonds. And if one achieved such perfection even in a handful of stories, despite the handicaps of a footloose life-style and hard drinking, one should be beyond the cavil of petty reviewers like yours truly.

NOTES AND REFERENCES

*This paper is based exclusively on translated Manto texts, namely stories rendered into English by Tahira Naqvi (*The Life and Works of Saadat Hasan Manto*. Introduction by Leslie Flemming, Lahore: Vanguard Books), Khalid Hasan (*Kingdom's End and other stories*, London: Verso) and Jai Ratan (*The Best of Manto*, Delhi: Sterling Publishers). While one has great respect for the translators, most Urdu scholars aver that these translations are just about adequate and at times do not do justice to the richness and resonance of the texts.

1. *The Life and Works of Saadat Hasan Manto*, Leslie A. Flemming. Lahore; Vaguard Books, 1985.
2. Ibid.
3. *Kingdom's End and Other Stories*, translated by Khalid Hasan. London: Verso.
4. *The Best of Manto: A Collection of his Short Stories,* translated by Jai Ratan. Delhi: Sterling.
5. Ibid.
6. Ibid.

Lord Shiva or The Prince of Pornographers: Ideology, Aesthetics and Architectonics of Manto

HARISH NARANG

Let me begin this paper by referring to a few incidents relating to Manto's literary life. When "Bu," a well-known story by Manto, was published in the annual number (1944) of *Adab-e-Lateef*, the daily, *Prabhat*, published from Lahore, observed that such stories "clearly corrupt the minds of young boys and girls and pollute public tastes."[1] In fact, the editor of *Prabhat* went on to demand a three-year imprisonment for the likes of Manto for writing 'dirty' stories. This was the typical reaction of a 'purist'. Writing in *Taraqqi Pasand Adab*, Ali Sardar Jafari observed that such stories were made of "stinking stuff" and that "it is their stink which makes them reactionary."[2] It was the typical reaction of a progressive writer.

When Manto resumed writing stories after migrating to Pakistan—it was quite an effort and after quite some time, as he himself tells us—his second story "Khol Do" was banned by the government of Pakistan—strange as it may seem—for "breach of public peace."[3] In fact, the cautious Pakistan government went on to impose a six-month ban on the magazine, *Naqoosh*, which had published the story.

"Thanda Gosht," which was written earlier than "Khol Do" but was published later, also attracted legal ire—this time on the usual charges of obscenity. However, Faiz Ahmed Faiz, deposing before the Press Advisory Council, of which he himself was the Convenor, while absolving the story of the charge of obscenity, faulted it for not fulfilling "those higher objectives of literature because in this (story) there is no satisfactory solution to the basic problems of life."[4]

Summing up Manto's life, Hanif Rane observed that Saadat Hasan Manto suffered from "as bloated an ego as that of Lenin or Muhammad Ali Jinnah."[5] Similar sentiments had been expressed about him in his life-time by Devendra Satyarthi in his story "Naye Devta."[6]

At the other extreme of opinion is Mumtaz Shirin, who stated that although, "In the process of internalising the poison of life in his stories, Manto had become a cynic, he had full faith in man; like Maupassant, he makes us aware that while man has filth, evil and ugliness in him, yet humanity is beautiful."[7]

There have been very few writers in the history of world literatures who have evoked—on second thought, I consider 'provoked' a more appropriate expression—such extreme reactions from reviewers and readers, priests and laymen, lawyers and judges, critics and creative writers. And as is evident from the above, these extreme reactions were completely contradictory as well. Manto has been, for instance, accused of being both a communist and a reactionary at the same time, and if that is not weird enough, by the same person and for the same piece of writing.[8] He has been called an extremely obscene writer who tried to corrupt young minds with cheap titillating descriptions (see quotation at '1' above) as well as a writer with "a spiritual experience"[9] who could pen a story like "Toba Tek Singh." His stories have been considered a threat to the national peace of Pakistan and have been banned (see quotation at '3' above), but he has also been hailed as the greatest story writer who did not only Pakistan but the entire Indian subcontinent proud. Strangely enough, Manto elicited similar extreme contradictory reactions even in his death:

> Manto is dead. Well, the world is rid of an obscene writer. However, I am at a complete loss to understand the reaction of these Pakistanis—organising meetings, passing resolutions, writing articles, bringing out special

numbers of magazines. And all this on the death of an obscene writer! Why all this hullabaloo...[10]

And if this confusion were not enough, Manto made it worse by calling himself "a fraud of the first order"[11] who could have done better by taking up a "gentleman's profession like serving the government, or selling ghee or inventing some miracle drug."[12] And on yet another occasion, he suggested that his grave carry the following inscription by way of an epitaph:

> Here lies buried Saadat Hasan Manto. And buried in his heart are all the secrets and techniques of story writing. Buried under tons of soil, he is wondering who is a greater story writer—God or he himself.[13]

Now, how do we discover the real Manto among these various Mantos? How do we find out which of the evaluations about him is closer to the truth? Is he really an obscene writer who is a threat to civilised societies? Or, is he really a great story writer who took upon himself the onus of exposing the hypocrisy behind the facade of civility? Well, to answer these questions and to understand the true significance of his art we need to examine—as is the case with all literary evaluations—Manto's ideology, aesthetics and architectonics. But this leads us to the next set of questions about him. Does Manto have an ideology—he who not only always denied having one but who denounced those aligned one way or the other? Secondly, and more significantly, does Manto have an aesthetics—he who relished writing on the filthy and the ugly, the sick and the stinking, the violent and the venomous? And finally, does Manto have a definite technique of story writing which makes him not only different from his contemporaries like Krishan Chander, Ismat Chugtai and Rajinder Singh Bedi but from other story writers of the Indian subcontinent?

Scattered amongst his non-fictional writings—defences and depositions, essays and epistles—are scores of statements, brief and elaborate, which deal with the definition of literature, its relationship with society, the responsibility of a writer, the role of didacticism in creative writing, the nature and significance of language and of literature, the significance of style and metaphor, and similar issues. It shall be my endeavour in the following pages to construct Manto's ideology, his aesthetics and his architectonics from these observations.

Manto considered literature to be something very serious and he defined it as the pulse of a nation, of a community. To quote him:

> Literature is not a dead body, which a doctor and his students can place on a table and begin to dissect. Literature is not a disease but is its alternative. Literature is not a medicine to be administered in a prescribed manner and quantity. Literature is the pulse of a nation, a community—literature gives news about the nation, the community to which it belongs, its health, its illness. Stretch your hand and pick up any dust-laden book from an old shelf—the pulse of a bygone era will begin to beat under your finger-tips.[14]

Discussing the subject matter of literature—any literature—Manto linked it up with the two most basic needs—he calls them hungers—of human life. The first one is for food and the second for the proximity and possession of the opposite sex. All human activities, Manto observed, could be reduced to these two kinds of hunger and the two types of relationships spawned by these hungers, namely, one, between food and the human stomach and two, between man and woman. These, according to him, have been the most ancient of relationships—since time immemorial—and are eternal. He observed:

> That's why whatever social, cultural, political and war-related problems there are around us today, these two "hungers" are at the bottom of them all. If we lift the

veil from the face of the current war then we shall see that behind mountains of dead bodies, there is nothing but "hunger" for nationhood.[15]

Manto believed that a writer—any writer—in any part of the world—progressive or reactionary, old or young—was faced with all kinds of social problems. "He selects from amongst those and writes about them. Sometimes in favour, sometimes against."[16]

How does a writer go about selecting, from amongst hundreds and thousands, those problems on which he wishes to focus his attention? Manto has commented on this aspect in detail, providing us with a significant opportunity to peep into his mind. "A writer picks up his pen only when his sensibility is hurt," said Manto while defending his story, "Dhuan," against charges of obscenity in the court of the Special Magistrate, Lahore. "I don't remember it clearly now since so much time has elapsed," observed Manto, "but surely I must have been hurt on seeing some situation, gesture or incident that provokes the pen of a writer."[17] Elaborating again on the choice of a subject, Manto observed in his lecture at Jogeshwari College, Bombay, that routine situations of life did not interest him:

> When a woman in my neighbourhood gets beaten by her husband every day and then cleans his shoes, she gets no sympathy whatsoever from me. But I feel a strange kind of empathy for a woman in my neighbourhood who fights with her husband, threatens to commit suicide and then goes away to see a film, keeping her husband on tenterhooks for two hours.[18]

Again, it was not just physical events which motivated Manto:

> A woman who grinds grains the whole day and then sleeps soundly at night can never be the heroine of my stories. Instead, a rank sinful prostitute who stays awake

at night but who while sleeping during the day, gets up suddenly from a nightmare in which old age is knocking at her door, may be the heroine of my story.[19]

Manto was to attract a lot of flak—Raja Sahib Mehmudabad was merely one of the many who criticised him severely[20]—for making prostitutes the principal characters of his stories. Referring to his choice, Manto observed:

> If any mention of a prostitute is obscene then her existence too is obscene. If any mention of her is prohibited, then her profession too should be prohibited. Do away with the prostitute, reference to her would vanish by itself.[21]

Defending his right to talk of prostitutes, he said:

> We can discuss lawyers openly. We can talk about barbers, washermen, vegetable sellers and inn-keepers. We can tell tales about thieves, petty criminals, dupes and those who way-lay. We can spin yarns about djinns and fairies...why can't we think of the prostitute? Why can't we pay attention to her profession? Why can't we say something about those people who visit her?[22]

Developing his defence further, Manto observed that it was a writer's prerogative to show society "the face of its weakness."

> The house of a prostitute is in itself a dead body which society carries on its shoulders. Until it is buried somewhere by society, there will be discussions about it. This dead body may be highly decomposed, it may be stinking, it may be terrifying, it may be frightening, but there is no harm in looking at its face. Does it bear no relation to us? Are we not related to it at all? Well, once in a while, we remove the shroud and peer at its face and also show the same to others as well.[23]

As I have shown elsewhere,[24] it is not just prostitutes, but most people on the periphery—the Mangus, the Bishen Singhs, the Neetis, the Sugandhis, the Shankars and the Thaila Kanjars—whom Manto chose to make the subjects of his stories. And his choice was no accident but a conscious socio-political act of empathy with those sections of society who survive on the fringes—those hapless victims of man's exploitation at the hands of fellow men. And these people on the periphery—as Manto believed and depicted—not only show a greater sense of humanist values than those who occupy the core, but also carry forward whatever is of permanent significance in a human society which finds itself in turmoil.

The question of looking for the intention of the author is significant in the case of Manto from another point of view as well. Manto repeatedly stated that he never resorted to didacticism in his stories. Referring to "Dhuan" again, Manto observed:

> In this story, I have taught no lessons, given no lectures on moral behaviour, since I do not consider myself to be either a preacher or a teacher of morals.[25]

In another essay—"Afsananigar Aur Jinsi Masail"—he stated categorically that "we writers are not prophets. We look at a phenomenon, a problem from various points of view in various circumstances and whatever we make of it, we present to the world at large but we never force the world to accept our point of view."[26]

Such statements by Manto led his critics to deduce—absolutely erroneously, of course—that Manto had no lessons to teach, and no morals to preach. Muhammed Hasan Askari, for instance, observed:

> Manto did through his stories what an honest (honest not in matters political but honest in a literary sense) and a true literateur ought to have done while writing in those circumstances and so immediately after the events. He puts the question of good or bad beyond the pale of

controversy. His point of view is neither political nor social, nor even moral but literary and creative. Manto only tried to understand the relationship between acts of cruelty and the various points of view of the perpetrator and the victim of cruelty.[27]

Not only does the above evaluation completely ignore the essential point of view expressed by Manto in his stories, it is full of the most obvious contradictions. It was Thomas Hardy who had once defined a good story as one which "slaps us into a new awareness." If there is one writer whose stories fit the bill, it is Manto. Not only his well-known stories like "Kali Salwar," "Bu," "Dhuan," "Khol Do," "Thanda Gosht," "Oopar, Neeche aur Darmian," "Babu Gopinath," "Hatak," "Naya Qanoon" and "Toba Tek Singh," but also scores of those really 'capsule' ones published under "Siyah Hashye" and "Dekh Kabira Roya" slap one—nothing less—into a new socio-political and, more significantly, moral awareness. The point to remember is that although Manto did not state his moral at the end of the story, he did have one which can be deduced from his intentions implicit as in his stories. As he himself put it, stories like "Kali Salwar," were not written for pleasure.

A work of literature being a social document, events—big or small—in the life of a society or a nation inspire its writers to create literary texts around them. Some events, however, are of such an intensity or a cataclysmic nature that instead of provoking a writer's sensibility into action, they shock it into a sudden numbness of complete inaction. His sources of inspiration appear to dry up suddenly and, however, hard he may try, he is not able to—at least temporarily—use his creative talent. This is precisely what happened to Saadat Hasan Manto when he migrated to Pakistan in the wake of the division of a single nation state—India—into two independent entities—India and Pakistan. Manto was completely confounded, not as much by the geographical divide as by the cultural chasm created by it. As he himself put it later, recalling those days of great confusion and crippling dilemmas:

> For three months, I could not decide anything. It seemed as if a number of films were being projected onto the same screen at the same time. All mixed up: sometimes the bazaars of Bombay and its streets, sometimes the small, swiftly moving trams of Karachi, and those slow-moving mule-carts, and sometimes the noisy humdrum of the restaurants of Lahore. I simply could not make out where I was. The whole day I would sit in my chair, lost in thought.[28]

This, directly and adversely, affected Manto's writing:

> ...I prepared myself for writing but when I actually sat down to write, I found my mind divided. In spite of trying hard, I could not separate India from Pakistan and Pakistan from India. The same puzzling questions rang repeatedly in my mind: Will the literature of Pakistan be different? If so, how? Who has claims to whatever was written in undivided India? Will that be divided too? Are the basic questions confronting the Indians and the Pakistanis not the same? Will Urdu go out of use there? What form will Urdu acquire here in Pakistan? Is our state a religious state? We will, of course, be loyal to the state but will we have the freedom to criticise the state? Will our circumstances after partition be any different from those under the British?[29]

Manto was responding to the debate initiated by Mohammed Hasan Askari about the status and nature of Pakistani *adab*. Apparently, like his own Bishen Singh, alias Toba Tek Singh, Manto found himself stranded on the no man's land between the "two streams. One of life and the other of death. Between the two lay the dry land where hunger and thirst co-existed with excessive eating and drinking."[30] Finally, Manto settled down to write light essays on subjects like "Types of Noses" and "Writing on

Walls" for *Imroz*. And as he himself tells us, gradually his style acquired a "tinge of satire." Manto did not feel this change in himself and he penned sharp and incisive essays like "The Question Arises" and "When I Opened My Eyes this Morning." He felt that his creative faculties had finally found a way out and he began to write with renewed vigour. Earlier, Manto had undergone another similar phase of literary limbo. In a letter from Bombay, written in October, 1945, to his friend Ahmed Nadeem Qasmi, Manto had observed that he had become "extremely lazy and idle" and that he found the act of writing "a meaningless physical exercise." Then he went on to explain the reasons for such a state of mind:

> The fact of the matter is that this atom bomb has shocked me out of my wits. Every activity appears to be meaningless.[31]

2

I would now like to shift the focus of this essay from the content of Manto's story writing to the form and style of his writing. Manto paid equal, if not more, attention to the form of story-writing as to its content. Let me begin with a few of his observations about the language of literature since it is not Manto's views but his language which came in for close scrutiny and criticism—not only by his critics but by the courts as well. Defending himself against the charge of obscene writing in his "Dhuan" and "Kali Salwar," Manto had made a very perceptive sociolinguistic observation:

> In language very few words are obscene in themselves, it is their usage which makes even the purest of words obscene. I believe nothing is obscene in itself, but even a chair or a bowl can become obscene through presentation in an obscene manner—things are made obscene on purpose."[32]

In fact, there is no limit to considering a word—any word—as obscene. Manto tells us about the observation by a witness for the prosecution—Lala Nanak Chand Naaz—who considered the use of the word *aashiq* by Ismat Chugtai in her story "Lihaaf," as obscene which elicited a smile even from the Special Magistrate, Rai Sahib Lala Sant Ram.[33]

Similarly, defending the use of some swear words in his story "Thanda Gosht," Manto had observed that "Ishar Singh has his own style of conversation. Thousands of people use the words which the writer has put in his mouth in their everyday lives. This act of his is not unnatural. The same can be said of Kulwant Kaur as well."[34] It is their everyday usage in non-belligerent situations which makes these so-called swear-words lose their abusive character. Manto gives us the example of the swear word *saala* which is considered an abusive term in north India. However, when it is used in the following situations, it is not abusive:

Hamaara baap saala achha admi tha
or
Saala hamse mishtek ho gaya[35]

However, Manto made a more significant and aesthetic observation, when he was asked in return—"How could we have expected sophisticated language from a crude and uncouth character like Ishar Singh?" "If the writer had put civilised and sophisticated words in his mouth," observed Manto, "the very basis of realistic writing would have gone; in fact, I would say, the story would have acquired a very crude form and art would have sunk low to the level of mischief."[36]

It is, therefore, quite clear from the above that Manto believed in the use of everyday language which he presented in a matter of fact manner:

If I want to write about a woman's breasts, I call them the breasts of a woman. You cannot refer to a woman's breasts as peanuts, a table or a razor.[37]

He went on to question the wisdom of not presenting a thing as it is: "Why should jute be presented as a piece of silk cloth...can denying reality help us become better human beings?"[38]

Manto was very particular not only about the language of his literary writing but about other literary devices as well. Here is an example of his use of euphemism. Euphemism, as we know, is a device used by writers to describe those taboos and events which are likely to offend the sensibilities of their readers. When Manto wanted to describe the sexual act between Ishar Singh and Kulwant Kaur in his "Thanda Gosht"—and this we know from the story is very crucial since it is during this act that Kulwant Kaur discovers his temporary impotence and suspects it to be because of some other woman in Ishar Singh's life—Manto sought the help of a game of cards. After Ishar Singh had gone on with the foreplay for far too long and without the expected results, an impatient Kulwant Kaur says: "Ishar Singh, you've shuffled the deck sufficiently well. Now throw the card."[39]

Such careful concealment, and yet he has been accused of obscene writing. Let us look at another literary device—the metaphor—which is an essential element of a writer's aesthetics. This is what G.C. Narang, an eminent critic of Urdu literature, has to say about the use of metaphor by Manto:

> No doubt, Manto's language can be highly suggestive but it cannot cast itself in the mould of modern expression which is replete with symbolism and metaphor.[40]

This observation, to my mind, is as much off the mark as another statement by Narang, who when drawing up a distinction between Manto and Krishan Chander, had observed that while the former was "interested in the seamy side of sex, the latter (was interested) in dramatising humanism."[41] It is really difficult to decide who is a greater humanist writer—Manto or Krishan Chander? In fact, the poser that those who write of 'seamy side' of life could not dramatise humanism is in itself wrong. But to return to my argument about Manto's use of metaphors, I reproduce below a passage from Manto's story "Kali Salwar" to show how effectively Manto uses metaphors to capture the predicament of the principal character, Sultana, who is a prostitute:

> There was a big, open maidan on the left in which were laid out innumerable rail lines. When these rail lines shone in the sun, Sultana would look at her hands on which were visible blue veins exactly like the rail lines. In the big, open maidan, engines and trains would move about the whole day. Sometimes hither, sometimes thither. The *chukk-chukk* and *phukk-phukk* of the engines would resound the whole day. Early mornings, when she got up and came to the balcony, she would see a strange sight. Thick smoke billowed in the mist, rising to the hazy skies in the shape of fat and heavy men. Big clouds of steam too which were emitted noisily vanished into thin air in the twinkling of an eye. Sometimes when she saw the coaches of a train that had been pushed loose by an engine, moving about on the rails, she thought of herself. She would think that she too had been pushed and let loose onto the rails of life by someone and she was moving automatically. Other people were shifting the points and she was moving ahead—where to she did not know. A day would come when the momentum of the push would gradually cease, and she would stop somewhere at some destination which she had not seen before.[42]

This is how Manto himself has commented on this passage: "What better symbols could there be for discerning readers? I have attempted to present the true picture of Sultana's life with the help of those symbols and metaphors."[43] This comment as well as the above quotation from "Kali Salwar," shows that Manto was quite capable of using the metaphorical mode of writing when it was called for.

Manto is a great stylist. His concern for style, besides presenting a character or a situation in its matter-of-fact realistic manner, as has been shown above, also includes precision and appropriateness of words and expressions. Replace one of them and the whole story may fall flat on its face. This is so obviously evident in the capsule stories in "Siyah Hashye" and "Dekh Kabira Roya." Even the so-called nonsense words and collocations in Manto's stories are not only indispensable but also memorable. Remember the expressions *dharantakhta* and *anti ki panti po* from "Babu Gopinath," or the expression *opar the gar gar the annex the bedhyana the mung the daal of the lalten* from "Toba Tek Singh." Manto—it may appear to be incongruous—is also a great votary of stylistic sophistry and he expected such suaveness even from those who abused him. Making fun of the crude style adopted by some of his critics, Manto commented:

> I say, if you want to throw stones at me, do throw them in a sophisticated manner. I am not ready to have my head split open by someone who does not know how to split open heads with stones. If you do not know how to do so, do learn it—if you can learn to say your prayers, learn to keep fasts, and learn to participate in literary meets, you should also learn the art of throwing stones at others...If you want to abuse me, do so gladly...but only in a suave manner. Don't ruin the taste in your mouth, nor hurt my sentiments. For me, the sophistry of style is the only touchstone.[44]

3

Finally, a few words about Manto's architectonics of story-writing. First, the physical environment in which he created his stories. Replying to a question—How do you write your stories?—Manto observed:

> I sit on the sofa in my room, get hold of a pen and paper, say bismillah and begin writing a story—my three daughters are around, making a noise. I talk to them, arbitrate in their sundry quarrels. I also prepare a salad for myself—look after the guest, if one happens to drop in—but go on writing the story.[45]

It is interesting to note here that when Buchi Emecheta, a renowned Nigerian woman novelist observed to an interviewer that she wrote her novels in the kitchen, in the presence of her five children indulging in their various activities, the interviewer, a lady, was shocked into disbelief and she protested against the choice of such a mundane physical environment for as serious an activity as creative writing. But, perhaps, both Manto and Emecheta wish to be in close touch with the routine physical reality of daily life while giving reign to the flights of their fancy. It does not, however, mean that Manto could always write at will—whenever, wherever and under all circumstances. I have already mentioned above that events like the partition of the country and the dropping of the atom bomb over Japan during the Second World War had almost paralysed his creative faculties, although temporarily. Similarly, he describes a situation when his inspiration simply refused to oblige him:

> I put pressure on my mind to bring out a story—I try to be a story writer. I smoke cigarette after cigarette but no story emerges from my mind. Finally, I lie down exhausted like a barren woman...I change sides, get up, feed my sparrows, swing my daughters around, rid the house of the rubbish, collect at one place all the small

shoes which are scattered around, but as for the damn story, which I feel is lying somewhere in my pocket, it refuses to shift to my mind and I feel miserable.[46]

However, Manto's inspiration is not something purely intuitive and irrational. It is a well thought-out activity. In another essay called "Manto," he sheds light on the same physical circumstances of his craftsmanship:

> When he wants to write a story, he'd think about it at night. He'd be confused, he'd get up at five in the morning and would like to extract it out of the morning newspaper but won't succeed. Then he'd go to the bathroom and would like to cool his head so as to be able to think. But he'd fail once again. Irritated, he'd pick up a quarrel with his wife for nothing; failing once again, he'd go out to buy a *paan*. The *paan* would continue to lie on his table and he'd be struggling—in vain—with the plot of his story...finally, in sheer retaliation, he'd pick up a pen or pencil and after writing 786 on the top, he'd begin the story with the first sentence that came to his mind..."Babu Gopinath," "Hatak," "Mummy," "Toba Tek Singh," "Mozel"—all these stories, he's written in the same fraudulent manner.[47]

In fact, after a lot of thought and effort, Manto had standardised for himself certain aspects of the architectonics of story writing and could produce reasonably good stories whenever commissioned. As he grew older, Manto wrote excessively, primarily to meet the expenses of his daily drink. The manner and the speed with which he produced some of these stories—not all of them are above average, although stories like "Aulad," are very good—provides us with ample evidence of his having honed the architectonics of story writing very well. Let me illustrate this through the analysis of one such story, "Aankhen," written during this period.

Towards the end of his life, Manto would often throw a challenge to all and sundry: "Give me a sentence and I will turn it into a full-fledged story, right here, under your very eyes." One day a young poet—Farhaad Zaidi was his name—gave Manto the following sentence:

In her whole body, I liked her eyes the best.

Right in the presence of half a dozen people, amidst the din and noise of the office of *Naqoosh,* Manto took a piece of paper, picked up his pen, wrote 786 on the top, which as we know is saying the Bismillah, and then wrote the title—"Aankhen." Then he copied the sentence—In her whole body, I liked her eyes the best. Here are some of the sentences which followed it:

Those eyes were exactly like the headlights of a car in a dark night, which we notice first of all. Please do not think that those eyes were beautiful. Not at all. I can differentiate between beautiful and ugly. Forgive me for saying so, but they weren't beautiful; despite that, they were terribly attractive.[48]

These sentences give us a very good insight not only into Manto's architectonics but also his aesthetics. First of all, he finds a very unusual simile for the eyes—like the headlights of a car in a dark night. It is a very modernist—or shall I say very post-modernist—simile. Secondly, he shocks us by observing that the eyes were not beautiful. The statement surprises us since it is in apparent contradiction to the statement in the opening sentence—In her whole body, I liked her eyes the best. But he resolves the contradiction in the next statement—that "despite that, they were terribly attractive."

Manto then goes on to weave quite a complicated plot, full of twists and turns, the culmination of which is that those attractive eyes have no seeing power in them—they are stone blind. And in the last sentence is also Manto's signature, namely the unexpected ending. It is interesting to observe here that as a part of his craftsmanship, Manto led his readers up the garden path by confronting them with unexpected endings story after story.

We get a similar insight into Manto's craftsmanship about story writing through a radio-play which Manto wrote under the title, "Aao Kahani Likhen." Lajwanti, one of the three recurrent characters in a number of plays by Manto, suggests to her husband, Kishore, another recurrent character, that they write a story jointly. Kishore says that he does not know how to write one, although he can narrate one. The story he chooses to narrate goes as follows:

> Once there was a girl named Naani. She had a sister called Nahani and her brother was called Bisaula. Naani set up three villages of which two were already set up and the third could not be set up. The one which could not be set up was visited by three potters. Two of them were physically handicapped while the third had no hands...The one who had no hands made three bowls; two were broken and the third had no bottom...the one which had no bottom was used for cooking three grains of rice...[49]

The manner in which the story proceeds gives us a chance to 'know' Manto's mind about the craft of constructing stories. At each stage an unusual element is introduced.

Of the three villages proposed to be set up, two were already set up and the third could not be set up, or of the three potters two were physically handicapped and the third had no hands, or of the three pots two were broken and the third had no bottom, etc. And then of the three choices offered, the last one which is the most unusual of the three is picked up to compound the bizarre elements: the village which could not be set up is visited by three potters or the potter who had no hands made three bowls or the bowl without a bottom is used for cooking rice, etc.

What follows in the play when they begin to construct a story is an interesting see-saw battle in which Lajwanti introduces an element or a situation which forces a certain kind of continuation, while in his turn her husband, Kishore, always manages to give it an unexpected twist to foil her expected continuation, so that towards the end Lajwanti grows really desperate and picks up a quarrel with Kishore for blocking all her attempts to make the story move in a certain direction and proceed in a particular manner. As stated above, this is what Manto always does with his own stories as well—he introduces an element which raises in his readers certain expectations. Then he gives the story an entirely unexpected twist. This he does in situation after situation, in story after story. His reader is ever hopeful of his making one false move and the story falling flat on its face but it never happens. In fact, Manto said as much when he compared himself with a rope-dancer:

> He is a person who never walks on a straight, smooth road but walks on a taut rope. People expect him to fall any moment but the shameless fellow that he is, he has not fallen to date.[50]

To sum up then, Manto is an outstanding story writer of our times who belongs not just to Pakistan or to the Indian subcontinent but to the larger heritage of world literatures. His story "Toba Tek Singh" could be counted amongst not only his best but amongst the best ever written. Manto's choice of prostitutes and pimps and people living on the periphery of society as subjects was not accidental. It was an essential part of his ideology—an ideology which foregrounded the lives of the marginalised and the subaltern with the clear objective of not only changing the course of the majority discourse but to subvert it. The use of matter-of-fact language, unusual similes and metaphors and an incisive, satirical style were a part of the same aesthetic strategy of subversion. The technique of giving his stories strange, unexpected and at times weird endings was not without premeditated objectives. Slapping his readers into a new social awareness for subverting the status-quo and bringing about fundamental changes into the societal set up. He is thus not, as made out to be by Muhammad Sadiq, "a prince of pornographers,"[51] but he is, as Krishan Chander put it, in a very telling metaphor, "the Lord Shiva of Urdu literature, who had drunk to the dregs, the poison of life and then had gone on to describe in great details its taste and colour."[52]

NOTES AND REFERENCES

1. Cited in Balraj Menra and Sharad Datt, *Dastavez*, vol. 4, New Delhi: Rajkamal Prakashan, 1993, p. 19. The translation of this and all subsequent quotations in this paper are mine. I am grateful to Professor G.C. Narang and M.G. Vassanji for going through the paper and making some very valuable suggestions.
2. Cited in Devinder Issar (ed.), *Manto Adalat Ke Kathghare Men*. Delhi: Indraprasth Prakashan, 1991, p. 51.
3. Ibid., p. 97.
4. Ibid., p. 107.
5. Devinder Issar (ed.), *Mantonama*. Delhi: Indraprasth Prakashan, 1981, p. 33.
6. Devendra Satyarthi wrote his, "Naye Devta," in retaliation to Manto's "Taraqqi Pasand" in which he had made fun of Satyarthi.
7. Ibid., p. 25.
8. Ali Sardar Jafari praised, among others, the story "Bu" in an article published in *Qaumi Jang* (Bombay) in February, 1945. The same Ali Sardar Jafari attacked the same story for its reactionary contents, a few weeks later.
9. Aga Babar, "Manto Aur Veshya" in *Mantonama*, op.cit., p. 36.
10. Cited in *Manto Adalat Ke Katghare Me*, op.cit., p. 9.
11. Saadat Hasan Manto in *Dastavez*, vol. 4, op.cit., p. 177.
12. Manto, "Pas Manzar," ibid., p. 133.
13. *Mantonama*, op.cit., p. 13.
14. "Kasauti" in *Dastavez*, vol. 4, op.cit., p. 61.
15. "Afsana Nigar Aur Jinsi Masail," ibid., p. 56.
16. Ibid.
17. "Tehriri Bayan," ibid., p. 41.
18. "Adab-e-Jadeed," ibid., p. 27.
19. Ibid.

Ideology, Aesthetics and Architectonics of Manto 89

20. Ibid., p. 26.
21. "Safed Jhooth," in *Dastavez*, vol. 4, op.cit., p. 50.
22. Ibid.
23. "Safed Jhooth," in *Dastavez*,vol. 4, op.cit., p. 50.
24. Harish Narang, "Images from Periphery: Politics, Manto and Morality," in *Studies in Humanities and Social Sciences*, vol. 1, Nov., 1994, pp. 62-78.
25. "Tehriri Bayan," op.cit., p. 41.
26. *Dastavez*, vol. 4, op.cit., p. 56.
27. Muhammed Hasan Askari, "Hashiya Aarai" in *Mantonama*, op.cit., p. 238.
28. Manto, "Zahmate-Mihre-Darakhshaan," in *Dastavez*, vol. 4, p. 77.
29. Ibid., pp. 77-78.
30. Ibid.
31. Reproduced in *Dastavez*, vol. 4, op.cit., p. 191.
32. "Tehriri Bayan," *ibid.*, pp. 39-40.
33. Ibid., p. 35.
34. *Dastavez*, vol. 4, p. 96.
35. Ibid., p. 97.
36. Ibid.
37. Ibid., p. 42.
38. Ibid., p. 97.
39. Manto, "Thanda Gosht," *Dastavez*, vol. 2, p. 270.
40. Gopi Chand Narang, *Urdu Language And Literature*, New Delhi: Sterling Publishers, 1991, p. 147.
41. Ibid., p. 133.
42. "Safed Jhooth" *Dastavez*, vol. 4, op.cit., p. 51.
43. Ibid.
44. *Dastavez*, vol. 4, op.cit., p. 62.
45. Manto, "Main Afsana Kyon Likhta Hoon," *Dastavez*, vol. 4, p. 175.
46. *Ibid.*, pp. 175-76.
47. *Dastavez*,vol. 4, op.cit., p. 179.
48. *Dastavez*, vol. 1, op.cit., p. 393.
49. Ibid., vol. 3, p. 19.
50. Ibid., vol. 4, p. 178.
51. Muhammad Sadiq, *Twentieth Century Literature*, Karachi: Royal Book Company, 1983, p. 305.
52. Krishan Chander, "Manto:Urdu Adab Ka Shankar" in *Mantonama*, op.cit., pp. 30-31.

The Theme of Piety and Sin in "Babu Gopinath"

VARIS ALVI

Love oscillates between piety and sin and, in the conflict between the two (that is, between commands and prohibitions), acquires multidimensional and myriad meanings. It is only in the best of romantic poetry that this tension manifests itself in its infinite variety. Otherwise in the common poetic tradition there is contempt for sin, glorification of love and ridicule of piety. "Babu Gopinath" not only exemplifies the metaphoric power of romantic poetry, it also possesses its own unique range of metaphors which add to this notion of love. It is essential to understand these metaphors in order the grasp the essence of the story.

Babu Gopinath is such a lover of ghazals, that he even has the courage to let the woman he loves spend a night with a stranger so as to hear a courtesan sing. He is a *dervesh* of the brothel and is completely immersed in worldly affairs—but it must be remembered that he also has the capacity to be detached from both. His attachments are not possessive. He admires the body, but does not exploit it. His sin is sin. Yet it neither exalts nor degrades him. He is neither a saint who worships a prostitute as a deity, nor is he a cynic like Mohammad Shafiq Tusi (another sinful character in the story) who cannot see a woman in a prostitute and goodness in a woman. Speaking about Zeenat, a prostitute, Gopinath says, "Zeenat is a very good woman, but alas she is too noble—I am not interested in women who look like wives." He is capable of understanding the womanhood and humanity of a prostitute. That is why he never exploits the body of a woman.

In Rajinder Singh Bedi's story, "Kalyani," Mahipat, who is a counterpart of Mohammed Shafiq, sees Kalyani only as a prostitute. When Kalyani shows him her child, he can neither tolerate the woman in the prostitute nor the mother in the woman. For Mahipat, when a brothel begins to resemble a home, it becomes hell and he runs away from it. Shafiq at least is possessed by the dark beauty of lust and he never exploits the woman he does not like. In contrast, Yasin, the owner of Nagina Hotel, is merely licentious. He neither loves a woman like Gopinath nor worships the body like Shafiq. In his debauchery there is the pettiness of an ignoble shopkeeper who knows how to exploit the goodness of others. Thus, while poor Zeenat waits for him at a hotel, he uses her car to take a Christian girl he has began to fancy out for a ride. Gopinath's comment on this incident is as follows:

> Manto Sahib! What sort of man is he? If he is fed up, he should tell her. Zeenat is also a strange woman. She knows what's going on, but she never tells him to arrange for his own car if he wants to make love to that Christian woman...What shall I do Manto Sahib! She is good and gentle. I don't know what to do. One should be a little clever.

He makes the effort to turn Zeenat into a clever prostitute. The problem, however, is that she is neither interested in love nor sin. She surrenders her heart to Shafiq with the same indifference with which she surrenders her body to Yasin or to any other customer. It is as if none of them is a part of her existence. She neither sees herself as a prostitute nor as a mistress. She needs someone who can make her aware of her innate goodness, who can awaken the woman in her. According to Gopinath, she needs a man who can protect her, take care of her and give her a sense of belonging. One who may or may not love her (she doesn't need love), but would never treat her as a prostitute or a mistress. In other words, she needs a husband and a home for only then can she discover her womanliness, her motherhood and her humanity.

Sin leads Gopinath towards sainthood and Zeenat towards domesticity. Shafiq and Yasin are content to be sinful. Zeenat, however, wants to reform. Gopinath revels in his life of sinful pleasures, yet he is not so completely absorbed in it as to want to make debauchery the goal of his life. But what is the goal of his life? Perhaps nothing. Because he regards everything as a fraud and an illusion.

Here we must consider Gopinath's existential condition. At some point in his life he realises that life has no meaning; that life is merely a dream and human beings shadows. That is why he either says nothing or feigns ignorance when Abdul, his servant, spends only ten or twenty rupees out of the hundred Gopinath gives him, and then either pockets the rest, or pretends to have dropped the money or asserts that his pocket was picked. Similarly, he knows that not everyone with a runny nose and a drooling mouth is a saint, yet he continues to seek the company of Ghaffar, who is a fraud dressed in saintly rags. He understands the reality of the society in which he lives and yet is detached from it. It is as if he lives in a dream and prefers to continue to sleep and dream. Other people are acceptable to him only if he can see them as shadows in a dream.

Gopinath is the son of a miserly *bania*. After his father's death he inherits ten lakhs of rupees. He doesn't hoard them. He receives them as if they have come to him in a dream; he squanders them as if he were living in a dream.

Gopinath doesn't have much faith in life. He is an intelligent man, but he doesn't use his intelligence to give a shape to his life. He wastes his life, just as he squanders his money. Life for him is as fleeting as wealth. To save money like a miser or to treat life's wealth prudently is against his *dervesh*-like nature.

He likes to keep the company of the poor and of vagabonds. Perhaps they are like him and make no effort to give a meaning to their life or to shape it. He feels that a man can live with them without pretence. For a man like Gopinath that is essential because he can't lead a life of duplicities. Even if he wants to, he can't be a hypocrite, for the dissolute life he has chosen for himself has already ripped off all masks.

The world of the respectable, the noble, the well-mannered and the influential is not for Gopinath. The duplicitousness that is required to live in it is against his temperament. He feels suffocated in such a world. In order to survive in it, the real self, which is a battlefield of idiosyncrasies, has to hide behind a rich and glamorous facade. In a brothel, however, there is no pretence, no demand to construct an artificial moral self. There men behave according to their innate natures. In a brothel, the measure of their goodness cannot be found in conventional morality. Indeed, Manto creates a figure like Gopinath not to pass moral judgements but to discover the sources of creative energy.

Gopinath is neither cunning nor a hypocrite. He cannot live in the practical world, because he has never been cheated by life. Indeed, a person like Gopinath can either be a cynic or a sanyasi; the idiosyncrasies of eros can either lead him to the brothel and the experiences of sensual pleasures or make him into a religious quester for whom life is a dream and the world an illusion. He is the kind of person who can either swallow the bitter truth of life's insignificance or set out in search of some transcendental truth. In any case, what he knows of the world is a result of his experiences in it. And experiences are all that really matter to Gopinath. He doesn't care whether they are base or exalted, physical or spiritual.

Manto is not interested in portraying him either as a Mahatma or as a romantic soul who worships beauty, elegant feelings and noble habits. Had he done so, he would have written a caricature of a romantic and a philosophical tale. Gopinath would then have sparkled in the story like a bright star and the marriage of Zeenat would have been an example of the most exalted idealism.

Further, the life of deception and deceit in the brothel would have acquired an aura of nobility. Gopinath would have, at the end, found peace and consolation. He would, however, have lost that energising restlessness which enables him to understand that it is the power of eros which refuses to allow life to be neglected even when it seems meaningless. He is genuinely interested in women and feels comfortable in the colourful atmosphere of the brothel. For him, pleasure is not an escape from life; it is, rather, an attempt to pounce upon life. He does, however, realise that while a woman may be like a lamp which can illuminate a night of pleasure, she can't keep the dark shadows of life away forever.

Gopinath, in his innocence, his openness, his longing for happiness, is the very antithesis of the moralist whose life is pure, good, principled and sterile. A moralist is dignified and responsible. No one can, however, tell with certainty if a moralist is really as straightforward and righteous as he pretends to be. Gopinath, on the other hand, is both a good man and a ruffian. By portraying him thus, Manto has called to question all our normative moral standards. Gopinath is not a pillar of society. He is merely a lover of ghazals, and as such is no more permanent on the path of life than a footprint.

Gopinath's ordinariness is in conformity with the realistic plot of the story. It is the very absence of real evil in him that saves the story from becoming either emotional or theatrical. It is also the absence of nobility in Gopinath that prevents the story from sliding into melodrama. Gopinath arranges the marriage of Zeenat, his mistress, to someone else. Had he done so out of noble motives, we would have wept with Zeenat and found consolation in tears. Further, had he arranged her marriage cynically, we would have seen it as merely another example of the evil perpetrated by feudal lords, who have no compunction in getting rid of their mistresses by marrying them off to their servants. Manto's story is, however, more complex. Here Zeenat's marriage seems like a satisfactory solution to Gopinath's problems. It enables Gopinath to help give Zeenat the kind of security he could not have her given. He knows that temperamentally he is not the marrying kind, and he is also aware that he is rapidly sliding into bankruptcy.

An interesting aspect of Gopinath's character is that in his relationship with the prostitutes there is neither the sophistication of the Nawabs of Lucknow nor the cheapness of the Mawalis of Bombay. He is, instead, an ordinary person with ordinary preoccupations. And he is happy as he is. He says:

> Manto Sahib! I am not interested in music, but I enjoy going out and waving a ten or twenty rupee note before a singer. I love to take out a note, show it to her, watch her get up with an elegant gesture, and walk up to me to receive it. It gives me pleasure to stuff the note in one of my socks and watch her bend down to get it. There are many such meaningless things which we libertines enjoy. Otherwise, who doesn't know that parents put their children in brothels and believers their Gods in tombs and graveyards.

It is obvious that Gopinath is quite aware of the reality of the world. He knows that a brothel and a Pir's tomb are fraudulent places, and that there can't be better sites for people who want to deceive themselves, and Gopinath deceives himself because at some juncture of his life, he realises that life is meaningless. Yet, his urge for life is so strong that he does not allow his knowledge of the meaninglessness of existence to so overpower him as to make him commit suicide. Camus says that people do not make rational decisions to kill themselves, because it isn't reason but the desire for life which enables man to carry on.

The paradox is, however, that it is precisely Gopinath's sense of life's deceptions that makes him fully aware of the romance of life. He is like a romantic artist who longs to live without inhibitions—although Manto portrays him as a person who is ignorant of poetry and literature, and as one who has little knowledge of music. Manto insists on showing that Gopinath is an ordinary man and not a bohemian artist in revolt against the constraints of a moral society. Had he been a bohemian rebel, Zeenat's marriage would have merely been an example of a decadent life. Manto is not interested in writing such a stereotypical story. For him a bohemian life, where sexuality is debased and cowardly, and where the power of eros is sick, tired and jaundiced, holds no interest. Gopinath's life in the brothel is robust and manly. An ordinary person, his erotic life has none of the hypocrisies, restrictions and neuroses of people in a cultured society. Gopinath loves Zeenat like a beloved, but he arranges her marriage as if she were his daughter. Love, he believes, can assume various forms.

At the first glance it appears that in this seemingly realistic story, Gopinath is a romantic character. But the moment one sees Gopinath, seated on a couch smoking his hukkah, bless Zeenat, one realises how far removed he is from a figure of romance. Here it is worth recalling Mary McCarthy's comment about *Madame Bovary*. She says that the only romantic character in the novel is the drab and uninteresting husband of Emma. The peculiarity of a great writer is that he doesn't convey romantic feelings through characters who are typically handsome, young and dashing.

Gopinath is a man of feelings and passions. He lives only for the sake of experiences—even if the experiences are as worthless as those of offering money to a singer and teasing her. He is an epicure. As he himself confesses, "When I am penniless, instead of going to a brothel, I shall go to the tomb of a Pir." He is not concerned about the reality of the brothel or the Pir's tomb. Both have interesting experiences to offer. He doesn't visit either as a supplicant. He visits them because in the sinful atmosphere of the brothel and the sacred ambience of a Pir's tomb, he finds comfort and delight. The fact that both are places of deception and fraud doesn't call into question the authenticity of his experiences there. Indeed, did Wordsworth never doubt that his experience of a sacred power throbbing behind the spectacle of nature was an illusion; yet for him the experience of the secret beauty of nature was real. Further, he conveyed that experience in such lovely melodies that it was also real and true for his readers. Of course, Gopinath's experiences are neither lofty nor sublime. They are utterly common. They are so mundane that Manto neither participates in them nor invites us to do so. We do, however, realise that Gopinath's life would be barren and meaningless without them.

In the last scene of the story, in which we see Zeenat sitting on a bed decorated with flowers, Manto enters the room and breaks the charming illusion. Seeing a professional prostitute dressed as a virginal bride, he can't stop himself from asking, "What kind of joke is this?" No one, however, laughs. Zeenat's eyes fill with tears, and she says, "Don't make fun of me, Bhaijan." Her quietly spoken plea, transforms the scene; instead of comedy, it turns into a scene charged with tragic irony.

What Manto himself considers deception, is real for Gopinath and Zeenat. For Gopinath, Zeenat is simultaneously a prostitute and a bride. In his eyes, she is a woman who had once played the part of a prostitute, but is now sitting before him as a bride. Who knows what the real character of a woman is? Anyway, the moment Zeenat dresses up as a bride, she ceases to be his mistress. Gopinath's romantic feelings as a lover are transformed into fatherly affection. As far as he is concerned, it is not his beloved's marriage he has arranged, but his daughter's.

Gopinath is a vagabond in the market place of beauty and it is essential for him to have money to spend. He is not a miser. He squanders money. In the brothel every transaction is made in cash. Anyone who has money can be a customer. Gopinath spends with abandon. He is not worried about the day when he would have no money left. He is a rake who is intoxicated by life; but he is also a realist who knows that the world is a mistress who is faithful to no one. He is familiar with the etiquette of a brothel; he knows how to depart elegantly.

Gopinath knows that he is a debauchee, but he doesn't demand faithfulness from Zeenat. Responsible to no one, he knows it would be wrong to ask Zeenat to sacrifice herself to him. The relation between the two of them is complex. They are attached to each other, and yet are aware of the fact that any demand for permanence would be fatal for both of them. That is why he finds a husband for her, and she agrees to the arrangement. The moment the marriage is arranged, Gopinath's love for Zeenat ceases to be blind and selfish, and becomes completely selfless. Perhaps, Gopinath is childlike and innocent. It is also possible to say that his celebration of the marriage of Zeenat, a prostitute, as if it were the marriage of a virgin, is no better than deceitful play, akin to the marriage of dolls which children perform; that it is fraud, an aspect of life's illusions. Yet for Gopinath, it is real, it is truthful. Gopinath is really a wise fool who knows that if life were a dream in which we were shadows, it would be better to live as if we were real and our actions had consequences. That is why he doesn't want Manto at the end to break the illusion. When Manto mocks at Zeenat dressed as a bride and she weeps, Gopinath caresses her affectionately, and looks at Manto with disdain. While Manto, the story writer, forgets that there is reality in the fictional structures he creates, Gopinath, the man who lives a life of illusions, is undeceived by the drama of Zeenat's marriage, which he enacts, and its reality.

The narrator of the story is Manto himself. He is involved in the events, but maintains a satirical distance from all that he observes. Considering the provocativeness of the story, the manner in which Manto participates in the story reminds one of an adroit ring master who puts his head into a tiger's mouth and still manages to come out alive. Manto is so successful that he describes the events without becoming sentimental or grandiose. His role in the story is complex. He refuses to give Gopinath and

Zeenat advice. Instead, he watches their lives take their own inexorable course. There are, however, times when he can't be a mere spectator. For example, when he is told that the real reason for taking Zeenat to Bombay is to help her to become a clever prostitute and allure a rich man, he is shocked. He writes:

> When I learnt from Gopinath the reason why he took Zeenat to Bombay, I was baffled. I couldn't believe that such a thing was possible. But later when I observed things more closely, my doubts were removed. It was Babu Gopinath's earnest desire that Zeenat should become the mistress of a good, rich man in Bombay and extract money from different people.

At first, Manto's sympathies are with Gopinath when he sees him being fleeced by worthless people. But when he realises that Gopinath is a weak victim of clever hunters, his sympathies turn into reproaches and irritable criticism. Manto's ironic and humorous asides add to the realism of the story without diminishing our sympathy for Gopinath. This is evident even in the following remarks in which he compares Gopinath unfavourably with the Zamindar of Sind to whom Zeenat is married :

> Ghulam Hussain was wearing an elegant suit. He acknowledged people who came to congratulate him with a smile. He was a large man. Beside him Babu Gopinath seemed like a quail.

Yet, despite this ironic description, our interest in Gopinath does not diminish. We wonder about him much after he caresses Zeenat affectionately and walks out of the room. Having completed his one mission in life, he leaves Bombay and we continue to wonder if he spends the rest of his days in the shadow of a Pir's tomb.

Manto's attitude towards the other characters is not neutral. He takes sides, expresses his likes and dislikes and passes judgements on them. Zeenat, for instance, is presented with great psychological insight. Instead of merely being an ordinary Kashmiri *kabutari* (pigeon), she emerges as a tender and graceful woman. When Manto sees her for the first time at Babu Gopinath's place, he describes her as follows:

> Her face was round and her complexion was fair. On entering the room, I at once realised that she was the Kashmiri *Kabutari* whom Sando had mentioned in the office. She was a very neat and clean woman, with short hair which seemed to have been trimmed but was not. Her eyes were bright and sparkling. From her countenance it appeared that she was extremely frivolous and inexperienced.

Apart from her frivolity, what Manto highlights here is neatness and cleanliness. In order to understand the reason for this emphasis, it would be useful to compare her with the prostitutes Manto describes in her two stories. The stories are: "Shanti" and "Siraj." The prostitutes in both are young like Zeenat. Shanti, who is also from Kashmir, is careless and indifferent towards the dress, make-up and manners. She only talks business, and walks away when it is over. Siraj smokes marijuana. She is ill-tempered and rude. She is also dirty and doesn't bathe for days. Zeenat, on the other hand, is described by Manto as "a woman of good social disposition; a woman of few words, who is simple, neat and clean." The fact is that both Shanti and Siraj are heartbroken. They have been deceived by their lovers. Zeenat has not faced any tragedy in life. Shanti and Siraj are aggressive and burn with the desire for vengeance against the man who betrayed them. Their rage destroys them.

In contrast, Zeenat is indifferent towards life. This is perhaps because she has achieved many things and had many experiences in a short span of time. She lacks the maturity which comes as one struggles to make a life. Everything has come much too easily to Zeenat. She is also frivolous. Frivolity is a charm in a young girl, but in an

Piety and Sin in "Babu Gopinath"

adult it is a sign of shallowness. Thus, when Manto rebukes her when he learns that she has been pushed into the trade by Sando and Sardar, she casually answers: "I do not know anything Bhaijan. I do what these people tell me." Manto's response is interesting:

> I wished I could sit with her and make her understand that what she was doing was wrong. Sando and Sardar would even sell her for their own gain. But I didn't say anything. Zeenat was so foolish, unambitious and lifeless that she irritated me. She was a wretch who didn't know the worth of her own life. Even if she had to sell her body, she could have been more discrete. Indeed, I was very sad to see her. She wasn't interested in smoking, drinking and eating; nor was she interested in telephone conversations or even the couch on which she often relaxed.

Watching her flirt with Shafiq, Manto says, "I did not like her flirtation with Shafiq. I found it vulgar."

Manto doesn't present her as an oppressed and afflicted woman. She is both pleasant and well-mannered, frivolous and inexperienced, disinterested and vulgar at the same time. This is what distinguishes her from the prostitutes represented in works by lesser writers.

Describing her relationship with Gopinath, Manto says: "Did she love Gopinath? I couldn't tell from her actions. It was, however, obvious that Babu Gopinath cared for her a lot and did everything to make her comfortable. But I didn't realise that there was some sort of strain between the two of them. I mean that despite being very close to each other there appeared to be some reserve between them." There is no secret bond between them that gives the story its final twist. Had they loved each other, the final wedding scene would have been sentimental in the manner of Hindi films. Zeenat would then have broken down and thanked Gopinath for his kindness and generosity with moist eyes.

The marriage of Zeenat to someone else at the end of the story is a proper and inevitable solution to the variety of complications in the story. For Zeenat, it promises a new life and new experiences. For Gopinath, it is a release from difficulties. He doesn't regard her marriage as either a moral or an immoral act. For him it is merely another occasion. He washes the hands of the guests and helps to feed them. Then, he quietly slips out of Zeenat's life. Beside the bridegroom, he looks like a quail. Had there been no humour in Manto's eloquent narrative, Gopinath would have seemed like a forlorn lover and the story would have been nothing more than a painful elegy on the death of romantic love. What ensures that the story does not fall into sentimentality are the last sarcastic words of Manto when he sees Zeenat dressed as a bride. Gopinath is hurt by them. Manto writes, "The faith which Babu Gopinath had in me seemed to break." It was with this assertion of faith between them that the story had opened: "The frequency of our meetings increased. I liked Babu Gopinath, but he had faith in me. That is why he respected me more than others."

The story "Babu Gopinath" is a brilliant exploration of the complex play of emotions between different characters. Manto refuses to stay confined within the conventional parameters of good and evil in his assessment of the characters, and thus succeeds in infusing them with such a living force that whenever we think about them they reveal new qualities.

Translated from Urdu
by Ahsan Raza Khan

Surfacing from Within: Fallen Women in Manto's Fiction

SUKRITA PAUL KUMAR

By now, feminist criticism has already popularized the need for voicing the absent, the silenced and the inarticulate. And it was nearly five decades ago that a significant writer in Urdu had the vision to present pulsating glimpses of the invisible and silent woman, the woman fallen from the mainstream society of honourable ladies and gentlemen. In a number of Manto's stories, there is an impending sense of immediacy with which one confronts a totally degenerate society, a world of enslaved women, of women commodified and consumed in accordance to the unquestioned fact of male sexual need and the principle of supply and demand. Indeed, one does not have to be a woman writer to creep into the inner terrain of the psyche of the oppressed or the exploited female. Manto demonstrates an androgynous sensibility in unravelling the existential stirrings of women with as much sensitivity as he does those of men. A writer of his calibre did not have to be a woman to perceive the dehumanization of a society which nourished the callous male exploitation of female sexuality. There is an inevitability in the narration of such stories as "Hatak," "Mummy," "Babu Gopinath," and many others. Manto just had to tell these stories, which gradually merged into a long confessional tale of human civilization recorded in literature. He did not have to weave any formalistic patterns, nor did the experiences of his stories seek the support of any mythology or romance. There is an unusual directness about his stories in which he presents a specific kind of consciousness of women sobbing without tears, remaining out of general sight; of women who are made to sell their virtue in the market before they are castaway. They live in an infernal underworld, invisible to 'respectable' society which pleads ignorance of its existence. Ironically, not only has this society produced this world, it also provides it full sustenance.

Society's hypocritical indifference to such a world is not just a quiet consent to its existence. In fact, it is due to the vested interests of patriarchal society that prostitution survives because it does not seem to threaten any of its fundamental principles. Let it be so then! But not so with Manto, a writer who could see through the pretension of a 'moral' law erecting its mythology of the good and the bad on a laissez-faire economics of male sexuality. He needed no masks of metaphors and symbols to construct the reality of that 'other', which has been pushed into the seclusion of a black world, if only to satiate men sexually so that they lead a so-called normal domestic life based, ironically, on chastity and the homely virtues prescribed for their women.

From amongst the not-so-talked-about Manto's stories is "Mahmuda," the story of a woman pushed into prostitution for sheer survival. Mustakeem is a sympathetic male witness, anguished but unable to do anything to save Mahmuda from slipping into her gruesome circumstances. He is drawn towards her extraordinarily beautiful big eyes on his wedding day. A keen attentiveness about her settles into his consciousness for ever and he follows her life with acute sensitivity through the news from his wife. A simple girl of a humble background, Mahmuda is married to a railway employee who turns into an eccentric maulvi within two years of his marriage, with poor Mahmuda left alone to fend for herself. Mustakeem finds himself getting more and more concerned about the fate of Mahmuda, but from a distance. The greater his sympathy, the greater the alertness of his wife. When Mahmuda is driven to 'bad ways' because of her husband's indifference and his lack of propriety, Mustakeem wishes to save her and bring her home. Kulsum, his wife, will not hear of it. He knows he could give her shelter, save her from falling into an abysmal world and marry her to a respectable man. But Mustakeem is incapable of action and like hundreds of other men and women of 'respectable' society, he becomes an accomplice in contributing to the degeneration of humanity. In his inaction lies his consent; and, with his consent, the fraudulence of his sensitivity is certified. Towards the end of the story, he introspects, "If only I could have resisted my wife...she'd have been upset only for a while and perhaps would have gone away to her parents for a few days. It would have saved Mahmuda from submitting to that filthy existence. Why did I not save her? Did I have honest intentions? Had I been honest and truthful, Kulsum would have come around soon enough. I have committed a great crime, I have sinned."[1]

His introspection makes him weed out the falsity of his position. But all such debating and confessions are like "the last dose of oxygen to a dying patient." He may be redeemed psychologically. But not Mahmuda. As fate would have it, two and a half years later, after the partition, at Karachi, Mustakeem comes face to face with the image of Mahmuda made up as a vulgar market prostitute surrounded by people cracking dirty jokes with her. Before he can run away and escape an encounter, Mahmuda addresses him, inviting him to a "first class paan" and announcing that she had attended his wedding. Mustakeem is absolutely and totally frozen. What seems to surface in him is the thought that Mahmuda was at one time very much a respectable woman of his own social set-up. And that she could have remained there if he had helped. He feels a guilty participant in her downfall. This is indeed a tragedy of inaction which is quietly enacted over and over again in society to make it possible for some people to continue abusing human existence. The mental proximity of Mahmuda and a growing abstract relationship with her could not elicit any action from Mustakeem, a typical middle-class person who could find cerebral avenues of escape and remain a coward.

Talking of Kulsum, Mustakeem's wife, Manto dismisses her as a woman typical in her jealousy and "possessiveness," incapable of transcending her self-centredness to help save a fellow woman. Perhaps her own insecurity is cause enough for her denial of shelter to Mahmuda. She may after all end up losing her husband to Mahmuda if she were to give her a place in the house! But that is obviously not the focal point of the story. Mahmuda's transition from being a modest, demure subject to a legendary object of consumerist passion, is perceived through the inert consciousness of Mustakeem. What is implied is the functional complicity in the brutalization of women in society.

From Mahmuda, sitting as an exhibitionist at a paan-shop, Manto takes us to the very centre of a prostitute's existence, to her dreary room in his story "Hatak." With Rajender Singh Bedi's complex story "Kalyani" as the backdrop, "Hatak" seems a simple, straightforward, but very powerful story of the alienated, deadened prostitute coming alive through a sense of utter humiliation. A stereotyped representation of Sugandhi would have merely yielded an anaesthetized picture of a prostitute with layers of social prejudice and obscurantist beliefs. For Sugandhi to breathe in flesh and blood in the story, Manto had to simply cut across all the pretensions of a hegemonic sexist approach. To cross the threshold and peep into the other's consciousness does not mean just a single step. It is a dive, a journey demanding commitment, perseverance, courage and stoicism, because to cross this threshold is not to step into safety but nightmare; it is a plunge into the vague unconnected territories of the mind.

Entering Sugandhi's room in the beginning of the story, one gets a sense of the macabre which is accentuated by the sound of the tingling silver coins tucked inside Sugandhi's blouse, vibrating as she breathes heavily "with the silver melting and dripping into her heart."[2] There is not just this one point, but a whole shifting subliminal line of thresholds to be crossed to reach the disjointed territories of the protagonist's mind. Sugandhi's chatter with Jamuna about the tactics and strategies she uses with various men, is merely a show of theoretical knowledge. In actual fact, the story tells us that she is intensely emotional, and that at the slightest suggestion of warmth from a man, she would melt into total submission and, yet, remain forever hungry for love.

She likes to remain suspended between a sense of being and non-being, and feels suffocated with so much air "above her, below her, and around her." The immensity of desire, and the need for a totality create in her an unending demand for love. She deliberately blinds herself to the lie uttered by her male customer every night, "Sugandhi, I love you." She slips into an illusion of love and believes she could love any man who comes to her. She wonders why men do not possess that kind of goodness. And yet at the height of her feelings, Sugandhi wishes to take her man into her lap and put him to sleep, patting and singing to him.

The make-believe world of love constructed by Sugandhi has within its folds Madho, who is very prominent in sustaining her dream. With a husband-like propriety over her, Madho provides nourishment to the starved Sugandhi through his regular visits, unfulfilled promises of material help and meaningless utterances. But Sugandhi is happy to live that lie since there is no possibility of living its truth anyway. In Mahmuda, the fact of prostitution is shorn of all myth or magic. The motivating factors leading to prostitution are indicated as economic exigency combined with the lack of a social structure for destitute women, and the callousness of so-called 'sensitive' fellow human beings.

In "Hatak," we are face to face with an already prostituted Sugandhi who sustains her essential womanhood by constructing a lie motivated by emotion and an urgent need to love. The depths of her womanhood remain intact. She is not a negativity, an absence or a 'deviant', because she has not internalized the inevitable social judgment pronounced on such women, that is "She is evil." The cleavages and the tensions operating at the various levels of her consciousness, converge into an intense moment of deep realization. Sugandhi is rejected by a mere "Ooun!" by the Seth; the male surveyor spits at the object on display. It's not as if she has never been rejected before. But this happens to be the moment when she has to face the reality of her existence, squarely staring at her. These moments of humiliation churn out the entire truth of her being; and, the myth of love has to explode.

Sugandhi's interior monologue at this point of the story strips her naked. She goes through an existential anguish precisely because she is capable of an intense inward journey. The requisite capacity to liberate herself from exploitation has been retained in her and she has kept her emotional and human self alive, even if it is with the help of a lie. But that lie, the make-believe has to be demolished—Madho has to go. Sugandhi acts from the centre of her being when she turns him out after articulating concretely the fraudulence of their relationship. But then, there is no knowing what is false and what is true! The vacuum and the horrifying silence surrounding her after Madho's departure has to be filled up—by perhaps another lie. She picks up her diseased dog and puts him on her bed, next to herself. I think of some lines from Amy Levy's poem *Magdalen* here:

> And there is neither false nor true;
> But in a hideous masquerade
> All things dance on, the ages through
> And good is evil, evil good;
> Nothing is known or understood
> Save only pain.[3]

It is the writer's sheer commitment to authenticity that makes the writer articulate such a minutely specific consciousness of an individual, in this case that of a woman who is a prostitute—so specific and yet so universally relevant. Such a literary discourse lends order to experience and makes possible the active participation of the reader. The intense moment of humiliation makes Sugandhi see herself as a victim, an object for the male to accept or reject. Inevitably, this throws open the possibilities of psychic rebellion, transformation and a new future. Life has to go on but only after its existent lie is exposed. The end of the story is the beginning of a fresh journey after crossing a series of crises. "Hatak" forges a forbidden social liaison across the divisions of moral law and sexual myth. Sugandhi, then, moves from dream to waking, establishing the autonomy of a woman's existence, after having made a definite choice of demolishing the make-believe world, so consciously created and maintained by her.

From amongst Manto's various female characters, the woman who emerges as one of the most potent, independent and androgynous personalities, is Mrs. Stella Jackson of the story entitled "Mummy." Pilar of Hemingway's *For Whom the Bell Tolls* and Gertrude Stein stand alongside Stella Jackson, not only in generating a sense of freedom around themselves, but also in initiating other men and women into a life of authentic action. Morally upright, strong of conviction and experienced in life, these women become the axis around whom a large number of people revolve, seeking psychological support, maternal care and emotional protection. Stella Jackson is "Mummy," a woman with an independent status which is a direct result of her own interaction with reality. She will, therefore, not fit into any prefabricated role model. Nor will she be a party to any complicity in the brutalization of women. All those men—Chadha, Ranjit Kumar, Ghareeb Niwaz, and many others who come to her are like her adopted children. With a cat-like attentiveness, she keeps track of each one of them; while in a drunken state, they are not allowed to take liberties with her young girls. Even her favourite, Chadha, is slapped and turned out of her house when he tries to get at Philis, a mere fifteen year-old girl. Chadha ultimately respects Mummy for having checked his animal instincts. It is she who spontaneously takes over the responsibility of nursing him when he falls seriously ill. The story lists a number of instances when Mummy comes to the rescue of one or the other, demonstrating her generosity, the capaciousness of her heart and readiness to help with all her resources. The entire credit for the triumph of truth, that of Ramsingh's confession and the subsequent burial of the murder case in the court, goes to Mummy's conviction and advice that Ramsingh should simply narrate the truth. But then, eventually, the same Mummy is turned out of the city for being a prostitute.

It is here that the writer gets carried away and blatantly makes Chadha indulge in sloganeering, upholding the character of Mummy and offering her to all those who may swim in the wave of perversion. She has, after all, the capacity to be everyone's Mummy! Contrasted with this is the sharpness of the indictment of the world which, in any case, keeps juggling truths and falsehoods, to and fro: Augusta Webster's poem "A Castaway" uses the language of the market:

> Our tradesmen, who must keep unspotted names
> And cheat the least like stealing what they can:
> Our...all of them, the virtuous worthy men
> Who feed on the world's follies, vices, wants
> And do their businesses of lies and shams
> Honestly reputably, while the world
> Claps hands and cries "good luck," which of these trades,
> Their honourable trades, barefaced like mine,
> All secrets brazened out, would shew more white?[4]

If an old 'harlot' can be compassionate and a universal mother in the story "Babu Gopinath," Manto locates a male counterpart of a similar temperament in the person of Babu Gopinath. Gopinath takes Zeenat under his wings. She is an inexperienced, almost naive young girl. She could very well have become a toy in his hands, an object for entertainment, exhibition and sexual exploitation. But Babu Gopinath cares for her with a paternal passion and wants her to settle down on her own. Love for Zeenat includes his care, respect and an anxiety for her well-being. He persists in making all efforts to introduce her to other men of means so that she may end up getting some support. His selfless involvement and sense of fulfilment when her marriage is fixed with a wealthy zamindar are evident. A lover turned father, Babu Gopinath does not allow anyone to insult or hurt her. The story ends with a touching scene in which Babu Gopinath becomes tearful when the narrator cracks a joke at Zeenat's expense.

A single example of fictional representation of how women became victims of male prowess in the holocaust of the partition is to be found in Manto's well-known story "Khol Do." Every man, be it her own father, registers as a sexually starved aggressive male to the woman who has gone through the horrendous experience of a series of rapes. The writer captures and reveals the damaged psychology of the woman-victim who has surrendered her sense of being and has become a mechanized sexual object involved in involuntary action.

By taking a few examples from Manto's fiction, this paper attempts to show how the writer succeeded in mapping a so-called 'fallen woman's' mind so authentically. It is not as if Manto had any conscious feminist agenda to present. But, in the selection of his subject for fictional delineation as well as in exploring the centrality of female consciousness, Manto's feminism is implicitly present. While this is one important aspect of his art, there is indeed a large chunk of his fiction dealing with male consciousness as well. Whether male or female, Manto is known for his perceptive delineation of the oppressed, the exploited and the victimized.

Manto's unusually alert antennae were turned towards authenticity in life and he subjected each human being to sensitive scrutiny. Human beings were not mere abstractions to him. His fierce commitment to life inevitably introduced the voice of dissension in his art as well as in his life, salvaging the dignity of human existence in the face of established systems and norms. In fact, the apparently gory world of his art records the aesthetic gesture of reclamation and solidarity by identifying intense moments of cognition of human anguish and by arousing compassion for the oppressed. The stories discussed in this paper betray the strain of that social morality which founds its whole system of good and evil on the sexual propriety of women. To impose any labels on Manto will undoubtedly limit the scope of his art. Given a feminist reading, his stories show how literature can become a potent weapon in disturbing the established modes of existence through a sensitive focussing on a generally 'excluded' aspect of human consciousness. As Helen Cixous remarks in *The Newly Born Woman*: "That which is not obliged to reproduce the system, that is writing...it invents new worlds."[5] Manto could just not accept pigeon-holed and straight-jacketed ideas and systems. That was the tragedy of his life, and was ironically also a point of salvation for his art which succeeds in truly sensitizing humanity.

REFERENCES

1. From Manto's story "Mahmuda." *Saadat Hasan Manto ki Kahaniyan*, ed. Narendra Mohan. New Delhi: Kitabghar, 1992. The translation into English is mine.
2. Ibid. From the story "Hatak." The translation into English is mine.
3. Amy Levy, "Magdalen," in *A Minor Poet and Other Verse*, London, 1984, p. 71.
4. Augusta Webster, "A Castaway," in *Portraits*, 3rd edition, London, 1993, pp. 38-9.
5. Helen Cixous and Catherine Clement, *The Newly Born Woman*. Translated by Betsy Wing. Manchester: Manchester University Press, 1986. Originally published in France as *La Jenne Nee* in 1975.

Manto and Punjabi Short Story Writers

TEJWANT SINGH GILL

1

The partition of India in 1947 has produced a vast range of fictional and non-fictional writings in Urdu, Hindi, Punjabi, Sindhi, English and Bengali. While the amount of work produced about those traumatic times is large, the quality is uneven. One can, however, assert that the finest short stories about the period were written by Saadat Hasan Manto. For him the partition was an overwhelming tragedy. His power as a writer lay, perhaps, in the fact that he found himself in opposition against those "forces of tradition, conservatism and especially religion,"[1] which he felt were responsible for the horrors. In Manto's case, however, the experience of defeat against cultural forces also brought with it new explanations and new perceptions. In contrast, other writers, particularly those in Punjab, where communal carnage was the maximum, rarely succeeded in writing stories which were capable of presenting anything more than realistic and graphic accounts of violence.

For Punjab the partition was a nightmare. In 1947, Hindus, Muslims and Sikhs slaughtered each other with a kind of ferocity that the land had never witnessed. What was shocking was that we had always looked upon Punjab as a place where people had been living within an integrated cultural community for centuries. The measure of the disruption caused by the partition can be gauged from the fact that millions of people were forced to migrate from Punjab, more than two lakh people were massacred and about fifty thousand women were sexually violated.[2] It is not surprising that for ordinary Punjabis, the partition was an incomprehensibly diabolical event.

2

In this regard Manto's writings are a rare exception for several reasons. First, his writings, from their beginnings in "Siyah Hashye" (Black Margins) to their culmination in the apocalyptic endings of his great stories "Thanda Gosht" (Cold Meat), "Khol Do" (Open Up) and "Toba Tek Singh," articulated all the terror, irrationality, brutality and inhumanity that the partition had projected in every sphere of life. In other words, multiple motifs went into the production of those writings. Second, they were couched in a bare, grim and ironic language that, with its Brechtian recklessness and down-to-earth bluntness, subverted the most settled of commitments. Third, its effect was to internalise the vision of a world that was no longer communitarian; caught in the labyrinth of communalism, it had in fact turned predatory.

"Siyah Hashie," in Khalid Hasan's English translation under the title *Partition: Sketches and Stories*,[3] comprises of thirty-two anecdotes of varying length. If a couple of them are of several pages each, then there are others which are not even one page long and in very many cases the sketches are not more than five or six lines in length. So overwhelming is their impact and chilling their effect that they leave, irrespective of their size, the reader with no option but to look for what lies beyond the texts. For example, in "For Necessary Action," a supposedly Muslim couple, seeks shelter in a house whose new occupants are Jains. Growing desperate at their confinement, the husband and wife come out of their hide-out and give themselves up to the new occupants. They are ready to be killed at the hands of their custodians who out of reverence for their peace-loving religion refuse to oblige them. All the same, they hand them over to the non-Jain residents of a neighbouring locality for necessary action i.e.

cold-blooded murder. This brief anecdote shows how during the partition cold-blooded murder had become the order of the day. More than that, it connotes how religious benevolence sanctified for ages, had turned malevolent. If, in this anecdote, professed non-violence becomes a ruse for practiced violence, then in "Mistake Removed" the security measures dictated by commonsense, invite calamity for the unfortunate person. A Hindu named Dharam Chand gets circumcised so that he can pass through an area occupied by the Muslims. This very subterfuge proves calamitous for him when he reaches a Hindu dominated area. The custodians of religion there chop off his penis with all the sadistic pleasure at their command. Likewise in "Jelly" all the innocence reserved for childhood in the local folklore and literary discourse, turns barbarous when the coagulated blood of the ice-seller looks like jelly to the child. How before the dance of the evil-spirits, the life of those who were spared, turns out to be a fate worse than death becomes evident in "Out of Consideration." In this three-lined anecdote a woebegone person's daughter is spared her life only to be raped.

In her otherwise circumspective study, Leslie A Flemming calls these pieces "intellectual jokes" which foreshadow his "later sarcasm" and suggests that Manto had yet to feel "deeply the pain of partition." There may be an element of truth in this objection if it is assumed that the message lies only in what the text denotes. If what its textuality connotes is received along with it, then this objection does not seem valid enough. Nevertheless, her objection to Mohammad Hasan Askari's contention that "man, even in his real shape, is acceptable to Manto, however he may be. He has already seen that man's humanity is tenacious enough so that even his becoming a wild animal cannot extinguish this humanity," is not without its grain of truth.[4]

Manto's celebrated short stories, are not open to objections of the type Flemming makes. If they are accountable, it is to a seamless and boundless counterpoint in which "various themes play off one another, with only a provisional privilege being given to any particular one; yet in the resulting polyphony there is concert and order, an organised interplay that derives from the themes, not from a rigorous melodic or formal principle outside the work."[5] In other words, it is their whole trajectory of production, reception and effect that can be challenged, but only by reckoning them with the contention that "there is no document of civilisation which is not at the same time a document of barbarism."[6]

The first story that comes to mind is "Thanda Gosht" (Cold Meat).[7] In this story Kulwant Kaur, the hot-blooded mistress of Ishwar Singh, flies into wild rage on suspecting that during his looting spree he has been with another woman. For all the fore-play in which he indulges through biting, sucking, smacking, kissing and licking, he cannot make love to her. Wild with rage, she calls the other woman a creature from hell. Provoked by his reluctance to reveal her identity, Kulwant Kaur takes his sword and mortally wounds him. In his last moments, partly out of penitence and partly to recompense for his mistress's rage, Ishwar Singh tells her that he had tried to make love to a young woman after killing six members of her family. At the moment of entering her, he had found out that she was dead, i.e. cold meat that he himself becomes at the end of the story.

Violence as the sole leitmotif of the story permeates every aspect of its structure and texture. If looting, plundering and killing comprise its nightmarish history, then impotence, hacking and blood-curdling screams are aspects of its catastrophic sexuality. Although the nightmarish and catastrophic message of the story is overwhelming, Askari reads hope in Ishwar Singh's remorse. Manto's own assertion that, "even at the last limits of cruelty and violence, of barbarity and bestiality, he does not lose his humanity,"[8] is a pointer in that direction. Whether this last glimmer of remorse can provide sustenance to a life convulsed with violence is problematic. To derive from it the possibility of a new range of experience and new horizon of hope is to transfigure a glimmer into revelation.

More excruciating than "Thanda Gosht" is Manto's story "Khol Do" (Open It)[9] in which the predatoriness that marked the formation of Pakistan under the ruse of Koranic dispensation is laid bare with brutal lucidity. The central character of the story is an old man who has lost his daughter Sakeena, while escaping from marauders. Feeling that his existence has lost all meaning and purpose, he trudges from one place to another in search of her. At last, he beseeches the razakars, who pretend to be social workers, to help him to recover her.

After ten days of praying and waiting, the old man finds himself by the side of the unconscious body of a girl whom the razakars had found on the roadside several days earlier. During those days they had presumably gang-raped her. No wonder when the doctor asks the old man to open the window, the half-dead girl automatically pulls her salwar down. Though the doctor is shocked and ashamed, the old man is beside himself with joy when he realises that his daughter is alive.

The story shows that Pakistani society, from the moment of its inception, had turned brutal despite the theological ideals held forth in its defense. By making Pakistan the locus for this horrendous incident, Manto does not exonerate the rest of India. The fate of Sakina was not exceptional. But for it to occur in Pakistan was an inexcusable crime. Manto believed that brutality could not extinguish human concerns, particularly those which drew sustenance from filial and fraternal feelings. Whether they could bring a derailed society back on the path of humanity is, however, a problematic question.

The most disturbing of Manto's stories is "Toba Tek Singh,"[10] in which an asylum is offered as a paradigm of the country. In actuality, the inhabitants of asylum emerge as better persons than the citizens of both Pakistan and India. As if eager to bring the treatment of the partition to the point of culmination, Manto begins this story with anecdotes reminiscent of "Siyah Hashye." Two insane persons. a Muslim and Sikh, pose as Jinnah and Master Tara Singh and wrestle with the ambiguity that stares them in the face due to the vivisection of the country.

Ultimately, the story focuses on an old Sikh, Bishan Singh, who can speak only in nonsense syllables. His whole effort is directed towards finding out whether Toba Tek Singh, a place in Punjab, has been allotted to Pakistan. No one can enlighten him on this score. At the border, learning from a liaison officer that the place has gone to Pakistan, he refuses to cross over to the Indian side. Left standing with his feet on both sides of the border, he collapses:

> Before the sun rose, a piercing cry arose from Bishan Singh who had been quiet and unmoving all the time. Several officers and guards ran towards him; they saw that the man, who for fifteen years had stood on his legs day and night, now lay on the ground prostrate. Beyond a wired fence on one side of him was Hindustan and beyond a wired fence on the other side was Pakistan. In the middle, on the stretch of land which had no name, lay Toba Tek Singh (p. 9).

For all the surreal identity that Manto constructs at first between the subcontinent and the lunatic asylum, and the disparity that he then inserts between the two, there is something in his critique that keeps it floundering. This lack is a result of his failure to visualise an alternative way of living, something at which the medieval *Guru-Kavis* and *Sufi-Shairs* were so adept. For example, in his memorable composition about Babar's invasion of India, Guru Nanak (1469-1539) exposes the predatoriness of the invaders, the impotence of the native rulers, the hypocrisy of the priests and the helplessness of the people. He even questions God for His accountability and thereby visualises a system in which violence will have no place:

Creator Thou art of all,
If the mighty beat the mighty
There is no cause for complaint.
But should the mighty lion fall on the herd
the owner has to answer.
The dogs have lost diamonds and jewels
And are unaware like the dead.
Thou Thyself bringest all together and then pull all apart,
All this is Thy greatness.[11]

Likewise, the great *Sufi-Shair*, Bule Shah (1680-1758), laments over the misery that has befallen the Punjab:

Come to me, O Love,
The gates of hell have opened,
Punjab has fallen on evil days
It is like the deepest hell.
The twelfth century has opened its jaws
Come sometime beloved of all,
Between the sky and earth,
Your woes are killing me.
Bulle, the beloved, will come to my house
And quench the fire blazing in me.[12]

For all that, he does not obliterate from his mind the feasibility of some alternative way of living.

With all his agnosticism, why Manto should have kept himself aloof from the influence of these medieval writers, particularly the *Sufi-Shairs* is very baffling indeed. All the more so because in his non-conformist way of living he was not unlike them. Indeed, Manto shared a structure of feeling with Ghalib, though his experiences were different. Perhaps he could not keep at bay the cynicism that Ghalib's agnosticism was free from. Maybe colonial rule had made all the difference and he had no option but to look with cynicism upon the people, with an element of compassion reserved of course for the fallen section i.e. prostitutes, pimps and the deprived ones.

3

Most of the Punjabi short stories[13] on the partition pale into insignificance before those of Manto. They either go off the mark or are inane as far as the laying bare of terror, brutality and inhumanity goes. Factors responsible for the partition are recalled or referred to in several of these short stories. Their treatment, however, nowhere matches the bewildering lucidity brought to bear upon them in "Toba Tek Singh" through strategies of identification and distinction, etc. In "Janam Bhoomi" (Native Land) written by Devendra Satyarthi (1908–), love for one's birth-place is held responsible for the indignities suffered by the people. Too much love, even if it is for one's place of birth, is sinful because it violates the notions of detachment sanctified by the traditional Indian ethos. In "Phatu Marasi" (Phatu, the low caste) by Gurbachan Bhullar (1937–) the responsibility for horror rests on a supernatural power seeking retribution. As the interlocutor recalls, "It was a deluge my lord, a dark deluge. The sanity of all vanished into thin air. None is to be blamed for that. It was some deluge that God had ordained (p. 155). Surely, this inane remark mystifies the reasons for the brutality of the partition. Quite the opposite of what Manto aimed at in his stories.

Other than these mundane factors, there are other factors that are held responsible for this horrendous occurrence. In Satyarthi's story, the blame is apportioned to the British who altered the complexion of life. No doubt they did that for their own interests but for the Indians first to approve the alteration and then to push the British out, was sinful. In another story "Chattu" (Mortar), written by a woman writer, Sukhwant Kaur Mann (1937–), the blame for all the ensuing dislocation is reserved for Jinnah and Jawaharlal Nehru in almost in equal measure. No wonder when the news broadcaster mentions their names, the aged woman in the story begins hurling abuses upon both of them. Here, the aim is to underscore the responsibility that rested on the political leaders. But instead of being made the leitmotif, it is only hinted at. As the partition became imminent, a sweeping change took place in the life of the people. There are several short stories in which the lineaments of this change acquire graphic description. At least two short stories are worthy of mention in this regard. One is "Bhua Fatima" (Aunt Fatima) by Balwant Gargi (1916-) in which the focus is upon the change taking place in the behaviour of the people: "The ditch of hatred between the Muslims and the Hindus was getting deeper. Leaders on both sides were raising slogans in favour of their respective religions. In temples and mosques, *kirtans* and *qawalies* were in full swing. Slogans were being trumpeted from both the sides...Fanaticism was at its height"(p. 215). The short story "Ulahma" (Complaint) by Kulwant Singh Virk[14] (1920-1987) takes into account the change that intrusively gets into the feelings and emotions of the people and segregates members of one community from those of the other. The basis for this change is laid by rumours of riots. Merging into the atmosphere, they begin to determine the environment itself. Thus begins the change that alienates the villagers from their hearths, homes, crops and even domestic animals that were once so inextricably a part of their lives. Driven by some unaccountable impulse, they have to find refuge in camps. The following description highlights the nuances this change involved:

> Within a day or so, ploughing came to a standstill. Those who used to sow seeds in the field, felt estranged. Of what use was the sowing of crops which they could not later on harvest? There was talk of burning down the houses which till then had been kept spick and span by them. They now thought of nothing else leaving the place. Gradually, all the Hindus of the area left for refugee camps as crickets fly to one side when water flows into the field from the other. Within a week or so, the Hindus and Sikhs had segregated themselves

from the Muslim population just as village women separate grains of one sort from those of another by winnowing them.

Only, the lucky ones were destined to get shelter in refugee camps. For others much horror was in store. "Bhootan Di Khed"[15] (Play of Evil Spirits) by Sant Singh Sekhon (1908) bears ample witness to the horror of the partition. The story begins with a graphic description of fifty Muslims, including women, children and aged persons, kept confined in the dharamshala of a village. They can go nowhere and even defecating and urinating is a problem for them. Then they are driven in groups of ten each to a nearby field to be done to death. In this case, the tide turns because there is amongst them a beautiful woman who charms one of the killers so much that when she consents to marry him, these helpless beings are reprieved. In Gurbax Singh Preetlari's "Mubina Ke Sukina"[16] (Mubina or Sukina) mortal panic grips the whole village, so much so that well-to-do persons have great difficulty in rescuing themselves from the wrath of the marauders. Here, a couple have to leave behind the infant daughter whose wailing could at any time jeopardise their life. Similarly, "Heera Mirg" (The Antelope) by Mohinder Singh Sarna (1926-) describes how hell breaks loose upon a village as a result of which innocent men and women lose their lives and become playthings for the murderous spree indulged in by the witch-hunters.

No less harrowing was the sexual violation of women often committed with impunity. Of course, the voracity of the rapists in these stories does not match what their counterparts embody in Manto's stories. Likewise, the affliction of the victims is not altogether as deadening or traumatic though it is depicted without any ambiguity whatsoever. A typical example is provided by Kartar Singh Duggal's (1916-) "Kulsum" (Kulsum)[17] in which an old man, supposedly a village priest, locks up a young girl in his dark house in order to offer her as a gift to the young school master. Tall, well-built and fair as she is, the school master tries to have sex with her forcibly. The young girl resists his advances, at first meekly and then ferociously, almost like a lioness. Then, she pleads with him to marry her with all the earnestness at her command. Grossly insensitive to her largely conventional but at the same time solemn feelings, he gets offended and walks out of the room in disgust. Taking umbrage over her alleged arrogance, the old man goes in and rapes her in no time. The school master enters the room again, this time to find her in a dishevelled state.

All these stories are replete with motifs which Manto has also grappled with. Wherever, as in Kartar Singh Duggal's story, the motif seems to be borrowed, it ends up as a pale repetition of Manto's masterly treatment. When it marks a departure, as in Sant Singh Sekhon's or Kulwant Virk's story, it does not go far enough to expose the horrors of the partition. The engagement they promise with the dramatic aspect of the partition does not offer any new perspectives and explanations.

4

The following stories, in which the primary leitmotif of fear, estrangement, ravishment and rape is held in counterpoint by the secondary motif of a new horizon of hope, seek to carry this engagement towards an alternative view of the partition. They, thus, aspire to go beyond Manto in the dissemination of a message if not in the whole trajectory of their production, reception and effect. The first story to come to mind in this regard is Kartar Singh Duggal's, "Pakistan Hamra Hai" (Pakistan is Ours).[18] This is the story of a young Hindu girl who, in order to escape the turmoil, seeks shelter with a Muslim family. Otherwise a desperado, the young man of the family falls in love with this girl and marries her. So powerful is the marital bond between them that she refuses to go to India when the armymen come to recover her for repatriation. Her forthright reply to them is: "I won't go, I shall never go. These trees are ours and so are their leaves. This plant that I have been watering is yet to grow"(p. 91).

In this plea is latent the effort to undo the partition through invoking a deep attachment for the marital bond and one's natal home that reclaims the natural ambiance for its support. Though a source of sustenance to the man and woman concerned, it cannot replace the political decision arrived at for malevolent reasons by the politicians. In Kulwant Singh Virk's short-story "Khabal"[19] (Perennial Grass) renewed kinship is visualised as a way of facing, if not of undoing, the disastrous consequences which the partition has brought in its trail. It concerns a young married woman from a Sikh family who is abducted by a Muslim and kept in a dilapidated house in a village which can't be easily reached. The recovery-officer, himself a Sikh, goes there against all odds so as to rescue her for her sake, if not for that of her community and country. The miserable condition in which he finds the woman almost bewilders him:

> In that house made of brick and mud, the abducted wife of another man lay helplessly before me on a cot. I could not think of an uglier image of man's inhumanity to man. Abducted, raped and humiliated, she lay quietly and still. There was not one from her caste, community, religion or village with her. No one had told her that she could once again be with the people who were dear to her. Perhaps, if some one had told her, she would have refused to believe him. After all, how could any one rescue her from such a big and strong country like Pakistan? It was foolish even to dream of such an attempt (p. 207).

When the recovery-officer tells her that he would come to take her after a few days, she pleads for quite a different sort of favour. Her plea to him is to put her in contact with her sister-in-law who had been abducted by persons of the nearby village. She wants that young girl, whom she had brought up like a daughter, to be with her. Only then would she be able to fine a good match for her and forge a kinship to sustain her through life.

In Sant Singh Sekhon's[20] two stories, historical memory and cultural heritage are sought to be invoked so as to make this sustenance not only veritable but efficacious as well. In his story "Jitt Te Haar" (Victory and Defeat), the central character, Mehardin, who is the chief of a Muslim village in the vicinity of the Sikh population, finds no heresy in persuading his brethren to convert to Sikhism. What disposes him to do so is not fear of the turmoil raging around at that moment of time. It is rather the retrospective feeling, that their ancestors had done something wrong by reneging their cultural patrimony several centuries back, which now strengthens his disposition in this direction. Added to it is his innate instinct that, in the absence of any kinship and cultural alignment, they as mohajirs, will not feel at home in Pakistan, the terrain of which is likely to be alien, and that too not just in a geographical sense. Further strength accrues to Meherdin's position from the example of Malerkotla where the Muslims and Sikhs lived peacefully if not amicably even during the dark days when killings and abductions went on in other areas. This was in gratitude to an earlier ruler of the state, who in the court of the Subedar of Sirhind, had raised his voice against the martyrdom of the younger sons of Guru Gobind Singh. How Mehardin's mind, although racked by conflicting feelings, arrived at a resolve of this sort is best conveyed through the following intricate sentence:

> In those days, swayed by mixed feelings, Mehardin, the village chief, thought about the varying historical stages and decided that it would be the undoing of a historic wrong if he could persuade his brethren to convert to Sikhism and repair the rupture since then undergone with the neighbouring Sikh nationality (p. 96).

His brethren readily agree to his suggestion and quickly begin to integrate with the Sikhs. Inter-marriages take place lending credence to the hope that the area between Delhi and Amritsar will acquire a new cultural configuration. This is the best illustration of society taking history into own hands not only to defeat the divisive tactics of the polity but to also organise a better future. However, the governments of India and Pakistan arrive at an agreement to repatriate Muslim, Hindu and Sikh women from both sides. Mehardin's own daughter, Zeenat, who had married a Sikh, is also repatriated. However, her husband, like the legendary Ranjha who assumed several subterfuges to recover Heer, also reaches Pakistan and settles with her there. Thereafter, their life passes peacefully and they occasionally visit India to see their relatives. They are happy that their marital bond is secure. But, the failure of Mehardin's dream of a cultural unity does not bother them at all.

In the next story "Amanat" (Trust), the same issue figures only to meet with a similar denouement. In this story, there is a Muslim girl who, as her family is getting ready to migrate, slips away and seeks shelter with a Sikh boy for whom she professes a fondness. They get married but she is soon forced to go to Pakistan. Delivered to her family there, she is married off to a collateral who for her beauty's sake, accepts her though she is pregnant from her first husband. A son is born to her and to entrust him to his rightful father, she returns to India under the pretext of visiting her relatives in Malerkotla. She meets her former husband who has so far kept his vow not to marry and who is gratified to get his son. As a token of gratitude and of further identification, he registers a legal deed to transfer his land to his son. The story ends with his tearful farewell to the woman who was earlier his wife and then the mother of his son, the rightful heir of his property.

The denouement of both the stories rests on a decision which does not take into account the cultural problematic that impelled the characters to take recourse to exceptional thinking and feeling. This shows that the egoistic and passional content which had animated their unconscious does not become a part of their political consciousness and ethical conscience. As a result the agenda that the good sense of these writers has projected for a national-popular unification of the Punjabi people is likely to be evanescent. This dilutes the texture of these stories, and the failure of the writers to infuse alternative richness is catastrophic a portent for the Punjabi imagination as the partition was for the history of the region. So true is Walter Benjamin's prescient observation here:. "Every image of the past that is not recognised by the present as one of its own concerns threatens to disappear irretrievably."[21] Whether the Punjabi writers will accept the challenge of this irretrievable disappearance into an irrevocable reality, is a question to which there is yet no viable answer.

REFERENCES

1. E.J. Hobsbawn, *The Age of Capital*. London: Sphere Books, 1977, p. 304.
2. *Millions on the Move*, Government of India Publications, p. 10.
3. New York: Viking, 1991.
4. *The Life and Works of Saadat Hasan Manto*. Lahore: Vangaurd, 1985, p. 74.
5. Edward Said, *Culture and Imperialism*. London, Chatto and Windus 1993, pp. 59-60.
6. Walter Benjamin, *Illuminations*, pp. 257-258.
7. *Stories About the Partition*. Volume I, II, III edited by Alok Bhalla. New Delhi: Harper Collins, 1994. "Thanda Gosht" figures in the first volume under the title "Cold Meat" on pp. 91-97.
8. "Riots and Refugees: The Post-partition Stories of Saadat Hasan Manto," paper presented at the 4th Punjab Studies Conference Columbia 12-14 April 1973.
9. Alok Bhalla, vol. II, pp. 69-73.
10. Alok Bhalla, vol. III, pp. 1-9.
11. Quoted in *A History of Punjabi Literature* by Sant Singh Sekhon, Patiala: Punjabi University, 1993, vol. 1, p. 208.
12. *A History of Punjabi Literature*, vol. I, 1996, p. 218.
13. Reference may be made to *Desh-Vand dian Kahanian*, edited by Jaswant Deed and published by New Delhi: Sahitya Akademi, 1995.

Most of the illustrations are drawn from this collection. The writer of this paper has himself rendered them into English.

14. Kulwant Singh Virk, *Merian Sharesht Kahanian* (My Best Stories). Delhi: Navyug Publishers, 1980, p. 54.

15. Sant Singh Sekhon, *Sekhon dian Kahanian* (Sekhon's Stories). Jalandhar: Central Publishers, 1966, pp. 181-187.

16. Its English translation is available in *Stories About the Partition of India*, vol. III, pp. 181-190. Included under the title "The Abandoned Child," it is wrongly attributed to Gurmukh Singh Musafir. Actually, the story is by Gurbax Singh Preetlari.

17. For an English translation see *Stories About the Partition of India*, vol. III pp. 91-95.

18. Jaswant Deed, *Desh-Vand Kahanian* (edited).

19. Alok Bhalla, vol. I, p. 207. His English translation of the title as "Weeds" is negative in its connotation and, therefore, seems inappropriate.

20. These two stories figure in his collection *Sianpan* (Sagacities). Ludhiana: Lahore Book Shop 1982. Its preface is written by the author of this paper.

21. Walter Benjamin, *Illuminations*, p. 257.

Manto's Philosophy: An Explication

ASHOK VOHRA

> I do not write on a black-board with a black chalk. I use a white chalk so that the darkness of the blackboard is more pronounced.
>
> —Manto

The corpus of stories, short stories, pen-portraits and other writings left behind by Manto continue to puzzle and surprise us. They are full of contradictions. Some of them portray an adolescent's dreams of the possible outcome of a stray affair with a woman, or the visions of a teenager in love which are thoroughly romantic and idealistic; others are down to earth in describing the stark realities of a cruel, strife-torn world broken into narrow water-tight segments by gender, religion, economic disparities, class and caste barriers. Some of his stories are compassionate and sympathetic to the oppressed and exploited sections of society, especially to prostitutes, who, for Manto, are the paradigms of the middle class exploitation. One can say that a prostitute in Manto's stories is a symbol of the oppressed and exploited class of society. She represents the hapless class of people who find themselves, by force of circumstances, in a given situation, and have such a weak will that they cannot even think of changing it, not to talk of revolting against it. They accept their fate and continue to believe that they are doomed to lead the life they are leading. In short, one can say that they are fatalists. Naturally, they are objects of our sympathy as well as pity. This can be demonstrated by taking the representative examples of Manto's portrayal of the characters of Sultana, Zeenat, Sugandhi and Sarita. Sultana in "Kali Salwar," whose brothel is near a railway yard, on watching "a railway coach that must have been given a push by an engine and was moving along the tracks by itself was reminded of her own life. She thought that someone had given her a push on the rails of life and left her, and that she was going along all by herself; other people gave the signals and she went along. Where she was headed for she did not know. She knew that one day, when the force of the push weakened she would stop somewhere, at a place which she knew nothing about." And Manto describes Zeenat in "Babu Gopinath" thus: "To the limit of annoyance, Zeenat was a woman without understanding, without desires and without life. The poor thing didn't even have a sense of value." She is depicted as a passive and dependent woman who is driven to the extreme. Sugandhi in "Hatak" is happy because she has to be happy though there is no reason for her to be happy. Her life is as eventless as ever. "Still she wishes that her days should go on passing the same way. She does not have to bother about making more money since she has no desire to construct buildings or improve her life." Likewise, Sarita in "Das Rupaye" entertains customers not because she wants to, but because others tell her to. And Mangu of "Naya Kanoon" traces the cause of Hindu-Muslim riots to a Pir's curse. He believes that as a result of this curse, India would always be ruled by foreigners.

While Manto's treatment of such lumpen characters in some of his stories is empathetic, his other stories dealing with the same section of society make fun of them and are thoroughly sarcastic. But irrespective of the genre to which the stories belong, they are thoroughly humanitarian and compassionate. His characters though egoistical, restless and rebellious show a remarkable combination of rebellious individualism and humanistic regard for their fellowmen. Some of his stories are full of the hope of a better tomorrow for mankind, whereas his anguish at the present state of affairs in many of his stories culminates in a kind of deep cynicism in which even the possibility of redemption is completely discounted. It is because of these contradictory traits in Manto that Abu Said Quraishi called him a *raham dil dahshat pasand,* a kind-hearted terrorist. The reason for ascribing this contradictory title to him can be traced to the fact that "in all his stories Manto seems to have struggled with two basic and opposing tendencies—a humanistic tender regard for other people and an anarchistic desire to rebel against all restraints. That neither tendency fully subdued the other, was perhaps the reason for his puzzling and contradictory behaviour and writing."[1]

This contradiction can be resolved if we look at the philosophy which lies behind his writings. At the outset it must be noticed that, unlike his contemporaries, Manto's stories are not set in the countryside, nor are they about poverty-stricken peasants or the problems of the rural folk. Instead they are about the working class urbanites. This is primarily because Manto did not write about things which he was not directly acquainted with, or had little knowledge of. But this should not lead one to think that Manto wrote only about matters which he directly experienced. Krishan Chander made this mistake. When commenting on Manto's story "Lalten," he observed: "Most of the story seems to me to be about Manto's own experiences. In its parts and in its final words, the sadness and weariness which are apparent seem themselves to be parts of Manto's romantic life."[2] Manto explicitly states in his article "Kasoti" that, "Literature does not portray the personal experiences of the author. An author picks up his pen not to write details about his own personal work-a-day life, or to give a description of his personal happinesses, sorrows, likes and dislikes, nor does he report on his personal health or sickness. His descriptions are likely to contain the tears of his sad sister, your smiles and the laughter of a poverty-stricken labourer." He is of the firm opinion that the moment a piece of literature is adjudged on the basis of the author's own experiences, achievements and failures, happinesses and sorrows, it becomes lifeless.

It was Manto's resolute conviction that literature is a mirror of reality. With changing reality there is a change in literature also. A writer picks one issue or the other with which society is confronted at a given time and he writes about it. He writes sometimes in favour of it and sometimes against it. Sometimes the writings are quite palatable to the society at large, and the powers that be in particular, but at other times they may be repulsive. An author is not a prophet. His main task is to depict reality as he perceives it with all sincerity. An author, Manto said, "sees one thing, one problem in different conditions and from different angles, and whatever he understands he presents to the world but he never forces the world to accept it."[3] That is why "literature" according to him "is not a sickness, but rather a response to sickness. It is also not a medicine which has to be used according to a prescription. Literature is a measure of the temperature of its country, of its nation. It informs of its health and sickness."[4]

Secondly, Manto, unlike his contemporaries like Premchand, Suhail Azimabadi, Ali Akbar Husaini *et al*, does not take a socially oriented view of literature as an instrument of social reform. His writings, therefore, are not reformist in character. They do not contain sympathetic portraits of the poor and the downtrodden. Nor do they make the fundamental problems of our life like hunger, poverty, social backwardness and slavery their subject. His works neither prescribe nor proscribe anything. In fact Manto in his "Afsana Nigar Aur Zinsi Masail," categorically asserts that "we (the litterateurs) are not legislators, nor do we prescribe or proscribe anything; legislating and administering is the job of others. We pass comments on the rulers but we are not the rulers. We draw maps of the buildings but are not ourselves the builders. We tell others what they are suffering from but we do not own the chemist's shop." It is precisely for this reason that Manto does not even explore the social problems created by poverty, oppression, caste and religious barriers.

Manto, on the other hand, makes man in his social setting the centre of all his stories. Like Locke and Rousseau, he believes in the essential goodness of man. It is social conditioning which robs man of this goodness. As he says: "One man is not very different from the other. The mistake committed by one can be committed by the other also. If one woman can set up a shop to sell her body, so can all the women, of the world. But it is not men who are the wrong-doers, the wrong-doers are the circumstances in which men commit mistakes and have to live with their consequences."[5] Like Sartre, he believes that men have an infinite capacity to transcend their given situation. All men and women, irrespective of their social-cultural-political-religious-economic standing, are equally capable of committing praiseworthy and blameworthy acts. Those who are high up in the social hierarchy can fall below their best moral standards. They can be hypocritical, dishonest, and insensitive to human needs. On the contrary, those who are at the bottom of the social scale can be honest and humane with pure and pious motivation. The character of Mammad Bhai shows that those who can kill a person without even batting an eyelid, those whom we consider to be dare-devils and paragons of courage, may at heart be really scared of even an injection needle.

We occupy different stations in life, sometimes because of our own peculiar social situations, and sometimes because of our innate capacities, but one thing is certain that each one of us, irrespective of our status in society, the culture and age we belong to, has the innate desire to be appreciated, admired and accepted. Manto recognised this desire as basic. His writings, therefore, provide reassurance to the oppressed, the downtrodden and the neglected that they are good. His story "Hatak" clearly demonstrates this. Askari, while commenting on "Siyah Hashye," wrote: "Man, even in his real shape, is acceptable to Manto, however he may be. He has already seen that man's humanity is tenacious enough so that even his becoming a wild animal cannot extinguish this humanity. Manto has confidence in this humanity."[6] Manto himself stressed this when defending the charge of obscenity levelled against him for his story, "Thanda Gosht," he said: "...even at the last limits of cruelty and violence, of barbarity and bestiality, he does not lose his humanity. If Ishwar Singh had completely lost his humanity, the touch of the dead woman would not have affected him so violently as to strip him of his manhood."[7]

Just as Manto believed in the perennial goodness of man, he also believed that there were certain aspects of human life which are universal and enduring. These according to him are: *"roti, aurat aur takht"* (bread, woman and the throne). According to him, "Man felt the pangs of hunger in the ancient days, and continues to feel them even now. He had the desire to be powerful earlier and even now. He continues to love wine and poetry as he did in the days gone by. Then what has changed?...Nothing. It is only when man is tired of bread, woman and power that he thinks of God whose nature is much more mysterious and difficult to grasp than any of these."[8]

Hunger, according to him, is the mother of all problems. It arose when Adam felt hungry for the first time. Another kind of hunger arose when the first man met the first woman. Both these hungers are at the back of most of the social, economic, political problems. They are also the cause of most crimes and follies. Manto was convinced of the fact that, "Hunger teaches us to beg, it encourages us to commit crimes, it forces us to become prostitutes. It teaches us to be selfish, lonely and isolated. Its attack is very fierce and all encompassing and it hurts us deeply. Hunger produces madness, madness is not the cause of hunger."[9] So, he concluded that all literature—whether modern, medieval or ancient, deals with the most ancient of relationships between bread and hunger, between man and woman. So much so that "even the religious books, some of which are said to be gospels, deal with the relationship between bread and hunger, between man and woman."[10] Manto was asked: if the relationship between man and woman and bread and hunger, is so perennial that it has been the subject matter of discussion from the most ancient religious books to the most modern writers, then why is there a need to take them up again and again? Manto replied somewhat elliptically: "Had the whole world stopped telling lies when it was told to do so once, one messiah would have been sufficient. But as we all know the list of messiahs is long."[11] He admits, though, that there is no fundamental difference between the problems faced by the litteratuers of today and those faced by the litteratuers of yester-years. Both of them write in the idiom and manner which is most suitable to their times. And that is what makes the literature of each epoch novel and unique.

Man, in whose humanity Manto has an inalienable faith, is invariably confronted with perennial problems. He has to make a choice. Man is, to use a Sartrian phrase, condemned to choose. "When he chooses to love a woman, the parable of Heer-Ranjha is made. If he chooses to love bread, the philosophy of Epicurus takes birth. He becomes Sikander, Chengiz or Taimur when he chooses to love power. And if he chooses to love God, he is transformed into a Buddha."[12]

Manto, probably under the influence of Freud, chose to write primarily on the man-woman relationship. He completely ignored the spiritual aspect of this relationship. Justifying his choice, he said, "Our age is an age of strange contradictions—woman is close yet very far. At some places she is fully dressed, but at other places she is completely naked. At some places she is seen in the guise of a man, and at others we are confronted with men in the guise of women."[13] He set before himself the aim of drawing a good and effective portrait of society and did not bother about his critics. In his own words: "I am only a painter (photographer) and those who have an ugly face do not like the mirror."[14] He took upon himself the task of painting a realistic picture of society. Literature, according to him "ought to present life as it is, not as it was, nor as it ought to be."[15] Manto's view of literature can be compared with Wittgenstein's method of doing philosophy. Like Wittgenstein, Manto too simply puts everything before us as it is and neither explains nor deduces anything. Since everything is open to view, there is nothing to explain either. And like him, Manto does not use lengthy narratives to describe either the settings of his story or his characters. Instead, he uses just a few words to describe them.

Manto disliked hypocrisy, pretence, and the double standards prevalent in society. Wherever he saw these he 'inwardly' fumed (cf. "Chughad"). His aim in his stories was to expose these evils. That is why he made prostitutes the subject of his stories. Thus, Manto, speaking through Babu Gopi Nath, in the story by the same title, replying to the question: "Why do you like prostitutes' houses and holy men's places?" says, "Because in those two places, from the floor to ceiling, there is nothing but deception. For the man who wants to deceive himself, there are no better places than these."

Manto presents a realistic exposition of the psychological states of the people found in these places. He also gives a detailed account of their human interaction and their social relationships. In all his stories, Manto emphasises that exploitation results from dependence. This can be seen from the characters of Sugandhi and Sultana.

He narrates in a down to earth manner, the helplessness of the poor, the downtrodden and the underdog and depicts realistically, "the mental and emotional states born under the influence of this helplessness."[16] To narrate this and to express his point of view, Manto does not hem and haw. What he has to say he says clearly, without any jargon and without any artifice, in the most direct manner. He does not try to make up with words what is not there in reality. In the words of Mohammad Ali Sidiqqui, "In his mind and ideas there is no holding back, no deceptive cover...there is no desire to impress or be impressed. He is not afraid of calling good good and bad bad."[17] Manto, talking about his style of writing, admits, "There is no equipment for beautification in my parlour, there is no shampoo, there is no machine to produce trinkets. I do not know how to do make up...I do not know the art of replacing expletives with nice and polite words..."[18] His sincerity of purpose and his love for putting what he sees in society in simple and plain words was responsible for his inherent dislike of classical poetry. Infact, he dislikes classical poetry so much that he calls it "mental masturbation," for it invariably camouflages even the most ugly reality under the cover of pleasant words and word constructions. Manto has the capacity to percieve and examine the bitter truth, and the courage to express it without any camouflage—either of words or of circumstances. He does not compromise at any level—whether it is in the use of expletives or the choice of common place words. Nothing is hidden, nothing is exaggerated. Everything, however obscene or unsayable it may be, is said in the most straightforward manner, that is, without subterfuge or exaggeration. There is no attempt at philosophising or artificial theorising. He is conciously revolutionary. In "Sarak Ke Kinare," he boldly asks the question: "Whose law is this? Earth's? Heaven's?...or that of those who made it?" He openly ridicules religion (for example, in "Mozel"); makes fun of God by saying that he is hungry for prayers, and points to the oppressiveness of traditional social institutions without any hesitation (as in "Ji Ayah Sahab" and "Khuni Thuk"). His capacity for calling a spade a spade does not even spare the dead. He reacts strongly when one Mr. 'Buniyadi' reminds him that it is customary, all over the civilized world, to talk about the dead, even if they were one's enemies, in reverential tones. He says, "I detest strongly the civilization in which it is customary to send the character and the personality of a person after his death to a laundry. So that after it is cleansed of its blemishes, it is hung in a corner at the mercy of God."[19]

Manto has been accused by some academic critics, like Rashid Ahmed Siddiqqui, of taking pleasure in giving lurid descriptions of a woman's physique and charged with erotic and obscene writing. Some critics have called him a man with a perverted taste who exploits sexuality as an end in itself in his stories. Nothing can be farther from truth than this. As far as Manto's description of sex is concerned, one has to note that he does not cut off sex from lived life. In his narrations sex is not detached from life, rather it is made an instrument for understanding and explaining life. For him sex is not an isolated event or an accident in a person's life. His descriptions of sex are matter of fact. They neither create a liking, nor a hatred for sex. They are neutral and objective. They do not tantalize us. Sex is seen as a natural urge. He uses sex both for understanding and explaining the beautiful as well as the ugly aspects of life. It is only after examining the sexual urge that Manto arrives at the conclusion that the suppression of this natural urge leads to many imbalances both in the individual and the society. His story "Panch Din" demonstrates this very effectively. In it the main character, the school teacher, who had throughout his life, in favour of a false public image, refused to acknowledge the attraction he had felt for the girls he taught, announces from the death bed, "I killed a desire, but I didn't realize that after this murder, I would have to shed a lot more blood."

As far as the physical descriptions of a woman are concerned, one can easily say that instead of arousing the passions, these descriptions produce a feeling of revulsion for sex. For example, who would, after reading the following description of Sugandhi in "Hatak," be ever aroused: "She slept on a large, teak bed. Her arms, exposed all the way to her shoulders, were spread out like the bows of a lyre from which the paper had come off after having been left out in the wetness of the night. Protruding from the left underarm was a heavy fold of flesh which had, from being squeezed excessively, turned a bluish hue; it seemed that a segment of skin from a plucked chicken had been applied to that spot." Only a pervert can be aroused by a description which uses analogies like "skin from a plucked chicken" for the description of a woman's skin, or "bows of a lyre from which the paper had come off" for the description of a woman's arms. This kind of description can only arouse a feeling of revulsion. It would be equally wrong to say that Manto has a gender bias. For he always wonders how 'he' could feel fulfilled when 'she' feels robbed.

In fact Manto's aim, as has already been said, was to expose the social evils, the loneliness and alienation prevalent in society. His descriptions are intended to expose the oppressors who demean women. Their object is not to titillate, but to arouse in the reader a sympathy for the victim and disgust for the perpetrators. The descriptions are focussed on the trauma and emotional turmoil of the oppressed in order to evoke sympathy for him and disgust for the oppressor and exploiter. Since his aim is to illustrate the consequences of social evil, he has to depict that evil.

Manto first expressed surprise when his story "Thanda Gosht" was termed obscene by saying: "It pains me to learn that a story, which tells that a human being, even after becoming a devil, cannot escape being a human being is thought to be obscene."[20] Later, Manto himself replied to the charge of obscenity by saying: "What can I do if this story is obscene? The event on which it is based was itself obscene. Today, the whole of society is obscene."[21] In fact, he beckoned people to read his stories if they wanted to be acquainted with society. He said: "If you find my stories unbearable then this age is unbearable...I am not seditious. I do not want to stir up people's ideas and feelings. How can I take off the blouse of a culture and civilization which is already naked? I do not even try to dress it because that is not my job. It is the job of a tailor."[22] Moreover, in "Mozel," he questioned, "Can there be any kind of dress in which one may not become immodest, or through which your gaze can't travel?"

In the enterprise of exposing society, Manto is not at all bothered about critics. He holds critics in low esteem and believes that "criticism can only destroy a flower by plucking its petals, it cannot put them together to make a complete flower."[23] He thinks that critics are redundant because, "There have been innumerable critics, but none of them could help remove the drawbacks of literature."[24] How right he was about the critics can be shown by taking the example of Hanif Rane, one of his critics, who like the prophet of doom had predicted that "Nobody shall be interested in the works of Manto after his death." This seminar and the continuous sale of Manto's works over the years prove how wrong Hanif Rane was. The prediction which Manto had made when he said, "...it is also possible that Saadat Hasan may die, but Manto will not die," is a reality today.

NOTES

1. Leslie A. Flemming, *The Life and Works of Saadat Hassan Manto,* Lahore: Vanguard,1985, pp. 1-2.
2. *Manto,* Bombay: Kitab Publishers, 1948.
3. "Afsana Nigar aur Jinsi Misail."
4. "Kasoti."
5. "Afsana Nigar aur Jinsi Misail."
6. "Hashiyah Arai."
7. "Byan:Thanda Gosht."
8. "Kasoti."
9. "Afsana Nigar aur Zinsi Misail."
10. Ibid.
11. Ibid.
12. "Kasoti."
13. "Afsana Nigar aur Jinsi Misail."
14. Mehdi Ali Siddiqui, "Manto Meri Adalat Mein."
15. In Manto's letter dated November, 1938 to Ahmed Nadeem Qasmi.
16. Ibadat Barelvi, quoted in *The Life and Works of Saadat Hasan Manto,* op.cit., p. 49.
17. Mehdi Ali Siddiqui, "Manto Meri Adalat Mein."
18. "Ganje Farishte."
19. Ibid. Among the modern writers, Khushwant Singh is the only one who follows Manto in this respect both in word and deed.
20. "Byan: Thanda Gosht."
21. Mehdi Ali Siddiqui, op. cit.
22. Quoted in Devendra Issar, "Urdu Ka Weh Yugantakari Kahanikar."
23. "Kasoti."
24. "Saadat Hasan Manto."

The World of Saadat Hasan Manto

SHASHI JOSHI

The three axis through which I would examine the relationship between the literary imagination and rendition of the history of Manto's times, as it pours into the narrative of the partition are: (a) the axis of cultural stereotypes; (b) the category of cultural visibility which these stereotypes impart to people; (c) the cultural power that they appear to acquire or negate through their visibility or invisibility respectively. We need a language beyond fixed categories of good and evil, of victims and victimizers, and an obsessive focus on violence as an act of insanity, barbarism, pathology.[1]

The very nature of language and narrative, which Lyotard views as agonistic, generating a discourse of conflicting oppositions revolving around a struggle, can be revealed in the words spoken by characters in the partition stories. How does conflict get deposited in, and in turn produce, cultural significations? Examining cultural stereotypes and their visibility as it is apprehended by those involved in conflict, may help us comprehend how the binaries evolve.

But first, I would like to comment on Alok Bhalla's critique of what he calls "communal stories." His basic point is that these stories do not condemn both sides equally and do not uphold the principle of "correct rememberance."

I would go along with Veena Das and Ashish Nandy when they speak of much of the literature on the partition as "inauthentic, because...violence from one side is equally balanced with violence from the other. Thus, the description of violent, inhuman acts perpetuated upon those travelling by train coming from Lahore would be matched by another description of similar, gruesome acts to which travellers coming from Amritsar were subjected. If a prostitute gave shelter to two women whose bodies had been mutilated by rioters then one could be certain that one of those women would be a Hindu and the other a Muslim."[4]

As for "correct rememberance," literature, I believe, cannot perform a balancing act like the legendary scales of justice. It must portray a slice, howsoever thin, of life viewed through the eyes of its protagonist. An act of rememberance is always partial, incomplete and fragmentary. There are conflicting versions of 'truth' and they have to be recounted in their one-sidedness and not inflict contrived resolutions on the readers' intelligence and sensibility.

I tend to view Manto as being almost alone in grasping the fragmentation of 'truth' during his times and that is why the authorial voice is absent from his partition stories. The victims and victimizers could belong to any community, but do not inhabit the same story and no attempt is made to establish parity between the monstrosities committed by all. Manto could well have identified with Masood Ashar's helpless conclusion: "Truth has so many faces. One man's truth can negate another man's truth. And when so many versions of truth clash, everything becomes an absurdity, loses all meaning, all sense."[5] The result is Manto's Kafkaesque stories, most of all, "Fundanen" (Pompoms).

More specifically, I read the three stories characterized by Alok Bhalla as communal narratives, rather differently. For him, Ahmad Nadeem Qasmi's "Parmeshwar Singh" seeks "to evoke sublime pathos for the Muslims as victims" and caricatures the Sikh character, Parmeshwar Singh. In my reading of the story, the bond betweem the Sikh and the Muslim boy is palpable. The love Parmeshwar offers to Akhtar, though initially rebuffed by fear in the child's heart, gradually breaks through to the child and the child begins to trust him. Yet, he cannot replace the child's lost world —the cultural world of his socialization of the Azan and the Koran. Nor can he substitute the child's mother, whose memory is not an abstraction for Akhtar but a warm, sensuous memory of a woman who read the namaz and gave him a drink of water with a bismillah.

Amar Kaur, Parmeshwar's wife, who cries for her own lost son, is as real as Akhtar in her rejection of the child. Instead of her Kartar with hair in a bun, with a comb in it, she has a child reciting "qul huwallah-ho-ahad" under her roof. Gradually, as the child's hair begins to grow, she begins to soften, and feels happy when she touches his hair, bringing out the strong physicality of the mother and child bond. The day he can tie his hair in a bun, she says, they would name him Kartar Singh. Nevertheless, she weeps: "Kartar is that wound in my heart which will never heal". And seeing the wildly powerful love between a mother and child in his neighbour's house, Parmeshwar begins to move towards the finale of his story in which he walks Akhtar to the border so that he can find his mother. At one level, the cultural stereotypes imbedded in the situation are too strong to be overcome easily, at another, the cultural symbolism that pervades our senses as we seek our emotional sustenance in the familiar sounds and images, is conveyed by the story.

In "Avtar: A Hindu Myth," Gulam Abbas, according to Alok Bhalla, "invokes Hindu myths to suggest that since the Hindus had over millenniums betrayed their gods by indulging in the most reprehensible forms of killings, their gods had now decided in disgust to abandon them and send a new avtar on earth in a Muslim household. There is, of course, no hint of the history of massacres by the Muslims."[6]

I was stunned to read this passage. The story, as I read it, poignantly brings home a truth, that within the God-filled cosmology of the Hindus there is no barrier of untouchability between Hindu Gods and Muslim victims. The evil unleashed into the midst of the Muslims in the lonely valley ends in a fantastic, messianic dream-fulfilling sequence of the new Avtar Kalki, born to a poor, besieged Muslim. It is an imaginatively constructed story that encapsulates the heartrending cry of Muslim grief in this instance: "What crimes had your victims committed? That they believed in a different form of worship than yours?

That their style of life was different? Is that such a big crime that they should be exterminated?"

The entire story could well have been narrated to us by Mohandas Gandhi and no one would have called him communal. Must Abbas, because he is a Muslim, square the circle of history by trying to balance his account of Hindu violence with accounts of "massacres by the Muslims?"

Krishna Sobti's "Where is my Mother" is accused of playing upon the popular Hindu fear of the Pathan as a mindless killer. But from the outset, the Pathan is shown to be in the grip of ideology-fighting to create a new country for which the self had to be sacrificed; he was tearing across the country, with no moment to look at the moon and stars, fighting a revolutionary war, a jihad. Where is the mindlessness? In fact, Sobti's Pathan is a stereotype ingrained as a deathlike fear in the girl whom he rescues. It reveals the power of the stereotype and of prejudice, despite the care the Pathan lavishes on her. All his attempts to reach out to her are met with paranoia. When she pleads: "Send me to the camp. They will kill me here—they will kill me..." the steel bands of his ideology snap and "Yunus Khan was forced to lower his eyes. He no longer felt like a brave, powerful and ruthless soldier. He felt miserable, helpless... weak." Compassion and pity break through his jihad. The image and memory of his dead sister, Nooran, which first compelled him to save the girl, re-emerges and fills his voice with kindness only to be met by the girl's terror of him.

To my mind, Sobti's Pathan is the counterpart to Parmeshwar Singh and the denouement of both stories leaves them equally tragic figures longing for relationships they have lost.

Parmeshwar Singh's heartbreaking longing for his son and the Pathan's tender memories of his sister have not prevented them from going on sprees of looting and orgies of killing. The critical moments in their lives are when both adopt children from the other community. These are seen as moments of individual weakness by those around them and, perhaps, also by themselves. Their strength is felt in their collectivity. Clearly, as long as the sense of empowerment and self-significance gets concentrated in the collective, the humane individual is in a minority. Thus, moments of "weakness" cannot change or obliterate the deep-seated fears generated by the stereotypes which, in turn, feed further terror.

"You are a Muslim—you will kill me," screams Sobti's girl child, while Parmeshwar Singh's wife and the child, Akhtar, exchange frightened shouts of: "You are a mussalla!" and "You are a Sikh!" What makes bodies of flesh and blood, with the same limbs and eyes, the repositories of collective identity? The cultural significations of their collective give them a sense of visibility and power, and the body bears their burden.

There is a close relationship between perceptions of collective cultural power, the symbols of cultural visibility and the cultural stereotypes in daily life. It is thus that the body becomes the repository of cultural symbolism because cultural visibility is possible only through the body. In sum: cultural power gets concentrated and deposited in the signification of collective visibility and this visibility is concretized in the body. Therefore, to violate and destroy the body is to make the culture of the other's collective invisible. Making it invisible appears to disintegrate cultural power and make it disappear. The mutilation and extermination of the body therefore is deeply implicated in notions of 'us' and 'them,' and the play of power between them.

The woman's body is the site of the fiercest, most brutal contest and women emerge in all narratives as trophies of victory or blots on collective honour. Simultaneously, women are the greatest threats to man's stereotype of masculinity—the biggest chink in his armour. A woman transgresses all codes of colour, race, religion and caste the moment a man controls her body. It is in the laboratory of her body that the real mixing of blood is accomplished.

Cultural power is maintained, asserted or negated by maintaining, asserting or negating cultural visibility. Since cultural visibility is inscribed on the body in terms of cultural significations, and inside the body in terms of cultural stereotypes, the violation of the body becomes the key to the destruction of cultural power.

Cultural power and honour is further heightened by castrating the masculine 'other' by violating and conquering 'his' women. Destroying the male may negate immediate cultural visibility but cannot destroy the potential for its resurrection. The metaphor of 'beejnash' is inapplicable as long as women are left unpossessed and undestroyed.

Women, in almost all the partition stories, exist between the fixed categories of communities, their own significations dependent upon the men who possess or violate them, and appear as truly liminal figures of communal ambiguity. (The daughter in Manto's "Khuda Ki Kasam," and Ayesha in Ibrahim Jalees' "A Grave Turned Inside-Out").

There is, thus, a basic conclusion to my disagreement with Bhalla and to my alternative readings of the stories: Literature cannot be "used" to "explain" a holocaust—it can only be felt as many truths, many fragments of painful reality and of actually lived lives. The most important feature of these stories that emerges, in my view, is the power of prejudice and cultural stereotypes. As I searched through other partition stories, to see whether those in which the authorial voice expresses dismay and pain in so many words, eschew all stereotypes, I discovered a fundamental commonality in them. All the authors, despite their own obvious sorrow and alienation from the macabre reality they described, employed the same stereotypes to portray the people and society around them. Thus, I reached another conclusion: society is made visible only through the prevailing stereotypes and the language of prejudice that prevails widely. Without this society becomes invisible.

Because these stereotypes do not help us build a moral ending to the stories, or to assert the basic goodness and love that we desire to experience and to overcome the difference from the 'other', they are of no less value to our understanding. In fact, they help us to penetrate the inner world of the victims and victimizers by providing the language of insight into the times and those who peopled it. Bhisham Sahni's "The Train Has Reached Amritsar," is a good example of how individuals thrown together, nevertheless, transmit messages of their collectives. Despite rioting in a few places, the train from Lahore to Delhi finds the author among passengers full of apparent camaraderie: "nothing had changed in the way people talked to each other or joked together." The stereotypes, however, continue their own existence: (a) the 'dalkhor' Babu is weak, says the Pathan; share our meat and become strong like us—else travel in the ladies compartment. (b) the Sardarji explains to the Pathans: the Babu won't take food from them because they didn't wash their hands (they are dirty people, goes the message). (c) when unwanted passengers clamber into the compartment, everyone shouts at them but "the Pathan, blind with rage" lands a kick on the woman's stomach. (d) when the train passes by a city in flames "each passenger was nervous and suspicious about his neighbour." When they discover the burning city was Wazirabad, a predominantly Muslim area, "the Pathans became less tense, the silence amongst the Hindus and Sikhs became more ominous." (e) when the Babu hid on the floor in fear, the Pathan mocked: "O coward, are you a man or a woman? You are a disgrace to all men!" (f) the arrival of Harbanspura and Amritsar—Hindu and Sikh areas—loosened the babu's tongue and he hurled abuses at the Pathans. "You dared to kick a Hindu women, you bastard ..." (g) in his "own area" now the Babu hits a Muslim trying to get into the moving train and knocks him off.

There was an all prevailing perception of 'our areas' and 'their areas' even in 'normal' times as we know from history. Literature is replete with such symbolism as well. Wazirabad or Harbanspura, Khalsa Mohalla or Islamabad Basti (in Ashk's "The Fodder-Cutting Machine'), Qadirpur or Jatunagar (in Intizar Husain's "An Unwritten Epic"). There was a notion of cultural hegemony in one's 'own area'—and it drew upon historical memory and myth. Intizar Husain's "An Unwritten Epic" captures this discourse sharply: "...friends put on their shrouds, asked for their mothers" blessings, committed their wives to God, and marched into the battlefield with such valour and majesty that they revived the memory of wars fought in ancient times...Nor were the jats wanting in character and ceremony. They came out mounted on caparisoned elephants, lighting up the night with their torches."

Khwaja Ahmad Abbas's story, "The Death of Sheikh Burhanuddin," is one of the most incisive descriptions of the stereotypes of cultural visibility. Sheikh Burhanuddin's narration of his hatred for the Sikhs racial characteristics, the habits and customs of this strange community bears no relation with any person's qualities or character. Both these are derived from the stereotypes imbedded in cultural symbols and their visibility: Sikhs were persons with long hair like women, but were bearded like savages, making a public exhibition of bathing in their underpants, they poured all kinds of filth, like curds, into their hair—curd from the shop of a dirty sweetmeat seller. They were incredibly filthy—they never shaved their heads. Naturally, the revulsion at their bodily culture led to Burhanuddin's view that "all Sikhs are stupid and idiotic." Yet, "they would not accept the superiority of the Muslim, and would strut about like bantam cocks twirling their mustaches and stroking their beards."

The denouement in the story comes with the physical death of Burhanuddin's Sikh neighbour and in the metaphysical death of the Sheikh's fixed notions of good and evil communities, as the Sardar cuts across communal, cultural and political boundaries by sacrificing his own life for the Sheikh's. Contradictory subject positions emerge in their relationship with the shifting power relations of communities as the backdrop.

The cultural symbolism of Sheikh Burhanuddin's "bantam-cock" Sardar is the epitome of cultural visibility. However, anything can become the carrier of the "enemy's" cultural assertion. "We can't tolerate any signs of Hinduism," yells Modabber and points at a tulsi plant that grows in the courtyard of a house he has occupied, in Syed Waliullah's "The Story of the Tulsi Plant." While, Sohrab, the horse owned by an old Muslim, turns into a sacrificial lamb in the chronicle of riots narrated by Ramesh Chandra Sen's "The White Horse."

The Pundit Chintaram, a scholar of Persian and Arabic, who calls himself a humble slave of Akka-e-Namdar, his spiritual teacher Hazrat Maulana, and had mastered every word of the Koran, must have his Hindu bodi chopped off with a sickle in "The Shepherd" by Ashfaq Ahmed.

Bhisham Sahni's child boy, Pali, in the story of the same name is, in the collective perception, a Hindu boy wearing a Muslim cap, while Qasmi's Akhtar in "Parmeshwar Singh," is a Muslim boy wearing a Sikh's kesh and turban. The pain in the heart of Parmeshwar, when he walks Akhtar towards the border and the tears in Zenab's eyes when she sends Pali away to India, are individual sorrows. They are culturally invisible in their collectivity. The caps, the kesh, and the bodi are public statements of this collective culture and are the signs and symbols of their visibility.

These stereotypes have not only a long history but are a part of reality we do not like to acknowledge: that the mass of people in the Hindu and Muslim communities have lived a back to back existence over centuries. When we ask poignantly: how do people forget and wipe out their past of living together, we often don't examine the nature of their life together, their discourses and mind-sets that build inclusion and exclusion deep into their psyches despite their shared daily lives. Real togetherness is a product of generations whose hearts reach out to each other, not when their bodies mingle together at the Pir's dargah or in the Dussehra mela.

The awareness of mortality, a common human fate, and the similarity of their relationships enable people to live side by side peacefully over long periods of time. Nevertheless, to live beside each other is not to live with each other. That comes only as a culmination of a conscious project to break through inherited stereotypes. However, the power narrative is extremely strong and exaggerated between the communities of the subcontinent. Collective assertions of power and bravery versus collective weakness and cowardice are the hallmark of their discourse and are imbricated in all literacy texts.

The dialogue of the partition stories is studded with the terms 'us' and 'them', 'we' and 'they'. The discourse of their characters frames the language of the writers as they paint the men and women who people their canvas. The language of these people, as much as the events they witnessed, stands testimony to the boundaries and divisions of the times.

Almost all the stories on the partition reveal that ordinary, 'normal' people are participants or, at the least, complicitous, in the acts of violence or bloodshed. Whether they are shaken to the core by their own bestiality as in Manto's "Thanda Gosht," or gloat bitterly when their 'own' people settle scores with the enemy as in N.G. Gore's "A Mouthful of Water, a Mouthful of Blood": "Did I disapprove of these things? No. Honestly, no. I myself did not look for anyone; didn't shove a knife between anyone's ribs; didn't drag any Muslim young women into my house—that is true...But what's the point in denying that I felt a sneaky joy in watching these neutering acts committed by others?...In every one of their acts, I was their partner in imagination."

Amrit Rai's train passengers exemplify the complicity of the spectator as they narrate with "pleasurable attention" stories of abducted women while employing the metaphor of the 'goonda': "whereas in the past, only Muslim goondas had been courageous enough to do such deeds, now even the Hindus and Sikhs had proved to the Muslims that they were braver goondas!"

Lakhs of men had died, lakhs of children had been orphaned, lakhs of women violated and, lakhs of people were vicarious participants through the discourse of the 'goonda's hooliganism'.[9]

The powerful depiction of conflict, based on cultural and historical differences, by various writers calls into question some of their stories' attempts at introducing compassionate, self-sacrificing and benign endings. Like all utopic moments, they leave us with a lingering question about how long it (the resolutions of their tales) can last in the 'real' world of separateness, stratification, mis-communication and silence. Categories of thinking and strategies of literary construction which present the desire to make connections across boundaries, are precious and moving. But they cannot erase the materiality of divisions. Writers who faithfully recount even partial, one-sided, culture-specific narratives, need to be taken seriously if we want to deconstruct the power of different discourses.

Does Manto's writing steer clear of all streotypes? The only story that describes the cultural visibility of his characters is "Mozel." Interestingly, it is also the only one which presents a utopic vision of a character sacrificing her life for another. We are made to recognize cultural symbolism and differences in this story: "I cannot marry you," says Mozel to Tirlochen, because "you are a Sikh." Mozel, in her short hair, ugly lipstick and frocks that barely hide her nudity, Tirlochen with his long hair, beard and turbal, Kirpal Kaur the virtuous, virginal, religious Sikh girl—these are all cultural stereotypes. But they are external to the bonds of love and compassion that exist between human beings.

Manto presents his characters' cultural symbols but immediately sets about transcending their visibility, and Sikh, Jew, Muslim, Hindu loose the burden that all systems of signification carry in society. Through apprehensive Sikh eyes, he gazes at 'Staunch Muslims', the "Miyan bhais who are mean and ruthless." Through Mozel's verbal assault on Trilochen, Manto tears into the cultural signification of Sikhs; their "silly underwear," their beards and hair. The same Trilochen who accuses Mozel of ridiculing his religion, gets his beard shaved and his hair cut and feels, "with absolute certainty that he had been carrying an unnecessary burden of hair which really had no meaning." Manto has not a shred of symptahy for cultural symbolism but he also has no insight into what makes people do what they do.

Nevertheless, when Mozel refuses to marry him, Tirlochen begins growing his hair again and slides back into the cultural visibility of his collective. I think Manto grasped the cultural signification in society though he despaired of it. To present the core sameness in the hearts and bodies of all human beings, Manto has only to remove Tirlochen's beard and hair, slip Mozel's dress over Kirpal Kaur's head, and in an act of defiant symbolism on behalf of humanity, against superficial cultural visibility, leave Mozel to die completely naked. The dying Mozel pushes away the meaningless essentialism of religion that is vested in Tirlochen's turban: "Take away...this religion of yours."

What system of signification, what world view, what discourse links the cultural symbolism of collectives to their mass consciousness despite the individual, personal trajectories of their lives, is not part of Manto's literary imagination. The fact that the course of his own life changed so dramatically when he felt compelled to move to Lahore also did not lead him to explore these questions.

The only sane voice inside a lunatic asylum while the world outside goes mad (Toba Tek Singh) is the most well known and most obvious of Manto's constructions. More ruthless is "Khol Do" in its rejection of the ideology of a religious community in the face of evil. The community of the trusted protectors is an illusion, a monstrous fraud, for the fence eats the field and the revolution devours its own children.

"The Dog of Titwal" is contested territory: it was hard to say whether "he died a noble death" or "he died a dog's death." Manto mocks at the foolish gullibility and mindlessness of people vis-a-vis discourses of power and authority. There is a constant tension between dream and reality: would those who killed the dog die as patriots or would they die the death of cruel fools for their country, religion or cause? The venom in Hindus and Muslims butchering each other did not lie outside of them, it was the result of a Pir's curse (Cf. "Naya Kanoon"). The term "curse" strongly implies an irrational force that takes over human beings. Manto's rejection of all ideology, religious or political (see his treatment of political activity as rhetoric in "Student Union Camp" and "Sharabi," his irreverence for nationalism: "Do or Die—Mein langot ka pakka Rahoonga"; and towards leftism: "whisky to aise gale se utar kar pet me inqilab-zindabad likhti chali gayi" (in "Babu Gopinath"); his contemptuous references to drooling dervishes and swearing by "Randi ka kotha aur pir ka mazar" in the same breath— assiduously created an absolute disbelief in any ideology of power or salvation. None of his stories offer solutions to evil, neither systemic, nor individual. At the most the characters of "Ji Aya Sahib" and "Khuni Thuk" employ subversive strategies—the weapons of the weak.

While other writers on the partition convey the evil and irrationality of their characters in their collective existence by treating them as distorted but recognizable beings, Manto's characters are surreal—they defy recognition because their inner worlds are hidden from us. Only their deeds bear witness to their existence. Manto's was an extremely individualistic, anti-status quoist literary intervention carrying the impress of angry radicalism even in his pre-partition stories. From the outset of his writing career, all his characters were lonely and isolated beings and connections between their evil and inhumanity, and their collective existence in society, were not part of his intellectual paradigm. Humanity—or the lack of it—was Manto's obsession, its sociology is left to us to decipher.

There was, and is, a tendency among literary critics to extract Manto's 'politics', his 'social concern' and his 'ideology' from his writing. A sensitive being and an insightful writer of life and its parables of existence such as Manto has no need of proving his social concern. All the 'progressive' writers around Manto were busy trying to connect men and women's social and economic status to their characters' lives and to provide systemic solutions to their problems. Many of them vulgarized their 'concern' by imbueing their writing and fictional characters with an ideology of 'commitment', political 'action' and 'intervention', often producing caricatures of life and people. They were, unlike Manto, not reflectors and philosophers on life but social engineers of existence turned literateurs.

The consistent theme underlying Manto's writing is, on the other hand, that one cannot find rational explanations for human actions. The impenetrable recesses of human souls offer no simple answers, therefore, he is not interested in going into them. If one man can rape and kill, all men can do so. If one woman can prostitute herself, all women can do so. The 'biological men' who exploit the women (the Seth in "Saugandhi" and the pimp Hamid) are not morally or emotionally identical in their maleness, in their relationships to women. For Manto, the human condition with its ugliness/beauty, vice/virtue, sharafat/badmashi, greed/generosity, cruelty/compassion is holistic and his concern transcends their sociological or political explanations. The drama/banality or heroics/tragedy of life are different colours on a moving screen—the cinematic imagination par excellence. It is in this sense that statements on Manto's 'politics' or his 'investigation' of society fall incredibly short of his creative and sensitive writing.

In "Tamasha," the terror that envelopes Khalid's father is juxtaposed against the innocent ignorance of Khalid—no 'politics', no 'ideology', no 'history' can displace or rationalise this terror. Likewise, an act of courage, spontaneous 'bravery' that is quintessentially an explosion of anger and moral rage, cannot be 'explained' politically and ideologically (Muhammed Tufail in "1919 Ki Ek Baat"). The narrator of "1919"—a political participant in the organized protest movement based on nationalist ideology, can only describe Tufail's "heroism." At most he can cherish it as admirable—an act of solitary courage in the face of bullets as "some fell and the rest fled." Just as Manto surely cherished the spark of Bhagat Singh's singular intervention while he busied himself in writing of dismal and dark lives.

Even in the overtly political theme in "Naya Kanoon," Mangu, the Tonga driver, transcreates the fragments of conversations he overhears, not into a political conception, but into a millionarian act of deliverance. The vision of Indian freedom and the liberation of the poor such as himself, flashes like lightening in his imagination only to be extinguished on the appointed day. Mangu had been made a monkey of, one hears Manto snigger, on the first of April.

What makes people leap from their existence as sons and fathers, husbands and householders, into a dance of death and destruction and become butchers and rapists before sinking back to an 'ordinary' life? The link between 'normality' and apparent 'pathology' is not one that he came to grips with. Far more incisive than others, with a cutting edge as sharp as the weapons used by his characters, Manto's stories provide little insight into the world-view and stereotyped prejudices of the killers who people his stories.

There are two, small exceptions. The brief, cryptic piece, "Khad" from "Siyah Hashye" and the title story from his collection *Yazid*, both penned after Manto's arrival in Lahore, show a glimmer of cultural specificity. "Khad" has insight into the inner world of a Sikh for whom the chopping of his 'kesh' and shaving of his beard were clearly worse than death, and he kills himself. The logical, pragmatic tone of his friend who narrates the episode in ten short sentences, on how he failed to persuade the 'stupid' Sikh to detach his emotion from such external symbols like hair which, nourished with curd, would grow back within the year, does not appear to have Manto's sympathy. The one word title Manto gives the story—"Khad" (Manure) is an ironic comment on the friend's superficial rationalisation of deeply felt wounds. The sarcasm of "Khad" lies in the friend's assumption that cultural symbols are external to the respect or humiliation of the self and leave no scars on one's being.

"Yazid," is the story of Muslim survivors in a Pakistani village who hear of India's tyranny in changing the course of the river which nurtures their fields and lives. Karimdad, the protagonist of this story, argues with logical coldness that everything is fair in war and all means legitimate against one's enemy. He contemptuously dismisses toothless fulminations against India as futile and impotent. A culture specific anger bares itself in Manto's ending to the story, when Karimdad names his newborn son 'Yazid' (tyrant) who would undo the tyranny of the enemy. Put together, "Khad," "Yazid" and Manto's "Open Letter to 'Pandit', Jawaharlal Nehru," suggest a new emotion and insight into the angers and feelings of collectivities which have been rent asunder.

Alok Bhalla's comments on Manto are most perceptive. Manto's world-view, as it emerges from his reading, and which I fully share, is the unrelieved, relentless journey of the damned. The stories, to quote Bhalla, "are written by a man who knows that after such ruination there can neither be any forgiveness nor any forgetting. Those who have seen the carnage can only stand and wait for death...the inhumanity of the partition has so obliterated the moral realm that there is nothing left to retrieve and nothing to hope for... language betrays, and ordinary people...become ruthless killers...horror is unflinchingly observed and recorded...to make us understand that we are all accomplices in the making of a barbarous world and that now nothing can save us."

The sad and weary message of "Siyah Hashye" is condensed in Manto's two line bitterness, titled "Aram Ki Jaroorat":

"Mara nahin...dekho abhi jan baki hai"
"Rehne de Yar...main thak gaya hoon!"

If there is any hope left in the world, it is this: the body will tire of blood-letting. 'Junoon', passion or violence, is expressed through the body, with cries of frenzy, running after victims, endlessly wielding the weapons of destruction and setting persons and homes on fire. When rape and pillage cross the threshold of exhaustion then, perhaps, there may be respite.

I believe that Manto's bludgeoning impact on our minds, and the emotional freezing we experience akin to the cauterising of our arteries, is because he is the voice of our times. Manto appears to belong less to the past than to the present, when all ideologies, beliefs and language reveal little about the 'nature of man' celebrated and discussed in centuries past. His stories are anti-ideology, anti-heroic, anti-salvationist; the figure of the amoral, Nietzchean man, prefiguring the end of all ideologies and the pitiless logic of the future, grows out of his words and challenges all reason and rationality. The world of a Sartrean nightmare from which there is no exit fills our unconscious.

Nothing is prescribed. Nothing is proscribed. To draw attention to the Neitzchean, amoral characters that people Manto's fiction is not to ascribe these characteristics to the author. Critics often collapse the personna of his fictional protagonists with the authorial value system or personality. Nothing could be farther from the truth. Manto's own bruised values and concerns, the acute observation of degraded lives and disintegrating morals, leaves the world with a tattered vision. It was not his business to patch the tear in the fabric of reality with his own visionary hopes. It is in this manner that he emerges as anti-ideological—not as the valueless artist but as opposed to offering 'ideology' as resolution of and salvation for individuals and societies.

A writer such as Manto cannot be a reference and a source for social scientists going about their rational activity of trying to understand the past. He can only be a reflection of the self-exiled consciousness. Manto's emotionless, dead pan, icily constructed stories testify to the iron that had entered his soul. The 'so-called homo-sapiens' that Manto refers to somewhere are recognizable in their physicality but not in any other moral feature of their anatomy. Such a perception of what was happening around him could only provoke mad laughter and sarcasm, as Hindus, Sikhs and Muslims chasing each other with knives and swords became hunters and prey, when blood and water mixed together on the road and reminded a child of jelly, when Sikhs were 'halaled' and Muslims were 'jhatkaed', when the division or 'taqsim' of loot was the first step to the 'taqsim' of bodies and when the tearing open of a sack of sugar disgorged human entrails.

NOTES

1. Concepts such as cultural power, cultural contest and cultural assertion have been worked out in the broader framework of a struggle for cultural hegemony in Shashi Joshi and Bhagwan Josh, *Struggle for Hegemony in India: Culture, Community and Power*, 1941-47, vol. 3. New Delhi: Sage Publications, 1994.

2. Lyotard, Jean-Francois, *The Post-modern Condition: A Report on Knowledge*. Minneapolis: University of Minnesota Press, 1979.

3. Bhalla, Alok (ed), *Stories About the Partition of India*, vol. 1. New Delhi: Harper Collins,1994, p. xv.

4. Das, Veena (ed), *The Word and the World*. New Delhi: Sage, 1986, p. 180.

5. Ashar, Masood, "Versions of Truth" in Khalid Hasan and Faruq Hassan (eds), *Versions of Truth*. New Delhi: Vikas, 1983, p. 51.

6. Bhalla, op. cit., p. xvii.

7. The stories referred to in the pages that follow are available in Alok Bhalla (ed), *Stories About the Partition of India*, 3 volumes. Leslie A. Flemming, *The Life and the Works of Saadat Hasan Manto*. Lahore: Vanguard, 1985, Khalid Hasan and Faruq Hasan (eds), *Versions of Truth*, and Satish Jamali, *Manto Ki Sarvshreshth Kahaniyan*. Allahabad: Satyam Prakashan, 1991. No separate footnotes are provided.

8. As Jean Paul Sartre wrote, "We cannot overlook the dialectical relationship between authorized, authorizing language and the group which authorizes it and acts on its authority." See my discussion of the activation and restoration of cultural memory and the connection between restored memory and its content of fantasy, in *Struggle for Hegemony in India*, vol. 3, pp. 77-86.

9. For a discussion of the stereotype of a 'Muslim as a Rapist' in Premchand's writings, see Shashi Joshi and Bhagwan Josh, op.cit. "Women and Sexuality in the Discourse of Communalism and Communal Violence," pp. 194-258. According to Sudhir Kakar, "The Litmus Test of Revivalism and Fundamentalism remains the attitude towards sex rather than power." See his *Colours of Violence*. New Delhi: Viking, 1995. His understanding of power is very reductionist and overlooks sexuality as a mode of acquiring power. See my review of Kakar, *The Hindu*, 17 December, 1995.

10. Alok Bhalla, "Introduction," op. cit., vol. I.

Manto in English: An Assessment of Khalid Hasan's Translations

M. ASADUDDIN

Manto began his literary career as a translator. Bari, his literary and ideological mentor, introduced him to the worlds of the English, the French and the Russian writers. He read, among others, Victor Hugo, Maupassant, Dostoyevsky, Chekhov, Pushkin and Gorky with passionate involvement. On Bari's suggestion, he undertook the translation of Hugo's the *Last Days of the Condemned* and called it *Sarguzasht-e-Asir*. Later, he translated Oscar Wilde's *Vera*, a collection of Russian stories and two plays by Chekhov into Urdu. It is reasonable to surmise that his apprenticeship as a translator made him aware of both the inadequacy and extraordinary power of words in conveying or communicating human experience. In his autobiographical essay, "Saadat Hasan," he alludes to his incessant, sometimes vain, search for the most appropriate word. No wonder that in his best writings one finds evidence of the writer's effort to exploit all the nuances and associations of words and even non-verbal elements of expression.

It seems that a resurgence in Manto studies is on the anvil for a variety of reasons. One of them pertains to the growing interest in the partition of India in 1947. Even half a century after this cataclysmic event, historians and social scientists are no closer to comprehending this phenomenon in all its complexity. They are now looking beyond the official historical documents to literary and semi-literary narratives which are sometimes much more insightful in illuminating critical human situations. If literature is supposed to mirror life, it is entirely valid to assume that the dominant attitudes, assumptions and the angst of an epoch will find expression in the creative writings of that period and social scientists will do well to take cognizance of this fact. A recent endeavour of putting together such writings can be found in the two volume anthology, *India Partitioned: The Other Face of Freedom* edited by Mushirul Hasan The one writer who has been given primacy in this anthology is Manto. However, besides the fact of the partition, about which Manto writes with searching insight and muted rage, the cult of violence that is raging around us today makes him increasingly relevant. With uncanny intuition, he reveals the darkness that sometimes lies at the core of the human heart and erupts in all its ferocity when the civilised values of restraint and discipline are thrown to the winds and men turn into brutes.

1

Translation may be considered as the reincarnation of a writer in a different language and culture; a bad and irresponsible translator can do great damage to a writer, falsifying his image and distorting the true import and spirit of his works. The politics involving selections from a writer and the translator's perspective can become crucial because a particular view of the writer may be projected which is not consistent with or may even be to the detriment of his whole corpus or his total image. One is reminded of the translations of Tagore's poetry into English by the poet himself and others in the early decades of this century, which resulted in building up his image as an oriental mystic and prophet, at the cost of his genius as a poet, playwright and fictionalist, an image which subsequent translators of Tagore have tried to dispel. The recent translations of Tagore by William Radice have been done from an altogether different perspective. A.K. Ramanujan's competence in translating U.R. Ananth Murthy's *Samskara* has remained undisputed, but some scholars think that his elaborate footnotes and the afterword, appended to the translation, tend to divert the reader's attention from the novel to anthropology. The translations of Ghalib's poetry by Ahmed

Ali, Yusuf Husain and Ralph Russell, and those of Faiz Ahmed Faiz's poetry by Victor Kiernan, Naomi Lazard, Agha Shahid Ali and Shiv K. Kumar have different degrees of competence and inadequacy. All this is mentioned here merely to emphasise the point that now, when Manto's appeal seems to be acquiring trans-national dimensions, one has to be very careful about the translations through which this appeal is being mediated.

The English translations of Manto's stories are scattered over innumerable literary magazines and anthologies. Among the magazines the most notable are—*Journal of South Asian Literature, Pakistan Review,* and *Thought.* The anthologies are truly numerous, sometimes representing Urdu short stories from the Indian subcontinent or South Asia, and sometimes arranged under some overarching themes. In the latter group fall three most recent works—the first one is the three volume compilation, *Stories About the Partition of India,* which contains four of Manto's stories and two short pieces from "Siyah Hashye." The translations are by Alok Bhalla and Tahira Naqvi. The second anthology is *India Partitioned: The Other Face of Freedom* (2nd edition) mentioned earlier, which contains translations of all the thirty two pieces from "Siyah Hashye" (Black Margins) by Mushirul Hasan. The third anthology is *Orphans of the Storm: Stories on the Partition of India* which has four Manto stories, one translated by Khushwant Singh and the three others by Khalid Hasan. Alok Bhalla's translations of Manto are, as he claims, quite close to the text except for some minor inaccuracies. Mushirul Hasan's translations had some blemishes in the first edition which have been removed in the second conveying, as they stand now, fairly adequately the splintered and fragmented quality of the original. Khushwant Singh's translation of "Toba Tek Singh" cannot compare favourably with some other competent translations of this classic Manto story, though one is pleasantly surprised to see that he has reverted this time to the original title from his earlier translation of it as "Exchange of Lunatics."

Apart from these translations spread in magazines and

anthologies, five collections, exclusively devoted to Manto's stories and sketches, have been published in English so far. The earliest among them is *Black Milk* translated by Hamid Jalal which contains six stories by Manto in English translation. This collection was quickly censored and very few copies survived the iron hand of the thought police in Pakistan. This was followed by Tahira Naqvi's translation of 17 of Manto's stories published in Leslie A. Flemming's book on Manto entitled *Another Lonely Voice*. Though Tahira Naqvi has achieved considerable fame in recent years as a competent translator of Ismat Chugtai's novels and short stories, her translations of Manto's stories belong to an earlier period and, though they are free from distortions and inaccuracies, they cannot be called very distinguished. In India, Sterling Publishers published the collection *The Best of Manto* which contains fifteen stories translated by Jai Ratan. Jai Ratan, a veteran translator who translates from Hindi, Punjabi and Urdu, has his own notions about translation and narrative logic and reorders his material making small changes here and there. Among all Manto's translators in English, the best known to date is Khalid Hasan. He has translated and edited two collections of Manto's stories and sketches—the first one is *Kingdom's End and Other Stories* and the second one is titled *Partition; Sketches and Stories*. Since both of them have been quite widespread in their circulation and have been extremely popular with scholars and general readers, I propose to concentrate on them and demonstrate how Hasan's translations raise important issues about the objectives of a translator, as well as the pitfalls and ethics of translations.

2

Khalid Hasan's English is good and idiomatic and his translations fulfil the criterion of readability in the target language. This seems to be the secret of the popularity of his anthologies. A non-Urdu reader will be immediately taken in by the lucidity of his prose and the clever turn of phrase and will be tempted to trust his competence and judgement as a translator. But as one compares his translations with the original, one is horrified by the kind of liberties he takes with the original and the distortions he makes in his translations. Hasan commits all the errors of an inordinately adventurous translator. He changes the titles of stories without any valid reason, leaves out big chunks of the original, summarises descriptive paragraphs and dialogues, changes the order of sentences, eliminates ellipses, flattens out uneven contours and cultural angularities of the original and sometimes, through not as frequently, adds his own bit for the benefit of readers not acquainted with Indo-Islamic culture and the history of the subcontinent. It will be my endeavour to substantiate these allegations with illustrations from his translations.

First, the change of titles. Hasan translates the title of the spine-chilling story, "Thanda Gosht," as "Colder than Ice." In fact, several translators have translated it either as "Colder than Ice," or "Cold, Like Ice," and one wonders what makes them do so. The story ends with the phrase "colder than ice" (Kulwant Kaur placed her hand on Ishar Singh's which was colder than ice) and if Manto had so wanted he would have retained it as the title. The euphemistic phrase "colder than ice" does not evoke the rawness and immediacy of Ishar Singh's experience as the phrase "cold meat" or "a lump of cold flesh" does. The keyword here is "meat" or "flesh" that serves as a metaphor bringing out the horrifying implications of man's descent into bestiality where a woman's body becomes the contested site for conquest, violence and sexual assault. Another instance of this kind of unimaginative change of title by Hasan is evident in case of the story, "Khol Do." Hasan translates it as "Return." It is crystal clear that the unbearable nature of the traumatic experiences of Sakina, Sirajuddin's daughter, has been telescoped in her gesture of lowering the shalwar following the utterance of the two words, "khol do" (open it). The neutral word "return" is not only insipid as a title divesting the original of its terrible impact, but changes the whole emphasis by shifting the focus from the daughter's trauma to the father's frantic search to find his daughter. Moreover, the change of the title in English to "Return" becomes more problematic if we remember that Joseph Conrad has a celebrated story by that name and Manto's story offers neither any parallel nor any counterpoint to it. Then Hasan translates "Sarkandon Ke Peeche" as "Wild Cactus" where the more literal "Behind the Reeds" would have been more appropriate because the preposition "behind" ("peeche" in the original) conveys the shady goings-on and thus brings out well the thematics of the story. Besides, Hasan's title lends itself to a kind of symbolic interpretation which Manto, in all probability, had never intended. Similarly, he translates the title "Saheb-e-Karamat" as "A Man of God" whereas "The Man of Miracles" would have been closer to the text and more appropriate. Hasan's unwarranted irreverence may be mistaken by an unwary reader for Manto's and if it is foregrounded in the title then the story will lend itself to an altogether different kind of reading. There are a few more instances of this kind in the two collections.

Secondly, the most serious of all Hasan's errors is his omission of large chunks of the original in his English translation. He leaves out not only sentences but paragraphs, even pages, doing great violence to the original text. For instance, in "Naya Qanoon" (The New Constitution), a story of about 3,500 words, the total omission amounts to about 500 words. In "Titwal Ka Kutta" (The Dog of Titwal), a 3,000 words story in the original, Hasan leaves out a total of about 400 words. In "Mozel" which runs into 7,500 words in the original, the omission totals about 700 words. And so on and so forth. However, the story that bears the brunt of Hasan's pair of scissors is "Swaraj Ke Liye" where he omits a total of about 1100 words of the original which also includes a full page in Urdu print. Now, if Hasan's omissions pertained to seemingly superfluous or supporting details of description or atmosphere building or interminably long character portrayal, though such omissions are certainly unethical and not permissible, one would at least try to make some sense of it. Manto is a writer who can by no means be called prolix. This makes Hasan's heavy dose of editing absolutely gratuitous.

In fact, some of the omissions by Khalid Hasan form an integral part, or essential elements of character portrayal, or the thematic core of the story. As an illustration of this, one can take up the story "Naya Qanoon." After introducing the protagonist Ustad Mangu, the tonga driver, in the opening four lines Hasan leaves out the following part:

> *Pichhle dino jab ustad Mangu ne apni ek sawari se Spain mein jang chhirh jane ki afwah suni to us ne Gama Chaudhry ke chore kandhe per thapki de kar muddabirana andaz mein peshan goi ki thi, "dekh lena Chaudhry, thore hi dino mein Spain ke andar jang chhirh jayegi."*
>
> *Aur jab Gama Chaudhry ne us se yeh puchha tha ki Spain kahan he, to ustad Mangu ne bari mtanat se jawab diya tha, "Wilayat mein, aur kahan?"*
>
> *Spain mein jang chhirhi aur jab bhai shakhs ko iska pata chalgaya to station ke adde mein jitne kochwan halqa banaye huqqa pi rahe the, dil hi dil mein ustad Mangu ki barai ka itraf kar rahe the.*

It is evident from the context that the above lines form an integral part of the character building process that goes on in the first page of the original story. They give the reader important insights into Mangu's unlettered mind which has its own logic and way of deduction. Then there is the scene where Ustad Mangu carries two barristers in his tonga whose conversation gives him the idea that they are opposed to the new law. In irrepressible anger, he mutters the word "toadies" under his breath. Manto elaborates further:

> *Jab kabhi woh kisi ko dabi zaban mein "tody bachha" kehta to dil mein yeh mahsus kar ke bara khush hota tha ke us ne us nam ko sahih jagah istimal kiya he aur yeh ke woh sharif admi aur "tody bachha" mein tamiz karne ki ahaliyat rakhta he.*

Hasan leaves out this part and thus robs Ustad Mangu of some of his interesting angularities. Yet another significant and long omission comes in the latter half of the story:

> Jab ustad Mangu ko kisi sawari ki talash nahin hoti thi ya use kisi bite wage par ghor karna hota to woh am tor par agli nishast chorh kar pichhli nishast par bare itminan se beth kar apne ghore ki bagen dain hath kar ke gird lapet liya karta tha. Aise mauqe par uska ghora thora sa hinhina ne ke bad bari dhimi chal chalna shuru kar deta tha, goya use kuch der ke liyen bhag dorh se chutti mil guy he. Ghore ki chal aur ustad Mangu ke khyalat ki amad bahut sust thi. Jis tarah ghora ahista qadam utha raha tha usi tarah ustad Mangu ke zehn mein nay qanoon ke mutaliq qiyasat dakhil ho rahe the.

These omissions have resulted in the following:

First, the context has been either muted or wiped out altogether. It is an axiom that the full significance of an event can be understood only with reference to its context ("context is all"). Similarly, a character derives his sustenance and signification from the context in which the author situates him. More so in the case of Manto who fine-honed the art of story-telling in Urdu and in some cases reduced narration and description to the barest minimum.

Second, in "Naya Qanoon" the narrator's descriptions and comments anchor Mangu firmly in a particular ambience and assign to him certain attitudes that make his character credible, contribute to the verisimilitude and prepare the reader for the final climax of the story. Hasan's omissions have alienated Mangu from that ambience and prevented readers from gaining an insight into his mental workings.

Third, linked with the above point, is the fact that though an ordinary and rustic tonga driver, Ustad Mangu is interested in the unrest in Spain; he has located the country in an imaginary space which he calls "Wilayat" and considers himself competent enough to forecast the Spanish Civil War. The translator ignores all this.

Fourth, the mutilation of the texts has severely reduced their textuality and interfered with their reception.

Fifth, the omissions have sometimes blurred the perspective of the narrator.

Like omissions, summarisation is also an omnipresent feature of Khalid Hasan's translations. He not only changes the order of the sentences but sometimes produces neat, if emasculated summaries of paragraphs and dialogues. This, besides eliminating details that contribute to the texture of the narrative, has resulted in inaccuracies. I have taken two examples at random, the first one is from the story "Siraj." The original runs as follows:

Mein ne ek din socha ke Dhondu ko batai bagher Siraj se milun. Wo Bikla station ke pas hi ek nihayat wahyat jagah mein rehti thi jahan kure karkat ke dher the. As pas ka tamam fazla tha. Corporation ne yahan gharibon ke liye jast ke be-shumar jhopre bana diye the. Mein yahan un buland bang imaraton ka zikr karna nahin chahta jo ghalazat gah se thori dur istadeh thin. Kiunke unka is afsane se koi taaluq nahin. Duniya nam hi nasheb wa faraz ka he ya rifaton aur pastiyon ka.

And this is how Khalid Hasan summarises it:

One day I decided to see Siraj without Dhondoo's good offices. I was curious. She lived in one of the filthiest slums of Bombay. The streets were almost impassable because of garbage heaps. The city had constructed a lot of tin huts for the poor. She lived in one of them.

Two things deserve notice here. First, in his translation of the passage, Hasan omits the place-name Byculla Station which gives the setting certain solidity, providing it, as it were, "a local habitation and a name." Second, by omitting the narrator's ironical understatement about the tall mansions fringing the shacks where Siraj lived, he has interfered with the perspective of the narrator by muting any evidence of his social conscience and awareness of economic exploitation. The second specimen of summarisation constitutes the ending of the story "Sau Candle Power Ka Bulb" (The Room with the Bright Light) which reads as follows:

Magr us ne choton ki parwah na ki aur haush wa hawas qaim rakne ki koshish karte hue wey mushkil apne ghar puhcha aur sari rat daraone khwab dekhta raha.

Hasan summarises it thus:

Like a mad man, he ran out of the courtyard and into the dark street.

We know that writers generally take the utmost care about the ending of their stories which gives them a certain design and sometimes offers interesting clues to the vision of the writer. The translator has no business to change it, even if it does not satisfy his subjective notion of the sense of the/an ending. In fact, the ubiquitous omissions and summarisations seem to spring from Hasan's patently western and mistaken notion of the English short story as something essentially crisp, sleek and precise as opposed to the free flowing oriental narratives invested with rich details that we are used to in this part of the world.

A successful translator needs inevitably to grapple with the problem of cultural transference. "Translation means, above all, an act of cultural information." Sometimes reference to a ritual, a song, a proverb, etc. illuminates essential aspects of a culture richly overlaid with a connotative context. A translator's endeavour should be to retain them as far as possible. In this connection one is reminded of the collection entitled *Classic Telugu Short Stories* which contains translations of 23 Telugu short stories in English. Ranga Rao, the translator and editor, pays special attention to this aspect of cultural negotiation. He rightly points out, "Translation is a discovery, by trial and error, of the right blend of English idiom and nativism: a good translation is a good, balanced text, balanced between, poised between a tolerable ballast of English idiom and a legitimate cargo of nativism." Khalid Hasan seems undeterred by any such considerations. He flattens out cultural contours, omits evocative place-names and either omits or mutes references to books, poets and artists in his translations. For instance, in the story "Babu Gopinath," he translates the following line:

Ghulam Husain ki farmaish per us ne Ghalib ki yeh ghazal, "Nukta chin he gham-i dil usko suna-i na bane" ga kar sunai.

as

She had even sung something for him which he had liked.

Now, it is obvious from the story that Zeenat's acquaintance with Ghalib's poetry and her singing skill reinforce the portrayal of her character as an accomplished courtesan, as distinguished from a commonplace whore. By muting this cultural nuance the translator has falsified the intent and spirit of the original. There is another aspect to it that relates to his omission of Ghalib's name. One wonders whether a European translator translating in oriental languages will ever feel constrained to omit references to Dante, Shakespeare or even a lesser poet. The surest answer is he won't. He will take it for granted that his readers are aware of these great writers or if they are not, they should make an effort to be so. Why then does Khalid Hasan feel coy to mention Ghalib's name? Is it from a sense of inferiority or a colonial hangover? The fact that the success of a translator also consists in how far he is able to provoke and stimulate the interest of his readers in the source language text should not be overlooked.

In contrast to the muting of cultural nuances mentioned above, Khalid Hasan sometimes goes to the other extreme and endeavours to transport an overflowing cargo of nativism. He adds information on his own and puts it in the body of the text as though it were written by Manto. The italicised parts of the following extracts from the story,

"Yazid" (The Great Divide), are purely Hasan's additions:

> The month of Muharram was drawing close. Jeena always loved to watch the procession they took out *to mourn the martyrdom of Hussain, the holy prophet's favourite grandson, and his companions, who had chosen death instead of allegiance to Yazid, whom they considered an unjust and illegitimate ruler.* She loved to see the devotees in black beating their breasts and walking with slow steps behind Hussain's riderless horse, the Zooljinnah.
>
> Bakhto's face went white *because no Muslim child is ever called Yazid as no Christian child can be called Judas. It is an evil name because it was Yazid at whose orders Hussain, the prophet's grandson and his companions were deprived of water and finally massacred.*

Needless to say, Khalid Hasan overshoots his brief as a translator who should resolutely resist the temptation to "improve upon" the original writer. He should not endeavour to expand, on his own, the textuality of the original in his translation. Yazid is a symbol for Manto and not a convenient peg on which to hang information about anecdotes connected with Islamic history or one's sociological knowledge about Shia practices. Khalid Hasan's translations of the pieces in "Siyah Hashye" are more accurate and closer to the original, precisely because they hold no scope for editing or additions, being themselves fragmentary and pared down to the bone.

3

Thus, what Khalid Hasan eventually presents to non-Urdu readers is a truncated, reductive and sometimes unreliable version of Manto. His command of the English language effectively camouflages the lapses in his translations. But the lapses are quite serious and defeat the very objective of translation. If the objective is to introduce a writer of great talent and insight to those who do not read the language in which he wrote, the translator should take utmost care that minimum sacrifices are made and no distortion takes place. An attitude of respect towards the writer and the original text is in perfect order. The translator's misplaced zeal should not lead him to add information for local colour or exotic appeal. Likewise, it should not lead him to sanitise the text, cleaning out all seeming warts, angularities and cultural nuances because in the ultimate analysis these may have been precisely the qualities which made the writer/the text unique and distinctive in the original language.

REFERENCES

Mushirul Hasan. *India Partitioned: The Other Face of Freedom*. New Delhi: Roli Books, 1995.
Alok Bhalla. *Stories About the Partition of India*. 3 volumes. New Delhi: Indus, 1994.
Saros Cowasjee and K.S. Duggal. *Orphans of the Storm: Stories on the Partition of India*. New Delhi: UBSPD, 1995.
"Exchange of Lunatics," Khushwant Singh (trans. and ed.), *Land of Five Rivers*. Bombay: Jaico, 1965.
Hamid Jalal. *Black Milk*. Lahore: Al-Kitab, 1956.
Leslie A. Flemming. *Another Lonely Voice: The Life and Works of Saadat Hasan Manto*. Lahore: Vanguard, 1985.
Jai Ratan. *The Best of Manto*. New Delhi: Sterling.
Khalid Hasan. *Kingdom's End and Other Stories*. London: Verso, 1987.
Khalid Hasan. *Partition: Sketches and Stories*. New Delhi: Viking, 1991.
Ranga Rao, *Classic Telugu Short Stories*. New Delhi: Penguin, 1995.

Saadat Hasan Manto: A Note

BHISHAM SAHNI

There is one aspect of Manto's writing to which little attention has been paid so far. It is that Manto invariably puts his characters in a world of make-believe. Sugandhi, craving for the steady love of someone, lives in a world of make-believe. In a way Gopinath, too, hoping to marry off his mistress and provide her a steady home, lives in a world of make-believe. The prostitutes live in a cruel world but their world of make-believe or their wishful thinking sustains them. In "Toba Tek Singh," even the lunatics live in a world of make-believe, although being insane, their wishful thinking cannot be taken seriously, and serves the purpose of a sharp comment on the partition of the country.

It is Manto's unique quality as a writer that he juxtaposes the world of reality with the world of make-believe. That is his special gift. It lends rare artistry to his writing, and adds immeasurably to the pathos of his stories.

Here and there he pricks the bubble of this make-believe world also. In "Babu Gopinath," at the end of the story when the narrator, on seeing the decked-up bridal chamber for the young prostitute who has been married to the Sindhi merchant, laughs and ridicules the pretence of marriage, the balloon of make-believe is punctured, and the girl begins to cry because she is deeply hurt. It would have been a safe and secure world for her if it had not been punctured.

Thus, to my mind, this fusion of the real and the unreal creates a unique world, a typical product of Manto's creative imagination. He is able to present life-like convincing characters, their inner world, their mental make-up and their cravings. The impressions they receive are also very human, since every human being, even in the worst of circumstances, dreams of a better future and indulges in a lot of wishful thinking.

It is a convincing world, though largely a world of make-believe.

But this very remarkable faculty becomes Manto's limitation.

The world of prostitutes is the world of crime, heartless exploitation, and the worst form of degradation and humiliation. Very rarely can a prostitute remain a normal human being in that environment. She either becomes a dull, stupid, passive and unthinking object of gratification, or develops into a cynical and a heartless professional. The world in which she lives is the world where man is wolf to man. Seldom can you find a prostitute with fine sensibilities. Such is the stark reality of brothel life.

Obviously, when Manto puts his characters in that context and humanizes them, he is creating a world of make-believe for himself and for his characters. His sensibility is that of a middle class artist.

Even in the milieu that he creates for his characters, it is possible that some girl would want to run away from the wretched life in a brothel and set up a home with a husband, have children, crave for a normal home life. And, it is also possible that impelled by this strong desire she would try to run away from that hell. It may be that she does not succeed. She is caught and brought back. But if she is determined, she can try to run away again. Her attempts may end in tragedy; she may either be locked-up or killed. Such a character would not be a romantic character or an idealistic character. She would only be striving to satisfy her inmost desire.

If the progressives found fault with Manto, it was on this score. During the forties, when the progressive movement in literature had over-zealous adherants, the main emphasis in literature was not on character realisation but on protest; its emphasis was on class strength; on highlighting the exploitation to which the weaker sections of society were being subjected. And the prostitute was the worst exploited of all. The progressives therefore expected that a sensitive artist like Manto, who was writing about the lives of the prostitutes, would also show the nature of exploitation to which the prostitute was being subjected. It would not have been idealistic or romantic on the part of Manto to show a character in the throes of a struggle to free herself from the shackles of this slavery. But, the fact that Manto should have totally ignored this aspect and concentrated on the softer humanistic aspects of her life, and in a way taken her brothel life for granted, disappointed the progressives.

Hence, while they acknowledged him as a master of the craft of short story writing and appreciated his deeply humane approach, they were also critical of his total lack of interest in the cruel subjection of the poor to exploitation.

This, I think, was the reason why they sometimes praised him, and at other times condemned him.

A Reading of 'Pandit' Manto's Letter To Pandit Nehru

ABDUL BISMILLAH

Manto and his writings have been assessed and evaluated from different perspectives. In the process they have both been admired and denigrated. The fact, however, is that Manto's stature has neither increased nor suffered any setback. Well, it is the same with all writers. Manto's stature, however, may be revalued if he is taken out of the world of his stories and assessed in the light of his other writings. However, it often happens that a writer whose identity is created within a particular structure, breaks the structure, and does something so different that he acquires a new identity.

Years ago the writer, Jerzy Kozinski, was born in Poland. He was separated from his parents during the Second World War. After some time, he reached America and settled there. He learnt English and began writing in English. For the Americans, he was an American writer who wrote in English and for the Poles, he was a Polish writer who wrote in English. For us, in India, Manto is an Indian writer in Urdu and for the people of Pakistan, he is a Pakistani Urdu writer. The truth is that, just as Jerzy Kozinski articulated the feelings and sensitivities of both the Polish and the American people, Manto captured the feelings and sensitivities of the people of India and the newly created land of Pakistan.

Manto has written many stories on the trauma of the partition and they have been studied fairly thoroughly. But the letter he wrote to Pandit Nehru, the Prime Minister of India, reveals some other facets of 'Pandit' Manto. The letter being alluded to here is the foreword to his book *Beghair Unwan Ke*. The book is dedicated to Nehru and the foreword to it is entitled, "Pandit Manto's First Letter to Pandit Nehru." This so-called letter addresses some grave issues related to the partition, throws light on some special facets of Nehru's personality and raises some controversial issues about Indian politics in such a manner that it can be the basis of meaningful debate today. This letter is dated August 27, 1954. Written about seven years after the partition of India, it is evident that the injuries caused during the partition had not yet healed. The people from *this* side had complaints against those from *that* side and vice versa. Manto now belonged to *that* side. That is why it is both interesting and important to know what he thought about *this* side.

During those days Nehru had acquired a mythical aura. Legends about him were legion which, though not recorded in history books, were a matter of popular belief. One of these was that foreign women were irresistibly drawn towards him. An example of such a belief can be found in Manto's letter:

> By the grace of God, you're considered very handsome by the Americans. Well, my features are also not exactly bad. If I go to America, perhaps, I'll also be bestowed the same status.

In other words, the secret of Nehru's charm is that he is considered handsome by the Americans. If an ordinary person like Manto reached America, he would also obtain the certificate of beauty. That is to say, beauty is neither the gift of God nor of nature, but is a slave of western ideas. Even if this remark lacks substance as far as Nehru is concerned, it certainly assumes significance when we consider how the titles of Miss World etc., are acquired now-a-days.

If the impact of Nehru's physique on others was great, his impact on politics was far greater. Even years after freedom, Pandit Nehru and Indian politics were synoymous. Manto admitted this, but in his characteristic way: "In politics, I can take your name with pride because you know the art of contradicting yourself well." Who can say whether the art of self-contradiction was peculiar to Nehru or has always been a common element in politics. However, Manto was sad, probably because he did not expect it from Nehru even if the others contradicted themselves. Nor did he expect that Nehru would stop rivers, *nehrs*, from flowing through his country. How could a Nehru, that is a person who was strong like a *nehr* (a stream), stop rivers? Manto was amazed and angry with him:

...I was surprised to hear that you want to stop rivers from flowing through our land. Panditji, you're only a Nehru. I regret that I'm just a measuring stone of one-and-a-half seers. If I were a rock weighing thirty or forty thousand *maunds,* I would have thrown myself into the river so that you would be required to spend some time consulting your engineers about how to pull it out.

If Manto had anything to do with politics, he would neither have been surprised nor sad. In economics land is considered to be a free gift given to man by God. It includes water, air, light etc. Then how can water be appro-priated by an idividual? But if land can be divided, why can't water? Therefore, it was not surprising to restrict the flow of the river Beas through the land of Pakistan (It may be noted here that this event relates to the controversy following the India-Pakistan pact).

For Manto, water may have been a free gift of nature, but in politics it has always been used as a potent weapon. It needs to be mentioned here that Manto was so upset by this that he wrote a moving short story, "Yazid," on this theme.

It is clear from Manto's remarks quoted above that on the one hand he was dissatisfied with the politics of Nehru, on the other he was so much attached to the land to which he had migrated that he wanted to be a rock and throw himself into the river. Undoubtedly, this 'act' of Manto may seem strange to Indians and Manto-lovers, but it is necessary to look at it from Manto's angle and against the circumstances prevailing at that time. May be Manto was right, or may be he was wrong.

Manto was a citizen of Pakistan, but prior to that he was a citizen of India. That is why he sometimes spoke in the present tense and sometimes his heart bled for the past:

> Panditji, there's no doubt that you are a great personality. You are the Prime Minister of India. You are the ruler of the country which was formerly mine. You are everything. But pardon me for saying that you have never cared for this humble person (who is also a Kashmiri).

These lines highlight two of Manto's agonies. One, he can no longer call his former country his own. Two, though a Kashmiri, he cannot do anything for the people of Kashmir. Nehru himself was an example of how much love a Kashmiri harbours for Kashmir. In Manto's words: "I know and believe that you've clung to Kashmir because, being a Kashmiri, you feel a sort of magnetic love for that land."

For both, Manto and Panditji, Kashmir was their homeland, but for others it was only a problem. It was a problem at the time of independence and continues to be one even today. Who knows how often the problem of Kashmir has been debated and how many solutions have been proposed. However, it seems that the problem has never been debated by the litterateurs of both the countries. They may do so in future. But Manto had already started the debate way back in 1954. One of his observations, about Nehru "clinging" to Kashmir, has been quoted above. Manto's remark is not simple, but is pregnant with deep irony. It expresses his disappointment over the fact that Kashmir was a part of India. The allegation regarding Nehru's "magnetic love" for Kashmir can be made against Manto as well. Manto's heart bled for Kashmir because he was a Kashmiri.

Many of Manto's Indian readers may be shocked by his views on Kashmir. But, as has been pointed out already, his observations were relevant to literature, not politics. That is why they are replete with contradictions. Perhaps, great writers harbour great contradictions within them. Manto, who accuses Nehru of "clinging" to Kashmir, adds in the same breath: "...I have only been upto Banihal. I have seen places like Kud, Bataut and Kashtwar. I have seen their poverty along with their beauty. If you have removed their poverty, then keep Kashmir to yourself." In other words, it was not important for Manto whether Kashmir remained in India or Pakistan. His real concern was the alleviation of its poverty. He only wanted Kashmir to prosper. He was ready to do everything for its well-being. One does not know if the following request to Nehru was genuine or an example of his prelidiction for tongue-in-cheek humour:

> Why don't you, since I am your 'Pandit' brother, call me back? First, I'll help myself to *shaljam shabdegh* at your place and then take the responsibility of Kashmir affairs. The Bakhshis etc. deserve to be dumped right away. Cheats of the first order.There is no reason for you to give them any importance, even if that suits you. Why must you...?

The students of history know that Manto's reference is to Ghulam Muhammad Bakhshi, who became the Chief Minister of Kashmir after the arrest of Sheikh Abdullah.

As far as the removal of poverty is concerned, Manto probably considered himself more competent than either Bakhshi or Nehru. The truth, however, is that an ordinary person like Manto could do nothing. However, the common people of Kashmir could have done a lot if they had been given a chance. And Manto, in any case, was one of those common Kashmiris. That is why Manto was thinking about Kashmir on behalf of its common people, while Nehru was thinking politically. Not only Nehru, but all the political leaders after him continued to believe that what had happened to Kashmir was just and fair. They have the same opinion about what is happening in Kashmir now. But if one were to make a survey of public opinion in Kashmir, would one come to the same conclusion as the politicians? One palpable injustice that was done to the people of Kashmir was that the Kashmiri language was pushed to the margins and Urdu was made the state language. It is important to stress this point because Manto was worried about the fate of Urdu, and his anxiety is recorded in this letter. I shall deal with it later.

Manto was sad that Kashmir was retained by India, but he would have had no complaints if India had eradicated its poverty. He was basically right. Manto, however, didn't ask the larger question: Had poverty been removed from other parts of India? Had Pakistan been able to alleviate the poverty of its people? Nevertheless, Manto had great expectations from Nehru with regard to Kashmir because Nehru was a Kashmiri. Of course, he was merely thinking like a poet.

But his outburst on Junagarh did not seem to spring from this kind of emotionalism. Manto's conclusion was: "You've illegally occupied Junagarh which can be done by a Kashmiri only under the influence of a Maratha. I mean Patel (God forgive him!)." Everyone is aware of the status Patel had in independent India. But the issue of Junagarh was different. Though it was a Hindu majority province, its Nawab intended to accede to Pakistan. As a result there was great discontent among the people and in February, 1948, the government of India had to send in troops and hold a referendum. The majority of people voted in favour of accession to India and the Nawab fled to Pakistan.

In Manto's eyes, this act was illegal. But his dissatisfaction seems to have sprung more from the fact that Nehru had done it at the instance of Patel. One wonders what Manto's reaction would have been if the decision had been taken by Panditiji alone? But the more important question here is whether Manto's indignation against Nehru was right. Obviously, it was right if one sees it through the eyes of the Pakistani citizen, Saadat Hasan Manto. However, if one looks at it through the eyes of a Kashmiri Pandit, then whatever the other Kashmiri Pandit had done was right.

Manto's grievances against Nehru were not only of a political nature. Basically he was a writer concerned about language and literature. One of his grievances was that Indian publishers had published his books without his permission. Alas, if only Manto was aware of how many authors from abroad were, and still are, published here without their consent! In this matter, things in Pakistan are no different. Another serious complaint Manto had was regarding Urdu: "You are a litterateur in English. Here, I write short stories in Urdu, a language which is in the process of being wiped out from your country." Manto emphasises two things in the above statement—one, India was no longer *his* country; it now belonged to others. Hence the sarcasm and the sting in the phrase, 'your country.' It is quite natural to feel distressed if something which once belonged to one is suddenly either snatched away from one or becomes strange. Two, Manto was distressed about the efforts to wipe out Urdu from India. There was a lot of noisy propaganda about it in Pakistan. The Indian Muslims were also affected by it. However, it now seems that Urdu faces greater danger in Pakistan. If one looks at the map of Pakistan, one cannot find a single province where Urdu is the local language. Urdu has been imposed on the people of that country just as it has been imposed on the people of Kashmir. Nevertheless, Manto offers an illustration of how Urdu was being wiped out from India:

> Panditiji, I often read your statements which indicate that Urdu is dear to you. I heard one of your speeches on the radio when the country was divided.Everyone admired your English but when you broke into so called Urdu, it seemed as though some rabid Hindu Mahasabha member had translated your English speech...

Here, it seems that Manto had no complaints about Nehru's language. His objection was to the purported shadow of a rabid Hindu Mahasabha member on his language. He had earlier commented on the influence of a Maratha on Nehru. By now it has been established that Sardar Patel's outlook was becoming communal. In his book, *Modern India,* Sumit Sarkar has quoted Mahatma Gandhi on the Sardar's alleged communal outlook, which runs as follows; "You are not the same Sardar who I knew once." This seems to be the reason for Manto's ironical comment on Sardar Patel. Likewise, drawing attention to the shadow of a rabid Hindu Mahasabha member, Manto probably wanted to say that the Congress, despite its secular pretensions, was not free from the influence of communal forces.

In this letter, Manto has focussed primarily on Nehru's personality as he did in his sketches on the personality of Jinnah, Agha Hashr Kashmiri and several protagonists of his stories. With due respect to Nehru, he revealed what he thought were the negative facets of his personality. There came an epoch in Indian politics when the slogan, "Indira is India," was given unseemly publicity. Even if one ignores this slogan, what cannot be ignored is the fact that after independence, not only Nehruji and Indian politics, as pointed out earlier, but Nehru and India were considered indivisible. The author of the book, *Edwina and Nehru*, written originally in French (in French the title is, *Pour l' amour de l'inde,* which literally means, "For the Love of India"), Catherine Clement has said in one of her recent interviews: "You cannot divide the two. it is both together —India and Nehru" (*The Hindu*, May 5, 1996). When a foreigner can think like this, one can easily understand the feelings of a person who was once a citizen of this country. Manto was sad probably because Nehru, who was not only a person but the 'state' itself, had with him or in his Congress party forces which were both communal and reactionary. Neither Nehru nor his Congress party were immune from their influences. Here, it would be appropriate to say—Manto could be right or he could be wrong. However, the truth is that deep down in his heart he felt an agony which made him restless. That is why he exploded at Nehru, Patel and Radcliffe at the same time. Commenting on Radcliffe's activities, he says:

> It was the time when Radcliffe had cut India into two slices of bread. It is regrettable that they have not yet been toasted. You're toasting them from *that* side and we

from *this* side. But the fire in our braziers has been lit by someone from outside.

The main reason for Manto's anguish and sadness was that India had been cut into two slices of bread. Another reason was that the fire in which the slices were being toasted was lit by someone from outside. As a matter of fact, it was both Manto's compulsion and his writerly obligation to ponder over the partition, its causes and consequences. Like many others, he was against the vivisection of the country, a fact which is substantiated as much by this letter as by the story, "Toba Tek Singh." The anger expressed against Radcliffe in his letter may have been at work while he was writing "Toba Tek Singh." For Manto, Radcliffe was the symbolic representative of those who drew boundary lines between countries, between hearts and between peoples. What was even more regrettable was that he was an "outsider." Manto could have borne the fire stoked from within but not the fire lit from outside. The reason perhaps lay in the fact that though India had been divided into two parts, the writer named Saadat Hasan Manto had developed a double self, one divided, the other undivided.

Manto, in any case, was Manto. For us, he may be great or small. But in reality he was just Manto. A measuring stone weighing one-and-a-half seers—neither one nor two.

Translated from Hindi
by M. Asaduddin

Manto: The Image of the Soul in the Mirror of Eros

DEVENDER ISSAR

You know me as a short story writer and the courts know me as an obscene writer. The government sometimes calls me a communist, and sometimes a great literary figure of the country. Sometimes the doors of livelihood are closed on me and sometimes they are opened for me. Sometimes I am declared a *persona non grata* and considered an 'outsider'; sometimes, when the powers-that-be are pleased, I am told that I can be an 'insider.' I am still troubled, as I have often been in the past, over the questions like: *Who am I? What is my status?* What is my role in this country which is regarded as the largest Islamic state?

You may call my concerns fictional, but for me the bitter reality is that in my country, which is called Pakistan and is very dear to me, *I have yet to find a place.* That is why my *soul is restless.* That is why I am sometimes in a *lunatic asylum* and sometimes in a *hospital.* I have still not found *my rightful place* in Pakistan. Nevertheless, I know that I am a significant person. My name is of great importance to Urdu literature. If I didn't have that illusion, my life would have been absolutely unbearable.

—Saadat Hasan Manto

These extracts not only reveal Manto's mind but also offer meaningful insights into the desires and aspirations of the characters who inhabit his fictional world. Manto's sense of himself and his circumstances, highlighted in the italicized parts of the extracts above, are also relevant for our understanding of his fictional characters. For him, contemporary man was restless and full of anxiety because he was trapped in the maelstrom of politics, religion and economics, as well as, the problems of social and personal identity. The result, Manto thought, was that contempo-rary man often found himself either in a hospital or in a lunatic asylum. Aware of his total irrelevance, and disoriented by his circumstances, Manto often found himself wondering: "Who am I? What's my position in society? What's my relevance and worth?"

These fundamental existential questions have, of course, always plagued man. What gives Manto's characters their special poignance, however, is the fact that they find themselves pushed out of their homes and towards the edge of annihilation. Exiled from their familiar places, excluded from all structures of social justice, they live a precarious existence. Standing at the brink of destruction, they are compelled to ask in anguish: "Who are we? Where do we belong? What is the purpose of our lives?" Characters like Sugandhi, Mamood Bhai, Bishan Singh, Fobha Bai, Janaki, Babu Gopinath, Tóba Tek Singh, Sharda, Mummy and Sahay find themselves either in hospitals or in lunatic asylums, in *chawls* or in whorehouses, on roads or on footpaths. They merely exist, victims of a world which is insensitive and barbarous. Their lives are steeped in sin and filth. Not all of them are, of course, lechers, pimps or whores. There are some, like Gulam Ali in "Swaraj Ke Liya," who could have enjoyed healthy and sexually fulfilling lives had they lived in different times. There are others like Raj Kishore and the Professor in "Panch Din," who are merely victims of hypocrisy and opportunism, or like Babu Gopinath, who are capable of sacrificing themselves for others. But a majority of them live in dark alleys or oppressive rooms, and remain lonely, friendless or depressed till the day they die.

1

Thus, my first proposition is that in the whole range of

Urdu literature, Manto is, perhaps, the only writer whose protagonists are drawn from the margins of society, and whose central concern is with the tragic loneliness of their lives. Indeed, one is struck by the fact that his stories are crowded with such characters. Manto is, of course, a social realist who is aware of the fact that social oppression and economic deprivation are responsible for the plight of his characters. It would, however, be reductive to read him merely as a realist. What gives him depth is the fact that he is profoundly concerned with the sense of isolation and absurdity, violence and evil which mark his characters.

2

My second proposition is that Manto presents, with artistic finesse and depth, the problem of the self and the other, or of the self divided. There is, in his stories, a profound interplay, not only between good and evil, but also between sex and violence, between the forces of Eros and of Thanatos. This interplay runs right from his early story about Jallianwala Bagh ("Tamasha") through his stories about the great killings during the partition, till his last tales like "Sarak Ke Kinare." Thus, Ishwar Singh in "Thanda Gosht," is simultaneously a sexually virile man and one who reaches the very depths of human baseness. And Toba Tek Singh, the lunatic, stands at the border separating two countries which have lost their capacity to think rationally and sanely. Manto's stories often take place in liminal spaces where borders are erased and consciousness loses its bearings, where sanity and insanity, health and sickness, moral goodness and sin cease to be sharply demarcated. The asylum and the hospital are apt symbols for life in such spaces.

3

My third proposition is that, while Manto never pretends to be a philosopher, he is concerned with questions of existence and the self, sin and evil, nature and culture. His preoccupations are always with the social and cultural man and not with man's essential nature. He, thus, simply accepts sex as one of the basic and instinctual aspects of human existence. His stories are attempts to explore the inner workings of those characters in whom instinct has either been repressed, distorted or exploited. In "Dhuan" and "Blouse," he writes, without apologetics, about the first confused awakenings of sexuality in the life of adolescents. While in a story like "Boo," he reveals how the erotic can be so distorted, and so lost in the labyrinths of lust as to become bestial. Stories like "Darpok," "Baanj," "Baasit" or "Sarkandon Ke Peeche," reveal the dark and destructive potential of the sexual instinct in human beings. Thus, Khan Bahadur Aslam Khan can, in a fit of uncontrollable depravity injure his maid, Shadan, with a *datun*. And, in "Sarkandon Ke Peeche," Shahina, alias Halakat, can in a bout of the anguish of sexual jealousy cut up innocent Nawab into pieces and cook her. Her wanton cruelty, a result of her savage eroticism, can be seen in what she tells Khan:

> I have decked up your Nawab...parts of her are on the bed, but most of her is in the kitchen..." There were pieces of flesh on the floor...someone lay on the bed covered with a blood-stained sheet...Shahina smiled and asked, "Shall I lift up the sheet and show you your decked-up Nawab? I have made her up with great care...I cut her into pieces with my own hands...

Perhaps, Manto's most horrific explorations of sexuality are in his stories about the partition. In "Thanda Gosht," Ishwar Singh copulates with the corpse of a young woman and becomes sexually impotent. Similarly, life-instinct turns into death, and sex is distorted into revulsion in the story, "Khol Do." Here, Sakina is repeatedly raped by men who profess to be social workers. These stories force us to confront terrifying questions about erotic violence and politics, religious fanaticism and social reason. Above all, they call into doubt all our assumptions about the nature of man and of violence in societies that are made by human beings. We are so appalled by what Manto reveals, and so bewildered, that we sympathise with Ishwar Singh, when at the moment of his death, he cries out, "What a mother-fucking creature is man!"

4

My fourth proposition is that Manto has a deep aversion to "coldness" in human beings. For him, coldness is always a sign of hypocrisy, insensitivity and death. This is another aspect of the human personality he has explored in his stories. If there is Babu Gopinath with his 'natural' warmth at one end, there is the cold purity and hypocrisy of Raj Kishore at the other. If Janaki or Mozel with their sensuality are at one end, Latika Rani's hardness is at the other.

Raj Kishore's claim to moral goodness hides the soul of an egotist, a sadist and a pretender. Society honours and respects him, but he is incapable of human sympathy. In contrast, Babu Gopinath is irresponsible and sexually indiscreet, but society laughs at him. Yet he is sincere, humane and full of kindness. He only deceives himself, not others.

Shyam, the film actor in "Murali Ki Dhun," is capable of genuine affection, even though he is an alcoholic and seemingly decadent. He exhibits neither cold regard nor deceit. He loves life and hates everything which is touched by the icy hands of death:

> How did Shyam die? Shyam who tasted death by sucking its lips, spat it out in contempt because the lips of death were cold and icy.

What all this suggests is that, while for Manto the conflict between Eros and Thanatos was an essential aspect of the human condition itself, he understood that sexual impulses, which were alienated from a sense of social responsibility and moral commitment, could become dangerous and lead to violence, hatred and war.

5

Unlike the stories of Krishan Chander, Manto's stories are strangely free from the noisy descriptions of a world where there is a surfeit of violence and loot. Maya Krishna Rao's choreography for a play based on "Khol Do," captures this particular aspect of his work rather well. Performed without the help of words, in Rao's choreographed version Sakina's abused body becomes the abode of Sirajuddin's soul. Having entered her body, Sirajuddin experiences the same pain and suffering his daughter went through. He endures all the torments of hell and the excruciating loneliness of her soul. He empathises with her sense of horror, for he realises that at the extreme limits of torment there is no one who can share one's pain. The soul has to experience its own desolation.

6

If we chart out the course of Manto's literary voyage using the above propositions as signposts, it would become clear that Manto was in the process of offering a detailed analysis of the causes of the collapse of all civilisational values in our country. Shocked by the massacres of the fascist and communist regimes, distressed by Auschwitz and Hiroshima and bewildered by the horrors of the partition, Manto's work is marked by an overwhelming sense of disaster. Given the world in which they find themselves, his characters are either morally destroyed, or intellectually paralyzed or sexually ravaged. Manto's imagination is apocalyptic; he is aware that he lives in times when man's claim to humanity is seriously in doubt. Yet, it is precisely such an awareness which makes him declare that man's salvation lies in rediscovering the spiritual:

There must be something called spirituality. In this age of science, atom bombs can be made and germs can be spread. For some, these things may be insignificant. But we cannot say that those people who derive spiritual joy from the *namaz*, *roza* or *kirtan* are mad. Certainly there is substance in spirituality, and for the wicked and the sinful spiritual education is the only road to salvation. They should be made to understand, not through any rigid religious code, but with the help of the principles of progress, that for God human beings are highest embodi-ments of nature. Once they understand the dignity of man, they will become aware of how far they have fallen, and their spiritual baptism will urge them back to their true nature.

As I pointed out at the beginning of this paper, the real and the most agonising question for Manto is about the salvation of man. He is convinced that as long as we don't try to answer it, the life of newborn baby, who is abandoned at Dhobi Mandi, on a cold winter night, wrapped in a wet cloth, would hang in balance. The overwhelming question for Manto is not merely the physical survival of the child, but its spiritual salvation.

Translated from Urdu
by M. Asaduddin and Alok Bhalla

Manto—The Person and the Myth

SHAMIM HANFI

The forty-two years since the death of Saadat Hasan Manto in 1955 have brought rapid changes in our lives, our literary culture and our short story. New attitudes have emerged about the short story, its meaning, its structure, its language and the writer's role and experiences. Critics have discussed modern sensibility in philosophical and theoretical terms at length. Many times the story has receeded in the background while discussions about its technique, experience and theoretical dimensions have taken centre stage. The writer has been marginalised by the critic, who has become more important.

The concerns of Qurratulain Haider, Intizar Husain, Zamiruddin Ahmad, their other contemporaries, and those of later writers like Nayyar Masud, Khalida Husain, Anwar Sajjad, who added new dimensions to the Urdu short story, are entirely different. But among Manto's contemporaries, Krishan Chander believed to be the best short story writer in Asia at the time, and better writers like Ismat Chughtai, Rajinder Singh Bedi, Hayatullah Ansari, Ahmad Nadeem Qasmi, Ghulam Abbas and Mumtaz Mufti, despite their originality and extraordinary creativity, have failed to provide in their work a frame of reference for their era. All of them were better educated than Manto. They led secure, comfortable lives and lived longer than him. But today, we either do not talk about them at all, or if we do, we refer to them as figures shrouded in history's mist. We do remember some of their stories for having made valuable contributions to the art of fiction. We also acknowledge their historical significance. Along with Premchand, they do form a part of our precious literary heritage. Yet we are not able to identify them as writers who dealt with the problems and experiences of a political era with creative responsibility.

Many of them may be considered great writers but they are not read any longer. Manto, however, still appears before us as a writer with valid questions. We ought to examine why his status is different from that of others. Is it because he is no longer the person who lived for forty-two years, eight months and seven days, but a legend and a myth? His own life story amazes and disturbs us. Many new writers see him as a mythic figure and insist that we can understand today's short story only by rescuing it from Manto's, and to some extent from Bedi's, shadow. They believe that unless this shadow is removed their accomplishments can neither be appreciated nor judged.

Every meaningful story that can stand on its own carves a niche in our consciousness. It determines how it is to be read and understood. It lays down the standards for its evaluation which cannot be easily rejected. It forges a permanent relationship between its vision and that of its audience. Purity of purpose, learning and the author's sincerity can hardly take a story too far. The significance of the story, like that of the social sciences, depends solely on our understanding of it. The writer does not want to prove anything to us nor does he want to produce pigeons from his hat. A story cannot stand on the strength of its intellectual arguments. In contrast to the progressive writers, Manto has endured because in his fiction he has not relied on learning, beliefs, ideology or trickery. His strength is not his scholarship and ideas but his genuineness and truthfulness, his experience and understanding. His story never tells lies and is thus disconcerting for the reader. Truth acquires in his story a new and amazing dimension. Marcel Proust had said that the universe is reborn with a new writer; this applies to Manto. He perceives every object and person of this universe with his individual eye and presents them before us according to the needs and concerns of his art. Hence, even when he disappears from his story, we do not lose sight of him. Manto's life can be seen as an unquenchable thirst and an unending quest. And his quest was ethical, social as well as artistic. The most important thing is that his quest does not originate in physical and materialistic sources. His story does not have predetermined and single-layered meanings and a purpose. We can segregate the magic of his personality and myth from his story and still discuss its fine qualities.

Manto's achievement is that he led the life of a full-time writer. He wrote his best stories just before 1947, and immediately after it, at a time when most writers were busy trying to be guides and leaders of society. They judged each other's literary worth on the basis of shared ideology and affiliations instead of true creative value. At the time, there raged a maddening conflict not only outside Manto but also within him. Hence, his stories are not merely social and political. We can understand his themes keeping in mind the social and political situation of the time. But in order to understand his stories, we should take account of the personal documents penned by Manto with a cold sense of indifference towards his own self. In this regard, his letters and articles can be quite helpful. A few excerpts from his letters to Ahmad Nadeem Qasmi follow.

> I'm myself very sentimental. But I believe that we should not suffuse our stories with sentiment. After going through your stories I feel that sentiment has overwhelmed you. You should try to suppress it (1937).
>
> I believe in a writer whose work makes us think for some time (1937).
>
> Life should be presented as it is, not as it was, or will be or ought to be (1938).
>
> Who is this Rajinder Singh Sahib? He also seems to be a lump of earth. Writes very well. You should read his stories carefully (January, 1939).
>
> Nadeem Sahib, I've not yet written what I've wanted to. I've so many problems that my ideas get mixed up. Besides, who is willing to listen to whatever I want to say. Day before yesterday, after seeing a man sitting on a

sidewalk in the market, the plot of a story took shape in my mind (August, 1940).

For long I've considered my existence in Turgenev's words— useless like the fifth wheel of a cart. I have wished to be of use to somebody. If a brick lying in a ditch can be used in the making of a wall, what else can it wish for (April, 1937).

Perhaps you don't know that I've never presented myself as a man of letters. I am a broken wall from which falling pieces of plaster keep making patterns on the ground (February, 1937).

My life is a wall whose plaster I keep scratching with my nails.

Sometimes, I wish to erect a building on this rubble. I keep thinking of this. Due to constant work, my mind remains on fire. My normal temperature is a degree higher, from which you can easily have an idea of the fire burning within me (February, 1939).

Manto is a spectator not only of life but also of himself. Without projecting himself in his stories, he presents a spectacle before us that contains his self also. Despite all this, he neither becomes sentimental nor does he impose a meaning from without. He reaches his truth with his whole being, understands his experience and depicts it. At the same time, he performs the duty of guarding the acts of his being, so that his story remains a story and does not become a pamphlet, an imposed manifesto, an announcement or a contract. In contrast to his contemporary progressive writers, he never allows a predetermined conception of reality to lead him; he knows that with changing experiences the meaning of reality also changes. His infamous and condemned stories, "Kali Shalwar," "Dhuan," "Bu," "Thanda Gosht" and "Khol Do," which were prosecuted for obscenity, are related to that experience and concept of reality which, not to mention ordinary people, even his contemporary writers did not have the courage to face. These writers held a conventional and traditional notion of reality, reached by unanimous agreement among themselves. For Manto, reality was his consciousness and the events conceived through it. His personality was as sensitive as his consciousness, apparently impressed by the smallest of things, appearances, objects and people, yet equally traditional and flintlike. The horrific reality in "Thanda Gosht" and "Khol Do" is still capable of splintering our senses and sensibility. The aesthetic restraint exercised by Manto, and the manner in which he saves himself from losing control in his stories, are qualities hardly found in the other writers of those savage times. None of his contemporaries, with the exception of Bedi, considered it necessary to think about the art of fiction. They did not pay attention to the distinction between a good and a bad story. Because of this we do not find the acute and intelligent insights of Manto in any of their stories. Some more excerpts from his articles follow.

Literature is either literature or something else. Man is either man or he is a donkey, a house, a table or something else.

Raja Sahib Mahmudabad and those who share his views say that it is utterly obscene. Whatever you write is filth. I say, quite right. Because I write about obscenity and filth only.

Today's writer is a dissatisfied person. He is dissatisfied with his environment, his system, his society, his literature, even with his own self.

A hardworking woman who works throughout the day and has a sound sleep at night cannot be the heroine of my stories. My heroine can only be a whore who remains awake at night, and while asleep during the day, suddenly wakes up after seeing a terrible dream of old age knocking at her door.

I don't want to whip up the emotions and ideas of people. How can I undress culture and civilization when they already have no clothes on. I also don't try to dress them up since it's not my job but that of drapers.

I'm a timid person. I'm terribly scared of prison. This life I'm leading, is not less painful than prison life. If another prison is built inside this prison, and I'm stuffed into it, I'll die within minutes.

I love life. I like dynamism. I don't mind being hit by a bullet in my chest while I'm moving around. But I don't want to die like a bed-bug in a prison. While reading out this paper for this forum, if I'm beaten up by you, I won't utter a sigh. But if my head is wounded in a Hindu-Muslim riot, each drop of my blood will cry out.

I'm an artist and don't like ungainly wounds. One can write on war and still die in a small dark room with the desire to see and touch a pistol remaining unrealized. Instead of such a death, it would be better if I gave up writing, set up a dairy farm and started selling milk mixed with water (*Adab-e-Jadeed*, Jan, 1944).

My stories are for healthy people, for normal people, who take a woman's breast for a breast and don't go further than that, for those who don't view a man-woman relationship with amazement, who don't swallow a work of literature at one go...

There's a simple rule about eating bread—every bit of it is to be chewed well and mixed with spittle so that, without overburdening the digestion, it still remains nourishing. The same rule applies to reading also—chew every word, every line, every idea in your mind. And stir well the saliva produced in your mind while reading, so that whatever you have read can be easily digested. If you don't do this, its result would be bad and you won't be able to blame the writer—how can properly chewed bread be held responsible for your indigestion ("Tahriri Bayan").

We can pick up a fight with others about beards, about pyjamas and about the length of one's hair. We can think up new ways of cooking *roghan josh, pulao* and korma. We can think about the colour and type of buttons to be stitched on a green dress. Why can't we think about the nation?

A whorehouse is itself a dead body carried by society on its shoulders. Unless society buries it somewhere, it's going to be talked about. The body may be rotten, stinking, impure, horrible and dirty, but there's no harm in seeing its face. Aren't we its relatives and friends ("Safed Jhoot").

We are not prophets. We see the same thing, the same problem from different points of view in different circumstances. Whatever we understand we present before the world. We never compel others to accept it.

We are neither lawmakers nor lawkeepers. These are jobs for others. We criticize governments but we aren't rulers ourselves. We draw maps of buildings, but aren't builders ourselves. We diagnose diseases but don't run a clinic.

You find my writing bitter and sour. But what has humanity gained from the sweetness that has till now been dished out to it? The leaves of neem may be bitter, but they do purify blood ("Afsananigar aur Jinsi Masail").

These assertions about the art of fiction, and about the role and responsibilities of a writer, are lucidly expressed. Manto freed the story from the mesh devised by academics and stressed the relations between the story, the writer and the reality that provides the experience for the story. He identified the concerns of his story in the light of these relations. These excerpts show that his concerns are not solely literary. His is a basic human predicament rooted in the aesthetics of the story and the social mileau. The process of learning, on which he has focussed our attention, does not belong to books, or philosophy or any ideology. The distancing of the reader from the standard bearers of the modern story, and the inability of the writers to impress the reader, result from their failure to strike a balance between learning and unlearning in their stories. Manto contemplates life in terms of real events and peoples. The denseness found in his work can be found in only a few stories by Premchand, Krishan Chander, Ismat and Bedi. His observation is very acute and does not miss even the minutest of details. He never ignores anything related to life and the people. Even in the midst of details and descriptions he never loses sight of the focussed centre and his creative purpose. He always avoids unnecessary words, details and descriptions. That is why a unity of impression is maintained throughout his stories. He neither allows himself nor his story to fall apart. In contrast to Manto, in Ismat, Bedi and the conventional progressive writers, we find glossing, commentary, emotionalism, rhetoric, exaggeration and disintegration. The reason for this is that they do not have a sense of the limits within which a story and a writer work. They do not know where they ought to stop. They keep an idealistic life in mind more than our problems, and they are so entangled in it, that they forget the form and role of the character. It is not that Manto did not believe in ideals and concepts, or was unable to view human sentiments and ideas as a part of reality. For him reality is both a sentiment and an awareness. If it had not been so, he would not have been so sensitive and vigilant about his moral views.

Alongside this, however, he never ignored the delineation of characters in his stories. Even if we take into account the nearly three hundred stories of Premchand and those of his contemporaries, none of them has created as many living and memorable characters as Manto. His characters are still capable of disconcerting us, of making us lose our composure. Manto could write such stories because he had a deep awareness of evil and did not look upon it as an abode of darkness. Babu Gopinath, Mammad Bhai, Sahai, Mummy, Sharda, Mozel, Ishar Singh, Sultana, Sugandhi—

all these are haloed faces peering over the boundary of darkness, filth and sin. In the words of Firaq, they are like plants growing alongside the river of sin. Manto knew the strength and value of sentiments but was more interested in human beings. He could never accept the conventional definition of human beings and humanity given currency by the traditional progressive writers and our middle class morality. His mind had devised a complex definition of humanity. In this the lines separating good from evil intertwine. He wrote:

> We are radicals, we perceive light even in the darkness of the world. We don't look upon anybody with contempt. If a whore spits on a passerby from the balcony of her brothel, we neither laugh at him as do other onlookers nor do we swear at her.
>
> People are not very different from each other. A person can repeat the mistake of others. If a woman can set up a shop in the market to sell her body then other women can also do the same.
>
> If a young, healthy and pretty girl from a good family elopes with a weak, ugly and poor boy, we hang her present and future in the noose of morality. But I try to untie the small knot that had made her treat all sense of propriety so callously.

Manto had tried to depict life and reality in all its hues. That is why he had to undergo such a long and trying ordeal as compared to others. His own life is full of horrors and grave physical and spiritual struggles. It is not possible for a hypocritical person to carry the burden of such profound experiences. In an era, in which small and insignificant personal goals have become so important in life, it is not surprising that Manto should appear to us as a legend. However, in this regard we should remember that Manto has been transformed into a myth by his admirers and his critics. These include his detractors who criticize him. In Manto's era, Meeraji was another personality who assumed mythical dimensions. Meeraji had made efforts, both consciously and unconsciously, to cultivate a deceptive impression of his personality. Manto, on the other hand, was honest both to himself and to the truth of his artistic experience. We should keep in mind that a living person is not a legend in himself. It is only others who make him into a legend.

Translated from Urdu
by Shikoh Mohsin Mirza

Saadat Hasan Manto: Ideology and Social Philosophy

TARANNUM RIYAZ

1

The literary achievements of Manto are spread over a wide canvas making the task of covering them in a brief article difficult. The appraisal of his literary works and the analysis of his political and social philosophy are equally ardous tasks. *Fatwas* were issued against him and he was even dragged to the courts for his writings. Manto did win the criminal cases against him in the courts. He was, however, always embroiled in controversies during his lifetime and continued to be so even after his death.

It is a curious coincidence that Manto, like Ghalib, was encouraged to continue to write by a group of his admirers. The number of his admirers has grown after his death. Manto's literary works are now the subject of research and critical evaluation from entirely new angles.

2

It is interesting to note that in many ways the socio-political context of the subcontinent in which Manto wrote his short stories is not much different from the social and political scenarios of India and Pakistan today. The issues raised in his short stories continue to stare us in our faces in the same manner as they did five decades ago. Poverty and deprivation, the gimmicks of politicians, the astute tactics of mullahs and pandits who divide people in the name of religion, the suffering of great scholars and success of mediocre writers were the themes of Manto; these are the troublesome issues of our times as well, and demand resolution. In this regard, the universal and eternal character of creative works of Manto and relevance of their analysis transcends time and space.

Manto's writings have certain features which accord them a distinct identity and a different complexion. Sometimes his writings seem to be full of contradictions. However, a careful reading of his works reveals that there is a philosophic continuity to his writings. Manto seems to be quite impressed with socialism, but he does not recognise it as the sole prescription for the political and economic problems of India. He refuses to endorse any particular political ideology. Nevertheless, he has a sharp political and social consciousness which helps him to develop his 'liberal' attitudes. Thus, he says: "The common complaint against me is that I do not write love stories. Since there is no flavour of love and romance in my stories, they are usually drab."[1]

Manto does not raise slogans, nor does he trade politics in the name of literature. He also does not recognise the imposition of political boundaries. This accounts for his confrontations with some of the prominent leaders of the progressive writer's movement in the country. It is a sad commentary on the history of Urdu literature in India that Manto did not receive the recognition which was due to him merely because some prominent progressive writers dismissed him as a reactionary. Manto's reaction to such pronouncements is sharp:

> I greatly detested the so-called Communists. I could not appreciate people who talked about the 'sickle and the hammer' while sitting in comfortable armchairs. In this connection, comrade Sajjad Zaheer, who sipped his milk in a silver cup, always remained a clown in my eyes. The true psychology of working labourers is manifested in their sweat. Maybe, the people who used this sweat to earn wealth, and used it as ink to write detailed manifestoes, are sincere people. However, you will pardon me, if I consider them to be impostors.[2]

This is indeed an acute observation, for it carries weight and has a certain logic in it. Manto essentially rejects the imposition of any alien philosophy on Indian situations. On the contrary, he believes in reaching the 'grassroots.' Manto has since been proved right, for genuine solutions to our problems will have to be found internally.

3

Manto was meticulous in observing the basic norms and technical requirements of short story writing. He rebelled against social and political bondages, but he respected the artistic and technical requirements of short story writing. One hardly comes across an extra word in his short stories. It is in this context that Manto's writings acquire a distinct identity. Describing his short stories, he says:

> The facts narrated in my short stories, dramas and essays are directly related to that part of the mind which is usually reserved for one's own self. Since these facts are fitted in the frame of short story, you come across them in the same very form.[3]

An analysis of Manto's writings raises certain questions. Answers to them can be found in his own writings. Was Manto writing short stories merely because he was a short story writer? Were his writings the result of his conscious or unconscious effort? Are his stories merely a collection of events and situations of his times? I understand that the answers to these complex issues cannot be found merely in his short stories. We have to consider his writings in their entirety.

An evaluation of the writings of Manto reveals that he consciously wanted to communicate his ideas to others. Therefore, to ensure communication, he took recourse to different forms of Urdu literature. In case the technical requirements of short story writing came in the way of communicating his ideas, he did not hesitate to write essays. His essays like "Mera Sahib," "Bari Sahib," "Murli Ki Dhun," "Nargis," and the caricature of himself are some of his noteworthy contributions to Urdu literature. Manto even used the technique introduced by Ghalib, i.e., letter writing, to communicate his ideas. "Chacha Sam Key Nam Nav Khatoot" is a good example of Manto's use of this form.

4

His famous short story "Toba Tek Singh" has been analysed from different angles. It seems that the main character of the short story, a mad person, is none other than Manto himself. At the time of partition, the piece of land, Toba Tek Singh, fell neither within the boundary of India nor of Pakistan. Manto asks who are the inhabitants of Toba Tek Singh? Are they Indians or Pakistanis? In fact, this was the dilemma of millions of Indians who never subscribed to the two nation theory. Toba Tek Singh is a metaphor for the abode of millions of Indians. Human beings who inhabited their own Toba Tek Singh, were happy in their milieu, and spoke their own dialects and cherished their historical traditions, suddenly witnessed the devastation of their habitats as a consequence of the partition. This harsh historical decision, in which these hapless people had no say, not only destroyed their homes and hearths, outraged their social and cultural relationships and perverted their value systems, but shattered their dreams too. Even their history was distorted. The lunatic asylum, around which the entire short story "Toba Tek Singh" revolves, alludes to the abode of millions of sensible and dignified people who were unable to understand the logic of the partition. This is how Manto beings the story:

> A mad person got embroiled in the syndrome of Pakistan and India to such an extent that he got further deranged mentally. While sweeping the floor, one day, he suddenly climbed a nearby tree. He delivered a long speech from the tree for about two hours on the delicate issue of India and Pakistan. When soldiers ordered him to climb down, he climbed further up the tree. When he was threatened some more, he said, "I want to stay on this very tree."[4]

Manto in the same story adds:

> "Molbi Saab (Maulvi Sahib), what is this Pakistan?" After deep contemplation, he replied, "It is a place in India where blades are manufactured."[5]

The fact remains, as Manto put it, that emotionally and mentally, even today millions of people scattered across India and Pakistan look nostalgically towards the lands they left behind. On the one side, beyond the barbed wires lies India, and on the other side, beyond the same barbed wires is Pakistan. For them Toba Tek Singh is a piece of land which has no specific national identity, it is a place where they make their lives.

Whenever I read the story, I am always confronted by a question: Has this process of the inhuman division of land come to an end? We thought that a tragic chapter of human history, in which about two million lives were lost, had been closed for ever. We believed that this illogical political process which resulted in the division of hearts, minds and human relationships, would never again be repeated in human history. It is sad indeed that this process is now being repeated again with the same barbarity. However, this time it is not Asia but Bosnia that is witnessing barbarism. Who knows, some Manto might be writing a "Toba Tek Singh" there.

Much has been written about Manto's two other short stories viz., "Thanda Gosht" and "Khol Do." Both these stories reflect the bitter social and political problems of the Indian subcontinent in a particular historic context. These stories show that human beings get transformed into monsters who hate each other once they are divided in the name of religion.

In "Thanda Gosht," the main character, Ishwar Singh who becomes a beast ultimately suffers the same agony which others suffered on account of his savagery. Similarly, in "Khol Do," a hapless woman who is the victim of human barbarity is unable to distinguish between the hounds masquerading as humans and a sympathetic humane doctor.

It is ironical that the brute characters and the outraged woman are both of the same religion. If religion is the cause of all the trouble, then why is the outraged Sakina not safe at the hands of fellow believers? Or is it that barbarism and savagery know no religion? It is amazing that both these short stories, which some found either obscene or artistically poor, in fact, highlight serious social and political problems which still confront us in cities like Ahmedabad, Bombay or Karachi.

5

The apprehensions which persuaded Manto to migrate from India continued to haunt him even in Islamic Pakistan. However, in Pakistan, a new and bitter reality dawned upon him. In India, he had apprehended discrimination on the basis of religion. But in Pakistan he had to face the predicament of being an outsider. This bitter reality became a major social and political problem for many in Pakistan. A great deal of death and destruction is taking place in Karachi these days because of this. In one of his essays, "Zaroorat Hai" (Wanted), Manto wrote:

> The Special Services Department invites applications for the following posts. The inhabitants of Pakistan alone would be considered for these posts. The migrants should send a money order of Rupees Twenty along with their applications instead of the (usual) Rs. Ten...[6]

The controversy between 'locals' and 'outsiders' is a perennial and intricate problem of south-east Asian societies. This problem has taken different forms at different times. The problem has not been solved by segregating people on the basis of religion. Manto highlighted this repeatedly in his writings.

Manto paid equal attention to other problems, which are common to India and Pakistan, in his writings. In his essay, "Zaroorat Hai," Manto satirically highlighted the issues of falling social values, the menace of nepotism, and the rising phenomenon of incompetence in government departments. In this essay a particular department wants to fill the vacancy of a research officer. The prerequisite qualifications of the candidates are as follows:

> One Research Officer; Pay-scale; Three-Hundred-Sixty-Five Rupees and quarter of Eight Annas monthly; Annual increment: Twenty-five Rupees, Four annas and one paise.
> The Upper Limit: Seven Hundred and Twenty Rupees, Eleven Annas and Nine paise.
> SPECIALISATION: The candidate should (1) Strictly follow the routine of praying five times a day; (2) Play the harmonium well; (3) Have worked in a railway workshop for at least two years and three months; (4) Speak through his nose; (5) Know how to cook Khamira of Gaw-zaban-anbari Wallah; (6) Have sufficient knowledge on how to breed buffaloes and be twenty-nine years and one day old. Preference will be given to a candidate who has been a teacher of theology in a girl's school.[7]

Manto also wrote a lot about dancing girls and prostitutes. Here, however, a careful study of his essays reveals that Manto viewed the issue of prostitutes and dancing girls quite seriously. He deliberated on it as a social problem and provoked his readers to ponder over it in the same vein. According to Manto:

> Begging is prohibited legally. However, nobody bothers to eradicate the factors which drive a person to indulge in this act. Women are prohibited from indulging in the flesh trade but no attention is paid to the motivations which force them into this trade.[8]

Does Manto offer a solution to these problems? In fact, he does not look for the solutions to these problems in any established social or political ideology. However, he does believe in interacting with the concerned people in order to find a solution to such problems. It seems that this approach resulted in his differences with the leading lights of progressive movement. For instance, the reaction of Manto to the news that the prostitutes of Rawalpindi were forming a trade union, is as follows:

> Recently we heard the news from Rawalpindi, the same place where the leader of the Nation, Khan Liaquat Ali Khan, was assassinated, that prostitutes were forming a trade union. Some people might have laughed it away or might have smiled on hearing the news, but I took it seriously. Any news that indicates the political and economical awareness of a prostitute or a housewife, of a drunkard or a Sufi, of a ruler or the ruled, I consider to be a good omen. The prostitutes of Rawalpindi would be in a position to project at least their view point. This would be their own view point, one which would emanate from their brains and be articulated through their mouths.[9]

It is important to note that Manto emphasised the personal viewpoint of the prostitutes in order to get to the root of the problem and find a solution. The essays in which he deals with social problems are neither narratives nor speeches. They are full of humour and satire. They might not be specimens of the highest forms of literature, but they do not reflect a mediocre mind. These writings are essential for any understanding of his social and political philosophy.

Generally, the characters in Manto's stories belong to the world of crime and the dens of prostitutes. Ironically these stories have been analysed only from one perspective giving a lopsided picture of Manto's motivation for concentrating on these themes. In fact, Manto not only represented their particular world in his short stories, but also reflected on the factors which nourished their world of crime. He even proposed some solutions. According to him:

> I neither believe in the death sentence nor do I believe in imprisonment. I believe that jail cannot reform a person. I believe in reformatories which show the right path to

wrong doers. We generally talk about dervishes and saintly people, a single word of whose can reform even evil characters. An ordinary mendicant can convert a devil into an angel. Spirituality is a reality. In this age when bombs are produced and germs are spread, this may appear absurd to some people. But those who attain spiritual bliss by reading Namaz, keeping fasts, performing arti and singing kirtans cannot be described as mad people.[10]

These observations of Manto on crime and punishment are highly pertinent. They indicate his awareness and knowledge of the different proposals made to deal with crime and reformation of criminals by various people around the world. However, Manto's ideas are drawn from the spiritual concerns rooted in our land. His prescriptions are indigenous and have been practised here over centuries.

Manto examines social value from two perspectives and interprets them in his own way. His first concern is with individual values which are the result of historical continuity. These values are cherished and preserved by individuals in society. Wherever Manto discerns ethical duplicity, he exposes it mercilessly. Manto had to pay a heavy price for his honesty, and face onslaughts from different directions. In his short story "Mr. Moinuddin," Zehra seeks a divorce from her husband Moinuddin so that she can marry her lover, the millionaire Ahsan. Moinuddin refuses to oblige her. However, he allows her to have sexual relations with Ahsan so that in the eyes of the world she would continue to be his wife. Moinuddin believes that the remarriage of his wife with a millionaire would bring disgrace to him. However, when Ahsan dies after transferring property worth millions of rupees in the name of Zehra, Moinuddin divorces her. His logic is as follows:

> I am doing all this because my honour is dearer to me. When people in my circle come to know that Ahsan left so much property in your name, they will spread stories.[11]

All those contradictory values of society where a Haji Sahib does not consider accepting a bribe, blackmarketing or smuggling of opium as being wrong, or where a prostitute overcomes many odds to have a black salwar to wear at *Moharram* and where a woman prays to *Bhagwan* (God) before selling her body, come within the purview of Manto's writings. Dividing human values, religious beliefs and challenges of existence into separate compartments and then seeking relationship between them is an interesting aspect of human nature. Manto enjoys watching this activity and invites his readers to watch it. He usually weaves his short stories around this very activity.

Manto not only exposes moral hollowness but also attempts to reverse the perceptions of common folk in society. This task is tantamount to burning one's fingers. For instance, in Islamic history, Yazid is remembered as a tyrant and a barbarous king who ordered that Hazrat Imam Hussain, the grandson of the prophet Mohammed and his family members should not be allowed to drink water from a nearby river in the scorching heat of the desert. However, in Manto's short story "Yazid," when a son is born to Karim Dad, he names him Yazid. Manto explains it as follows:

> Jeena's voice became feeble, "What are you saying Kemay? Yazid." Karim Dad Smiled, "What is in it. It is just a name." Jeena could not merely say, "But whose name?" Karim Dad replied seriously, "He may not necessarily turn out to be the same very Yazid. That Yazid stopped the river, this man will release it."[12]

In a way, Karim Dad's action is both rebellious and innovative. Manto wants to change the stereotypes embedded in the psyche of his Muslim readers.

Manto examines the value system from the perspective of political and economic changes in society. These changes do have an impact on society, its cultural norms and values. Manto's response to the progressive movement and communism has already been discussed briefly. However,

Manto is not satisfied with the American influences on the society and polity of Pakistan. Drawing a profile of the Pakistani society in the aftermath of US military and economic aid to Pakistan, Manto writes satirically:

> We will have buses fitted with American tools. We will have Islamic pajamas stitched from American machines. We will have clods of earth 'untouched by hands' from the American soil. We will have American folding stands for the Holy Quran and American prayer mats. Keep watching, you will find everyone singing your praise.[13]

Manto's writings reveal that though he was not completely averse to alien political ideologies, he did not get carried away by them. He drew upon these ideologies but did not recognise them as the last word. According to him:

> I felt sorry for the activists of the progressive movement who unnecessarily meddled in politics. These charlatans were using the prescription proposed by Kremlin and were busy preparing a mixture of literature and politics. Nobody bothered about the temperament or pulse of the patient for whom the mixture was prepared. The result is for every one to see. We are brooding over the stagnation in our literature.[14]

6

Manto emerges, in the light of his writings, as a humanist. He seeks answers to the problems from his own land and its history. He is a free thinker, who sees the reality clearly and analyses the events independently. He is not interested in being labelled. He is fully aware of the contradictions and other complications of the Muslim mind in the subcontinent. These contradictions got further accentuated with the creation of Pakistan. In the aftermath of the partition, the inner contradictions and emotional crises of the Muslims were further deepened. Manto boldly projects them in his writings. He even chooses unusual and potentially dangerous themes for his short stories. In one such story, he writes:

> Earlier everyone fought against one common enemy, since they were made to believe that he was an enemy and they accepted this as a truth because they had to earn their livelihood and win the medals and rewards. Now they themselves were divided into two parts. Earlier they were all known as Indian soldiers; now one was an Indian, and the other was a Pakistani. Rab Nawaz's brain would fail him whenever he thought about this issue. Was the Pakistani Army fighting for Kashmir or Kashmiri Muslims? In case they were prodded to fight for Muslims in Kashmir, why were they not sent to Hyderabad and Junagarh to fight for the Muslims there? In case it was a purely Islamic war, why were not other Muslim countries joining this war?[15]

The extract from his short story "Akhri Salute" (Last Salute), which was written in October, 1955, a few years after the Indo-Pak war over Kashmir and another excerpt from the very same story reveal the clarity of Manto's thoughts :

> During these intervals he asked Rab Nawaz, "Do you really want Kashmir?" Rab Nawaz replied with all sincerity, "Yes, Ram Singh." Ram Singh shook his head and said, "No! I don't believe it, somebody has incited you." Rab Nawaz in turn tried to reassure him, "No, you have been incited. I swear by *Panjtan Pak* (five holy persons of Muslims, viz. the prophet Mohammed, His son-in-law, daughter, and two grandsons)." Ram Singh held Rab Nawaz's hand and said, "Do not swear my friend. Everything will be alright." However, his expression clearly indicated that he did not believe Rab Nawaz.[16]

"Akhri Salute" is still relevant because it vividly reveals the contradictions in the Muslim mind accentuated by the partition. It portrays the mental, psychological and emotional state of the Muslims caused by the political games played in the name of religion.

In the final analysis, Manto does not appear to be completely free from ideologies. He might have stressed that he was not bound by any particular social or political ideology, but his writings reveal that he was influenced by at least some. He analysed the social realities, debated the social problems in the perspective of these very ideologies. His characters are engaged in the struggle for existence. These characters are angels as well as devils; they are kind hearted as well as cruel. One of his characters, who is himself scared of the needle of a doctor's syringe, brutally murders another person. This is how Manto viewed life around him and introduced his characters in his short stories.

The canvas of Manto's writings is too wide to be covered in a brief appraisal. I conclude this brief analysis with an excerpt from Manto's own writings which offers a succinct profile of the man:

> I am scared of jail. The life I am leading is no less painful than an imprisonment. If another jail is created within the jail I am already in, I will die of suffocation within seconds. I love life. I believe in action. I can face a bullet in my chest while I am on the move, but I do not want to die in jail like a bug. I can receive a good beating from you while narrating my essay from this platform and will not even heave a sigh. However, if somebody breaks my head in a Hindu-Muslim riot, every drop of my blood will cry. I am an artist. I do not like shabby wounds (on my person)...[17]

Translated from Urdu
by Riyaz Punjabi

REFERENCES

1. Saadat Hasan Manto, "Ishqiya Kahani," in *Manto Namah*. Lahore: Sang-e-Meel Publications, 1990, p. 74.
2. Saadat Hasan Manto, "Gunah Ki Baityan, Gunah Ke Bap," in

Opar Nichey Darmiyan, Delhi: Saqi Book Depot, 1989, p. 128.
3. "Jaib-e-Kafan," in *Manto Namah,* p. 221.
4. "Toba Tek Singh," in *Manto Namah*, p. 12.
5. Ibid. p. 11.
6. "Zaroorat Hai," in *Oper Nichey Darmiyan*, pp. 122-23.
7. Ibid.
8. "Gunah Ki Baityan, Gunah ke Bap," *Oper Nichey Darmiyan*, pp. 127-28.
9. Ibid.
10. "Qatal-O-Khoon Ki Surkhiyan," in *Opar Nichey Darmiyan*, pp. 74-75.
11. "Mr. Moinuddin," in *Manto Namah,* p. 65.
12. "Yazid" in *Manto Namah*, p. 108.
13. "Chacha Sam Key Naam Choutha Khat," in *Upar Nichey Darmiyan*, p. 80.
14. "Jaib-e-Kafan," in *Manto Namah,* p. 108.
15. "Akhri Salute," in *Manto Namah*, p. 126.
16. Ibid.
17. "Lazat-e-Sang," in *Manto Namah*, p. 621.

A Note On Some Myths About Manto

INDRA NATH CHOUDHURI

The Indian literary scene of the thirties, forties and fifties was the period of short stories. In every Indian language, great short story writers made their mark with their unconventional treatment of middle class values, the plight of women and the poor in particular. Saadat Hasan Manto was one of those writers who did this with great artistic skill. Manto's work, however, has always invited ambivalent responses from his critics. Thus, Upendra Nath Ashk, one of his biographers, candidly says that Manto's artistic skill ultimately looks rather fake because the endings of his stories seem contrived. This is apparent when one compares Manto with writers like Chekhov whose stories are simple yet profound. But surprisingly, Ashk also praises the structure of Manto's stories and their precise attention to detail. Ashk says that Manto received from Gorky his love and compassion for mankind, especially for the underdog, and from Maugham and Maupassant his unique craftsmanship (cf. *Manto Mera Dushman*).

Since ambivalent views of this kind are to be found among Manto's critics it is very difficult to create an authentic image of him as a writer. Thus, Leslie Flemming, in her comprehensive biography of Manto, has a difficult time in reconciling many things about the man. Take for example, Manto's decision to leave for Pakistan in 1948. She says that he left because he was afraid of the growing intensity of communal riots. Contradicting this, Ashk emphatically says that Manto left Bombay and went to Pakistan because he was an egotist and was quarrelsome by nature. When his film-scripts were put aside for those of Nazir Ajmeri, Kamal Amrohi and Shahid Latif, Manto's ego was hurt. Ashk puts it metaphorically when he says that when Manto found the main road blocked, with no chance for his car to get through, he took the side road and left Bombay. Ashk further says that while there was no doubt that there were some letters threatening to set Bombay Talkies on fire unless its Muslim employees were dismissed, they had no effect on Shahid Latif, Sadik Wacha and Ajmeri. Only Manto used them as an excuse to leave. The fact, however, was that Manto could not stand the lack of recognition.

Manto always provoked contradictory responses. He was a difficult man to understand. He was touchy, introverted and egotistical, and that often made him lonely. He frequently complained of being depressed. Some say that his desire for reassurance and approval were the real causes for his depression.

Manto carefully avoided making any direct references to historical events and personalities. There is hardly a writer who belongs to the same period who does not mention Gandhi or feel indebted to him. Manto makes an oblique and ironic reference to Gandhi in "Swaraj Ke Liye." Here, the narrator, an enthusiastic and idealistic activist, details the career of his friend, Ghulam Ali, who is imprisoned for his political activism during the Independence movement. Nigar, whom Ghulam Ali is to marry, stays at an ashram which is run by Babaji, who is modelled on Gandhi. Once Ghulam Ali is released from prison, the Babaji marries the two of them, but only after obtaining from them a vow that they will not consummate their marriage until India is independent. However, Nigar finds a technicality under Islamic law that allows them to break their vow. Manto ends the story with the wry comment on the unnatural manner in which family planning is enforced for the sake of fake idealism. In fact, according to Ashk, the story is based on a true incident. Manto's story is an attack on such purity and hypocrisy in the name of a cause. He exposes the fake idealism of people who are at the helm of affairs and have no concern for the sentiments of human beings, their urge for life and its demands.

Manto's short stories convey an "intense awareness of

human loneliness." As a result there is more of twilight and darkness than of daylight or brightness to be found in his stories. In 1939, Manto wrote, "I consider myself incomplete. I am never at peace with myself. I feel as if whatever I am, whatever is inside me, ought not to be. In its place there ought to be something else." This kind of dissatisfaction with himself was responsible for his lack of involvement with the cultural and political activities of his times. Of course, in order to write his stories, he had to take up political themes, but he did so without any real desire to comment on them. At the same time, however, he was certain that literature reflected changing social realities, and could offer an accurate diagnosis of the ills of society.

Manto's partition stories are a grim reflection on the tragedy that engulfed the subcontinent. One of his stories in *Siyah Hashye*, entitled "Karamat," reads as follows:

> The police started conducting raids to recover stolen goods.
> There was panic and fear. Under the cover of darkness people got rid of the stolen goods. Some even put away their own possessions to avoid a possible encounter with the police.
> There was one man who was greatly agitated. He had looted two bags of sugar from the local grocer's shop. Somehow he dumped one into the well nearby. While trying to do the same with the other bag, he fell into the well.
> People heard the noise. They gathered at the well. Ropes were lowered. Two sturdy men hauled him up. But he died a few hours later. Water drawn from the well the next day tasted sweet. That night candles were lit at the man's grave.

Most of Manto's stories dramatise the absurdity of the partition. Manto ironically asks: "Will Pakistani literature be different, and if so, how? Will literature be partitioned also? What I could never resolve was the question: What country did we now belong to, India or Pakistan? Whose blood was being shed so mercilessly everyday? And whose bones, stripped of the flesh of religion, were they being cremated or buried?...A terrible chapter was added to history, a chapter without precedent." This was the only direct comment he made on what turned out to be a "nationalism of mourning." Otherwise, Manto was never at the centre of events. He always stood at the margins and commented. As he himself says:

> For a long time I refused to accept the consequences of the revolution which was set off by the partition. I still feel the same way. But I suppose, in the end, I came to accept the nightmarish reality without self pity or despair. In the process, I tried to retrieve from this man-made sea of blood, pearls of rare hue, by writing about the single-minded dedication with which men killed men, about the remorse felt by some of them, about tears shed by murderers who could not understand why they still had some human feelings left. All this and more, I put in my work, *Siyah Hashye*.

One must conclude that even if Manto didn't have a great sense of history, his partition stories combine a fine degree of awareness and detachment, analysis and observation. They movingly record the sorrow of a whole generation in India and Pakistan who watched their historical fate helplessly.

The contradiction in the literature of his time was that on the one hand it came under the influence of Western progressivism, and included writings about prostitutes, primps and alcoholics. But on the other hand, it could not always conform to the ideological demands of Marxism, social realism and ideological purity. The Marxist critics disavowed any connection between progressive and obscene literature. Manto, in fact, unlike the majority of the Indian writers of his time, described fallen women realistically. He did not, like Saratchandra Chatterjee, romanticise them as victims of circumstances or as women who were chaste of heart. He was not interested in exploring the reasons why women became prostitutes. Manto never sat in moral judgement over his characters. He did, however, present prostitutes with empathy as well as detachment. Manto's stories like "Thanda Gosht" and "Khol Do" portray the macabre in humanity, and demystify human relationships and sexuality. In fact, a similar trend is also noticeable in the novels of writers in Bengali and other Indian languages. In Tarashankar Bandhyopadhya's *Agradani*, the helplessness of a poor, greedy professional priest has been brought out with remorseless irony. His change in fortune is so dramatic that ultimately as an *agradani* Brahmin, he has to swallow the ritualistic *pinda* (rice-ball) at the *shradda* ceremony of his own son. Similarly in Manik Bandhyopadhyay's "Pragoitahasik" (Primeval), the reader shudders at the stark, bare, naked realism which at times reaches the limits of an unbearable poignancy. The beggar, Bikhu, has so much love left in his heart for the beggar-woman, Panchi, that he commits a murder in order to earn the money they require to begin a new life somewhere else. As they flee the locality, a bright moon shines in the sky. In yet another story by the same writer, a daughter takes to prostitution under the devastating economic effect of the partition, only to be solicited one day by her own father. Tarashankar's *Jana Aranya*, made into film by Satyajit Ray, deals with a similar theme. The inability to find employment turns a brother into a pimp and his sister into a prostitute. Initially, they have no knowledge of each other's professions. But the dehumanising conditions of the society they live in turn the brother into his sister's agent.

To conclude, even though Manto and his contemporaries present human beings as cruel and ugly, they present humanity as kind and generous. Their writings reveal an undercurrent of man's elemental humanity even in his apparently inhuman postures.

Contributors

VARIS ALVI retired as a Professor of English from the University of Allahabad.

M. ASADUDDIN teaches English Literature at Jamia Millia Islamia, New Delhi.

ALOK BHALLA teaches English Literature at the Central Institute of English and Foreign Languages, Hyderabad.

ABDUL BISMILLAH teaches Hindi at Jamia Millia Islamia, New Delhi.

INDRA NATH CHOUDHURI is Director, Nehru Centre, London.

KEKI K. DARUWALA ia a poet and a short story writer in English. He lives in delhi.

TEJWANT SINGH GILL teaches English Literature at Guru Nanak Dev University, Amritsar.

SHAMIM HANFI teaches Urdu languahe and literature at Jamia Millia Islamia, New Delhi.

DEVENDER ISSAR is an Urdu short story writer. He lives in Delhi.

SHASHI JOSHI is an historian. She lives in Delhi.

SUKRITA PAUL KUMAR teaches English Literature at delhi University.

MUHAMMAD UMAR MEMON teaches Urdu at the University of Wisconsin, U.S.A.

GOPI CHAND NARANG retired as a Professor of Urdu Literature from Jamia Millia Islamia, New Delhi.

HARISH NARANg teaches English Literature at Jawaharlal Nehru University, New Delhi.

TARANNUM RIAZ, N-23B, Jangpura Extension, New Delhi.

BHISHAM SAHNI is a novelist and a short story writer in Hindi. He lives in Delhi.

ASHOK VOHRA teaches Philosophy at Delhi University, Delhi and is the Secretary of the Indian Council of Philosophic Research, New Delhi.